An Atlas of Irish History

D1319668

The history of Ireland and its people is one of extraordinary richness and variety. Combining more than a hundred beautifully crafted maps, charts and graphs with a narrative packed with key facts and lucid analysis, *An Atlas of Irish History* provides coverage of the main political, military, economic, religious and social changes that have occurred in Ireland and among the Irish abroad over the past two millennia.

The authors use the combination of thematic narrative and visual aids to examine and illustrate such varied issues as:

- Continental invasions
- the Irish diaspora
- land and the people
- Catholicism in crisis
- Ireland in the EU
- paramilitaries.

This third edition has been comprehensively revised, updated and significantly expanded to include an account of the startling changes that have occurred in Ireland and among its emigrants in the last few decades – from the impact of the Celtic Tiger to the peace process.

An Atlas of Irish History is an invaluable resource for students of Irish history and politics and the general reader alike.

Ruth Dudley Edwards is a prize-winning historian and biographer. Her many books include biographies of Patrick Pearse and James Connolly, and *The Faithful Tribe: an intimate portrait of the loyal institutions*.

Bridget Hourican is an historian attached to the Royal Irish Academy where she is working on the forthcoming *Dictionary of Irish Biography*. She is also literary editor of the *Dubliner* magazine.

Reviews of previous editions

'The sheer wealth of information assembled here makes this a priceless aid for anyone interested in Irish history.'

History Today

'Anybody seeking understanding of events in the country today will find this a very useful guide. It is a mine of useful and fascinating information.'

Universe

'An excellent general reference work. ... Recommended for academic collections both graduate and undergraduate.'

Choice

'An excellent reference book. ... The amount of information in this book is amazing.'

Irish Echo

An Atlas of Irish History
Third edition

Ruth Dudley Edwards

With Bridget Hourican

Routledge
Taylor & Francis Group

LONDON AND NEW YORK

First published 1973
by Methuen & Co. Ltd

Second edition published 1981

Third edition published 2005
by Routledge
2 Park Square, Milton Park, Abingdon, Oxon OX14 4RN

Simultaneously published in the USA and Canada
by Routledge
270 Madison Ave, New York, NY 10016

Routledge is an imprint of the Taylor & Francis Group

© 1973, 1981, 2005 Ruth Dudley Edwards and 2005 Bridget Hourican

Typeset in Bembo by RefineCatch Ltd, Bungay, Suffolk
Index compiled by Indexing Specialists (UK) Ltd, Hove, East Sussex
Printed and bound in Great Britain by
The Cromwell Press, Trowbridge, Wiltshire

British Library Cataloguing in Publication Data
A catalogue record for this book is available from the British Library

Library of Congress Cataloging in Publication Data
Edwards, Ruth Dudley.
    An atlas of Irish history/Ruth Dudley Edwards; with Bridget
    Hourican.—3rd ed. p. cm.
    Includes bibliographical references and index.
        1. Ireland—Historical geography—Maps. 2. Ireland—History. I.
    Hourican, Bridget. II. Routledge (Firm) II. Title.

G1831.S1E3 2005
911′.415—dc22

                                                              2004045008

ISBN 0–415–33952–9 (hbk)
ISBN 0–415–27859–7 (pbk)

Contents

IV Politics   71

V Religion   105

VI The Irish abroad   124

VII Land   155

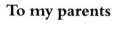
To my parents

Foreword

There is an inevitable arbitrariness about attempting to represent history or politics cartographically. It becomes necessary to concentrate on those aspects which can most usefully be displayed visually. Therefore, while I have attempted to deal with the more important features in the development of the Irish people, the medium lends itself to the portraying of facts rather than ideas, and some bias will be discernible. Any imbalance in the choice of material is conditioned by the aim of using the medium as effectively as possible, rather than forcing a strict pattern.

Let the nature of the beast therefore be the excuse for inadequate treatment of areas of Irish history that could claim extensive coverage in any general survey. By way of compensation, the cartographic format lends itself to a less insular approach. If one defines Irish history as being the history of the Irish people rather than simply of the island, one must look to most of the world for material. The Irish abroad merit a complete section within this book, as does Irish trade, since they are both susceptible of visual representation.

My debt to historians of Ireland will be evident throughout the book, and will be acknowledged in the bibliography. I owe many other debts. Mr W. H. Bromage drew the maps; his skill and forbearance in the face of enormous odds made the project possible. Professor G. R. Elton bears the responsibility for involving me in this venture, and has been my teacher and friend. My parents have given me moral, intellectual and practical support at all times; the book could not have been written without their help. Miss Vanessa MacErlean has been a precociously efficient assistant and a constant provider of moral support. Mr Patrick Taylor has been a model among publishers and Mrs Vanessa Mitchell a most helpful editor. Many others have rendered assistance, including Dr Patrick Cosgrave, Dr Ronan Fanning, Dr Dermot Fenlon, Mr Liam Hourican, Mr James McGuire and Mrs Una O'Donoghue. To them, and others, I extend my gratitude.

I have sectionalized the book with the object of increasing its coherence. All but the final section are prefaced by a general introduction. Cross-references shown by an Arabic numeral in brackets refer to the relevant map and its accompanying text. Roman numerals refer to sectional introductions. Each section, and indeed each map and accompanying text, is intended to form an independent unit, but cross-referencing to other parts of the text should not be ignored.

R. D. E.

1973

Note on second edition

In preparing a new edition I have acted where possible on the constructive criticisms made by reviewers and users of the first. The scope of the book has been enlarged, new maps, graphs and charts have been added, several others have been improved, updated or replaced, and the text has been extensively revised. I am grateful to my publishers (particularly my encouraging, constructive and efficient editor, Miss Mary Ann Kernan) for agreeing to substantial expansion and alterations.

I am grateful to Dr Michael Laffan for some very helpful suggestions; to Mr Oliver Snoddy for map 78a [now Figure 84a]; to Mr Neil Hyslop for so ably taking over as cartographer; to the staff of the Irish Embassy in London who answered promptly, efficiently and courteously my many requests for information; to the Northern Ireland Office and the British Library.

My father deserves a paragraph to himself. He spent over a week reading and annotating the book in fine detail, spotting errors and anachronisms, bringing me up to date on the past decade of Irish historiography, making countless useful suggestions for improvements and generally giving me that selfless and invaluable help which I am lucky enough always to have on call from my parents, husband, household and friends.

R. D. E.

September 1980

Note on third edition

After almost a quarter of a century – a period during which Ireland changed dramatically and scholars published prolifically – without the help of three historians, I should not have known where to start. Lawrence W. White meticulously went through the second edition and pointed out errors and lacunae and out-of-date facts and analyses, as well as making innumerable invaluable suggestions about new material. Bridget Hourican then stepped in. She was supposed to be my research assistant, but while I have done a great deal of text revision and updating, Bridget has been the main author of most of the new material relating to the Republic of Ireland and I am profoundly grateful for her brilliance, doggedness and good humour. It was James McGuire, editor of the Royal Irish Academy's *Dictionary of Irish Biography* for which they work, who recommended Larry and Bridget, and my publishers, Vicky Peters and Alex Ballantine, who finally made the third edition happen. Alex, my editor, was both relaxed and painstaking – a wonderful combination of qualities. Máirín Carter ticked me off for ignoring Irish sport, about which Bridget and I know nothing, so Eamonn Rafferty and Colm Carter, who know plenty, filled that gap.

R. D. E.
January 2005

I   Reference

The six maps in this section have been included primarily for reference pur-poses. In addition to the political and physical maps, which follow a traditional format, there are included maps of the provinces of Ireland split into baronies.

1   POLITICAL GEOGRAPHY OF IRELAND

The political geography of Ireland can be traced with some accuracy from the seventh century. At that time the country was divided into about 150 units of government, or small kingdoms, called *tuatha*. A *tuath* was an autonomous group of people of independent political jurisdiction under a king. Larger units, comprising several *tuatha*, were built up by local kings whose families main-tained their ascendancy traditionally. Some thirty such larger units existed by the early twelfth century when the diocesan system was established, and it was upon these that the new ecclesiastical organization was based (V).

   Larger historic units developed, dominated in the north-west by the Uí Néill and in the south by the Dalcassian descendants of Brian Ború (IV). In the twelfth century this led to the proposed division of the whole country into two ecclesiastical provinces – Armagh and Cashel. When the Uí Néill and the O'Briens failed to maintain their hegemony in the west and east, two other provinces – Tuam and Dublin – were added. In this way four greater kingdoms came to be distinguished which were described by ancient titles as Ulster, Leinster, Munster and Connacht. In fact the Uí Néill and the O'Briens had previously held no territorial rights to be rulers of Ulster and Munster: the areas of these provinces comprised those territories not claimed by the newly expanding kingdoms of Connacht and Leinster. Clare was conceded to Munster and Breffny to Ulster, and Leinster was confined to the historic Laigin lands to which Ossory and Dublin were conceded. On the other hand, the Viking towns of Waterford and Limerick appear to have preferred to be associated with Munster.

   The Normans adapted their methods of government to suit the conditions they found in Ireland, and therefore did not interfere with the provincial divisions. They were, however, concerned to superimpose on those parts of the

Figure 1 Political geography of Ireland: present county divisions and major towns.

country over which they had control over the political divisions that had obtained in England since the Anglo-Saxons. During the Norman period, therefore, began the division of Ireland into shires, later called counties. Although only Dublin was a shire before 1200, by the early fourteenth century there were twelve (Dublin, Waterford, Cork, Kerry, Limerick, Tipperary, Kildare, Carlow, Louth, Roscommon, Connacht and Meath) and four liberties (Wexford, Kilkenny, Trim and Ulster). After the Bruce invasion, some of the shires became liberties.

To correspond with the subdivision of shires known in England as the hundred, Irish counties were subdivided into cantreds – later known as baronies – which in turn were subdivided into townlands. Although the baronies initially denoted feudal and military jurisdictions, eventually they were used for fiscal and administrative purposes only. These divisions proved an essential administrative aid to the process of colonizing land, and later provided the basic units for the collection of census statistics.

Mainly because of political weakness, there was little attempt to extend the shiring of the country during the late Middle Ages. Apart from Mary's colonization of Queen's County and King's County (54), there was little opportunity for the Dublin government to extend its control until the military and political advances of the Elizabethan period. Between 1570 and 1585 Munster was divided into counties and Connacht, which in the fourteenth century had been called a county, was subdivided. During the reign of James I, Ulster was shired at the time of its plantation (55).

The divisions of the four provinces of Ireland are described in the following parts of this section.

The main contemporary political feature of Ireland is partition. Northern Ireland covers an area of 5,452 square miles, or about 17 per cent of the whole island. The border with the Republic is about 250 miles long, which has often posed severe problems of security. The Republic covers a total area of 27,136 square miles. For purposes of local government the country is divided into twenty-nine administrative counties (Tipperary being split into the north and south ridings and Dublin into the administrative counties of Fingal, South Dublin and Dún Laoghaire-Rathdown) and four county boroughs, and the Department of the Environment supervises local administrative bodies. In Northern Ireland the position is more complex and fluid (XI).

The original constitution of the Irish Free State was enacted in 1922. In 1937 a new constitution set up a de-facto Republic; it was so worded as to allow the External Relations Act of the previous year to cover relations with the British Commonwealth. Therefore, although the King retained certain prerogatives in external relations, these were not mentioned in the constitution. The Republic of Ireland Act 1948 repealed the External Relations Act and stated the terms under which Ireland would cease to be a dominion and become a republic outside the Commonwealth – 'on such day as the Government may by Order appoint'. By government order the country formally became a republic on 18 April 1949 and the Ireland Act of the Westminster parliament on 2 June 1949 delineated the citizenship and entry-residence status of Irish nationals within the UK. Irish citizens, however, did not become aliens in the UK: anyone born in Ireland before 1948 was granted the automatic right to opt to be a British subject and any Irish citizen has the right to enter Britain without a passport.

Partition came about via the Government of Ireland Act of 1920, which provided for two devolved parliaments of Northern and Southern Ireland (and for a Council of Ireland for consultation on common interests); elections for both parliaments were held in May 1921. A Boundary Commission was provided for in the Anglo-Irish treaty of 1921 to examine the boundaries of the two states and to recommend any necessary rationalization; the UK act that gave legal force to the terms of the treaty and thereby formally established the Boundary Commission was the Irish Free State (Agreement) Act of March 1922.

As a result of the Irish Civil War (22), opposition from the Northern Ireland government and dilatoriness in London, the commission did not begin work until 1924. Although its members had reached internal agreement on border changes in 1925, its report was suppressed. Its recommendations were to have been the transfer of 183,000 acres and 31,000 people from Northern Ireland to the Free State and the transfer of 50,000 acres and 7,500 people from the Free State to the North. Before the commission could publish its report, a leak of information to the *Morning Post* caused Eoin MacNeill, the Irish government's representative, to resign. The boundaries of the two countries therefore remained as they had been in 1921.

2   ULSTER

Ulster covers 26.3 per cent of Ireland and consists of nine counties: Londonderry, Antrim, Tyrone, Armagh, Fermanagh and Down, which are within Northern Ireland, and Cavan, Donegal and Monaghan, which are in the Republic.

3   MUNSTER

Munster covers 29.3 per cent of Ireland and consists of six counties: Cork, Kerry, Clare, Limerick, Tipperary and Waterford.

4   LEINSTER

Leinster covers 23.4 per cent of Ireland and consists of twelve counties: Louth, Dublin, Kildare, Carlow, Kilkenny, Laois (formerly Queen's County), Offaly (formerly King's County), Meath, Westmeath, Wicklow, Wexford and Longford.

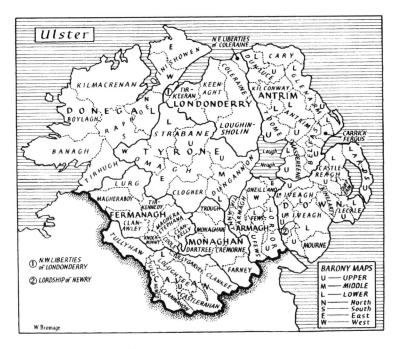

Figure 2 Ulster: counties and baronies.

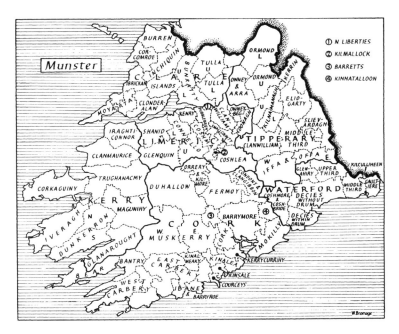

Figure 3 Munster: counties and baronies.

Figure 4 Leinster: counties and baronies.

5 CONNACHT

Connacht covers 21 per cent of Ireland and consists of five counties: Galway,
Leitrim, Mayo, Roscommon and Sligo.

The only difference between the contemporary divisions and those of the
sixteenth century is that Connacht, as befitted its historical importance, was
then much larger, comprising in addition to its modern counties those of Cavan
and Longford.

Figure 5 Connacht: counties and baronies.

6   PHYSICAL FEATURES OF IRELAND

Ireland is remarkable for a topographical variety disproportionate to its size. The coastline is dramatic and often inaccessible. Its most notable features are the high cliffs of north Antrim, famous for the legendary Giant's Causeway, a promontory made up of pillars of basalt, some nearly 40 feet wide and 20 feet high, and the spectacular cliffs of Donegal, Mayo, Clare and Kerry. Most of the south-west coast is an alternation of sandy bays and high cliffs.

Many of the coastal waters are dangerous, which is why the main harbours have all been established in river estuaries – Dublin on the Liffey, Wexford on the Slaney, Waterford on the Suir, Cork on the Lee, Limerick on the Shannon, Belfast on the Lagan and Derry on the Foyle. (Nationalists and unionists tend to refer respectively to Derry and Londonderry; those wishing to avoid giving offence say Derry/Londonderry; humorists refer to Stroke City. The town was known as Derry until altered in March 1613 to Londonderry, but in 1984 Londonderry District Council was officially renamed Derry City Council. In this book, following academic convention, the county post-1984 is called Londonderry and the city Derry.)

Near the coastline are situated most of the uplands of Ireland, although the so-called 'Central Plain' of Ireland is dotted with numerous low hills, known as drumlins (8). Much of this land is uneven and diverse, varying in quality from rich pastureland to bare peat bogs.

Ireland covers an area of 32,588 square miles, averages 110 miles in breadth and 220 miles in length. The climate is bland, there being relatively little seasonal variation in temperature, but there is a great deal of rain, averaging 30–50 inches annually over most of the country, with precipitation on up to 250 days in the wettest parts. R. A. Macalister contended that the climate in all but the north-eastern corner was the most enervating in Europe, and claimed that 'To this quite irredeemable vice of the Irish climate is due the notorious fact that Irishmen always do better in any country but their own.'

Much of the history of Ireland is the story of how invaders coped with the physical problems posed by the island. The Norse, for example, were uniquely equipped to adapt to the demands of the environment, and made generous use of the rivers and lakes of Ireland to penetrate its inner fastnesses (11). Other invaders found the country more inhospitable.

More significant perhaps than the physical problems of the country is its location. The close physical relationship between Ireland and Great Britain is symbolized by the fact that the minimum distance between the two is only 13 miles. An ocean away from its western neighbours, and protected from the twelfth century by the intimate interest of its nearest neighbour from attacks from the north, south or east, Ireland has nevertheless been locked in a struggle for some kind of independence for the past thousand years. Immune from the Homeric clashes raging across the Continent over the centuries, since

Figure 6 Physical features of Ireland.

the twelfth century the Irish people have concentrated on one enemy, not recognizing that without that enemy, Ireland would have been faced with unwelcome advances from others (10).

II Cartography

The development of cartography owes a great deal to many disciplines. The early map-makers could not have functioned without the material provided to them by traders and travellers. Later map-makers were given encouragement and an impetus towards accuracy by the increasing military requirement for scientific maps. Early maps were concerned mainly to indicate routes and landmarks: they were visual representations of itineraries. Accuracy in indicating direction or distance was of lesser concern. Imagination played an important part in map design, and artistry was a necessary feature.

Soldiers, however, needed to have an accurate idea of distances and locations, and the skills of mathematicians and astronomers were incorporated into the science of cartography; trigonometry aided the establishing of distances and elevations. Astronomers established that the earth was spherical and that any location could be pinpointed by the use of concepts of latitude and longitude; at a later stage, scientists found ways of accurately finding longitude.

Map-making began in the Middle East, notably with the Egyptians, but by the sixth century BC the Greeks were pre-eminent. From an early stage they constructed maps of their trading routes, including descriptions of the coasts known to their sailors, but since myth and hearsay formed a major element in the material brought back by travellers, accurate data were in short supply. But by the second century AD the science of cartography had advanced considerably; Claudius Ptolemy of Alexandria and Marinus of Tyre made dramatic contributions.

Although no examples of Ptolemy's work remain extant, alleged copies exist, and his writings give enough information to enable maps to be based on them. Ptolemy did not gain recognition in Europe until the fifteenth century, but his influence was then profound for over a hundred years. Of the maps illustrated on the next page, the first is based on the findings of Ptolemy in the second century, and the second was drawn 1,400 years later by a cartographer known as the Argentinian Ptolemy.

The discovery of Ptolemy in Europe in the fifteenth century heralded a cartographical renaissance. Hitherto, map-making had consisted largely of inaccurate copying of earlier maps, although Italian navigators and cartographers introduced portolans or sea charts to aid traders. Simultaneously with the

Figure 7(a) Ptolemy, 2nd century.
Figure 7(b) The Argentinian Ptolemy, 1513.

Figure 7(c) John Norden, *c.* 1608.

discovery of Ptolemy came the increase in data forthcoming from the great explorers, the Italian, Spanish, French, Dutch, Portuguese and English sailors who reached India, Brazil, the West Indies, southern Africa and many other undiscovered parts of the globe during this period. Subsequently, the advance of the science was steady. Crucial advances in instrument-making led to the creation of maps of real accuracy during the late eighteenth and early nineteenth centuries. Britain – which had hitherto followed rather than led cartographical advances – illustrated this new development in 1791, by establishing the Ordnance Survey. This formalized the work being done in surveying by army engineers. From 1745, when the army initiated scientific surveys of the Scottish Highlands, its contribution to map-making was considerable, and engineers took a leading part in the whole Ordnance Survey enterprise. By 1870, one-inch-to-a-mile maps for the whole of England, Scotland, Wales and Ireland had been produced.

7   IRELAND AND ITS CARTOGRAPHERS

As far as Ireland was concerned, its isolation restricted cartographical activity. For a considerable period it was considered to be the westernmost outpost of the world. However, the map constructed from Ptolemy's data, Figure 7a, shows that some trading contacts existed even in the second century which enabled an attempt to be made at describing the Irish coastline and the location of some of the tribes. By the fourth century, there were no longer any attempts to record tribal distribution; the inhabitants of Ireland were known simply as Scotae (43).

The later map shown here, Figure 7b, indicates that although cartography had advanced little by the early sixteenth century, trading knowledge of Ireland had become much more extensive (65) and important contemporary ports such as Drogheda, Dublin and Limerick were located with reasonable accuracy. In fact French, Spanish and Italian seafarers show in their maps a better geographical knowledge of Ireland than does the first English map of Ireland, produced in about 1483, which greatly exaggerates the importance of the Pale.

Detailed maps of Ireland were produced during the Tudor period, many of which, though beautiful, relied more on hearsay than on facts, on imagination than on investigation. The Elizabethans took a more pragmatic interest in cartography, largely because of the contemporary concern with exploration, and the maps produced in the late sixteenth century were a considerable improvement on earlier work. Technical developments improved the accuracy of surveying, and – with the recognition of the important contribution to be made by cartography to political and military activity – the science was encouraged. The work that ensued, though hampered in Ireland by war and appalling communications, is nevertheless a tribute to the dedication and ability of the map-makers.

The Elizabethans had practical, political and military reasons for encouraging good map-making. Inspired by the greatest map-makers of the age, the

Flemings, and by the publication of Mercator's map of England and Wales in 1564, English surveyors and draughtsmen worked together to produce maps of great artistry and increasing accuracy, though they excelled more in the former than in the latter. Ptolemy is said to have believed that a map without artistry did not convey any message, and Elizabethan cartographers too were preoccupied with the beauty of the finished product. Two of the great cartographers of the period were John Norden (Figure 7c) and Richard Bartlett, both of whom produced fine maps of Ireland. Bartlett was employed to produce a series of military maps, many of which had to be researched and drawn during the Nine Years War (15). He made use of information gathered by the English army during this war and incorporated it into his maps. His knowledge grew with the increasing success of the English forces.

The major breakthrough in accurate cartography in Ireland was made by Sir William Petty in his atlas of Irish maps, published in 1685. In 1654 Petty proposed to the commissioners responsible for the land survey that would provide the basis of the Cromwellian land settlement (56) a scheme for mapping the relevant parts of the country. This survey, known as the 'Down Survey', because the results were being noted down, formed the basis of his later atlas. He used soldiers to do the necessary surveying fieldwork, and the resultant maps were pioneering in their accuracy. His maps were not surpassed until the Ordnance Survey maps of Ireland in the 1840s, which were surveyed by army engineers and drawn by draughtsmen, using techniques that ensured accuracy and good representation.

III Military developments

G. A. Hayes-McCoy calculated that there were more than 200 military engagements of varying degrees of importance and size in Ireland from the medieval period to 1798. The more important of these are shown in Figure 9; they demonstrate that with the coming of the Norman invaders (12) the Irish began a military struggle that was to continue over four centuries. Before the Norman invasion, Irish military history was dominated by confrontations with the Norse invaders (11), although internecine strife between Irish aspirants to kingship was a feature of Irish life from the beginning of recorded history.

The major engagements of the medieval period are, however, those of defenders against invaders: most were fought in an attempt to prevent further Norman penetration of the country. That the Irish succeeded in preventing the Normans from completely overrunning the country was due not only to stout resistance but also to the isolation of the invaders from their homeland and the impossibility of their securing sufficient reinforcements to maintain and consolidate their position. Additionally, the importation by the Irish of Scots mercenary soldiers called galloglas (from *gall óglach* – foreign warrior) from the thirteenth century onwards was to strengthen their resistance considerably. At first confined to Ulster, galloglas later spread throughout Ireland in the service of the great families. These mercenaries prolonged the life of the independent Gaelic kingdoms for more than two centuries after the defeat of Edward Bruce (14). Four centuries after the conquest, the O'Neills and O'Donnells were still ruling most of Ulster according to the customs of their ancestors. It was not until their defeat in the Nine Years War (15) in 1603 that all of Gaelic Ireland finally fell to the invaders.

During the seventeenth century, Irish military history was to a considerable extent an offshoot of events in England. The alliance between the Catholic Old English and the Gaelic Irish was to develop in the 1640s into a confrontation with the English parliamentary forces (16). When James II landed in Ireland in 1689 in a desperate bid to regain his throne, he was using the island as an outpost in an English struggle for supremacy between Stuart and Orange (17).

With the triumph of William of Orange and the emigration of many Irish soldiers throughout the last decade of the seventeenth century (17) and much of the eighteenth, any serious resistance was finally crushed. Ireland was totally subdued, and any future resistance was to take the form of rebellions of varying ineffectiveness. Despite the setbacks of the sixteenth and seventeenth centuries when Ireland had looked to Spain, France and the papacy for help against England, the dissident elements of the Irish people continued to hope that ultimately foreign intervention would give them independence (10). During the sixteenth century, Ireland had become a country whose fortunes were of interest to Continental powers, and to some extent it became a pawn in the military and ideological conflicts of Europe. During the reign of Elizabeth, three invasions occurred in support of the Munster rebellion and the Nine Years War. The Continental confrontation between William of Orange and Louis XIV had its echo in Ireland, whither Louis sent men, arms, ammunition and money. He was concerned less to secure a decisive victory for James than to deflect William's attention from the Continent by facing him with a long drawn-out war in Ireland.

After William's victory there was no further Continental intervention in Ireland until after the French Revolution. The United Irishmen leaders, inspired by concepts of universal brotherhood and republican solidarity, managed to involve the French in the 1798 rising (19). This new defeat deterred the Continental powers from giving any further help, and during the nineteenth century Irish revolutionaries had to go it alone, their only foreign help being financial support from Irish-Americans (51).

In 1803 Robert Emmet led an abortive rising that in many ways was merely a continuation of that of 1798. Bad communications led to a confusion of orders, and when the rising eventually broke out on 23 July 1803, instead of involving 3,000 men as planned, Emmet was left with a rabble of only eighty. He and twenty-one others were executed.

Even more ineffective was the Young Irelanders' rising in 1848 (31). They had made few preparations or plans for a rebellion, which was precipitated by an acceleration of government coercion and the arrest of many of their leaders. The main organizer was William Smith O'Brien, but no amount of rhetoric could persuade the starving Irish peasantry to reject the advice of their clergy and fight for intangible political ideals. The country scarcely noticed either the rebellion or the subsequent transportation to Van Diemen's Land of its leaders, who included Smith O'Brien and Thomas Francis Meagher; even before the rebellion, John Mitchel had been transported there.

The other Irish rebellion of the nineteenth century owed something to that of 1848. A number of Young Irelanders – including James Stephens and Charles Kickham – were later to become Fenian leaders. Although their rising in 1867 (51) affected only a few scattered areas of the country, until independence the Fenian movement was to be a potent force in Irish revolutionary circles.

Irish revolutionary activity during the twentieth century again brought in a Continental element. The 1916 leaders (20) received help from Germany, and during the 1930s and 1940s IRA groups negotiated for German aid. As was the case with earlier Continental help, German aid was given with the object of harassing Britain rather than of helping the Irish. Over the past few decades, the IRA has received money, equipment or moral support from a variety of sources, including Libya, international terrorist groups and unofficial Irish–American sympathizers (51).

There is a coherent pattern in Irish military activity. Until the seventeenth century, when the woods were cut down and roads improved, military

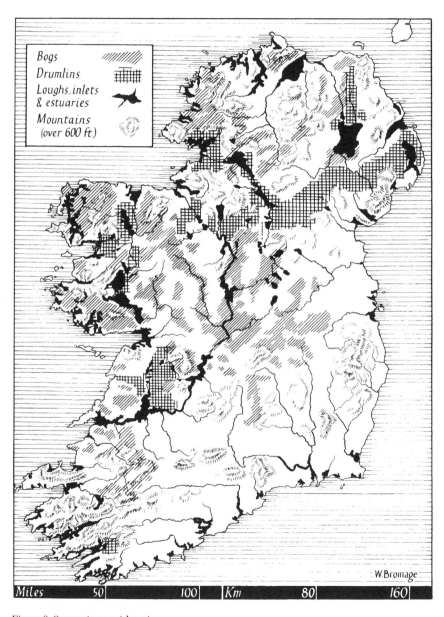

Figure 8 Strategic considerations.

encounters were dominated by physical considerations (8) – problems of terrain. For almost four centuries there was a continuous struggle between invaders and defenders, which broadened during the late sixteenth century to involve Continental armies. During the seventeenth century, military activity was mainly a consequence of what was going on in English politics. From the eighteenth to the twentieth century militarism was restricted to no more than a tiny section of the population. Not until the Anglo-Irish war of 1919–21 did a significant minority become involved in any of the various armed rebellions, which until 1916 had little political impact (although an unintended consequence of the 1798 rebellion was the Act of Union). With the outbreak of the Civil War in 1922 there developed an ugly confrontation that would prove a divisive force in Ireland until the present day (34). Since the 1970s, the IRA, its offshoots and its loyalist paramilitary opponents have introduced a pattern of random violence and destruction into Irish military activity.

8   STRATEGIC CONSIDERATIONS

Ireland's natural barriers have always posed problems to invading forces. Only the Vikings, with their skilful command of rivers and lakes (11), were equipped to meet competently the physical hazards of the country. For other invaders, a country so liberally supplied with rivers, lakes, mountains, bogs, drumlins (small hills) and an inhospitable coastline posed almost insuperable difficulties. Additionally, until their commercial exploitation in the seventeenth century, vast areas of woodland covered the country, forming virtually impenetrable barriers to effective progress. In the early seventeenth century, about 15 per cent of the total area of the country was forested. Vast tracts of woodland made most of north-east Ulster and south-west Munster almost totally inaccessible, while extensive detours were necessary to reach many parts of Connacht.

Ulster posed the most serious problems of accessibility, and its physical defences explain why Gaelic rule continued throughout most of the province until 1603. There were only three entry routes. Two were close together in the south-west, where Ulster and Connacht are separated by the river Erne, one approach being over the river near Ballyshannon and another between the lakes at Enniskillen. In the south-east of Ulster there was the Moyry Pass, the gateway to Ulster known as the Gap of the North and said to have been defended by the mythological Cuchulainn. Moyry is the gorge in the hills between Dundalk and Newry through which the Slighe Mhidhluachra (61) ran, 'where the Irish might skip but the English could not go'. From a military angle, the importance of commanding these vantage points was obvious: the earlier neglect of forts in Ulster had severely handicapped the English army in the Nine Years War (15).

In the west of Ireland, although it could be forded in a few places, the Shannon posed a formidable obstacle to an advancing army, and the country beyond was inhospitable and unfamiliar. Leinster was familiar territory, but even there, before the seventeenth century, the English were never at home in the mountainous and wooded areas of Wicklow from which the Irish chiefs launched frequent attacks on the Pale (28). From the military point of view, the most favourable part of Ireland was south-east Munster, which had rich land, numerous towns and good communications.

The Irish were successful in resistance while they used the Fabian tactics suitable to their difficult terrain. The Normans settled in good land, and while the Irish avoided direct confrontation and stuck to forays from their mountains, woods and bogs and used guerrilla tactics, they could hope to compensate to some extent for their inferior military skill and equipment. O'Neill was successful as long as he stayed in Ulster; it was only when he moved to Munster that he met defeat.

The English learned well the lesson taught them by O'Neill, and by 1610 a chain of garrisons and forts had been set up around the whole country. Twenty-six garrisons and thirty forts established government control throughout Ireland, and guarded trading towns and landing places from foreign invasion.

9   BATTLE SITES

Figure 9 is a reference point for the main battles or sieges in Irish history. So many different protagonists are found in Irish battles, including Irish, Norse, Normans, Old English, Scots, English, royalists, parliamentarians, Protestants and Catholics, and there is such a bewildering mixture of these elements, that it is impossible to convey more than a general indication of the main bodies on each side.   None in Antrium

1014

Clontarf

Victory of the High King, Brian Ború, over his challenger, Máel Mórda, king of Leinster, the Norse of Dublin and Norse allies from Orkney, Scandinavia, Iceland and Normandy (11).

1171

Dublin

Strongbow and Dermot MacMurrough took Dublin in 1170, but in 1171 were threatened from the east by a fleet of 1,000 Norse under the displaced King of Dublin, Asgall, and from the west by a much larger army led by the High King, Rory O'Connor. Instead of launching a united attack, the Norse attacked in May and were decisively defeated by the Normans. The High King continued to build up his forces and besiege Dublin, but in September a surprise raid on his camp by a small Norman army resulted in a complete rout (12).

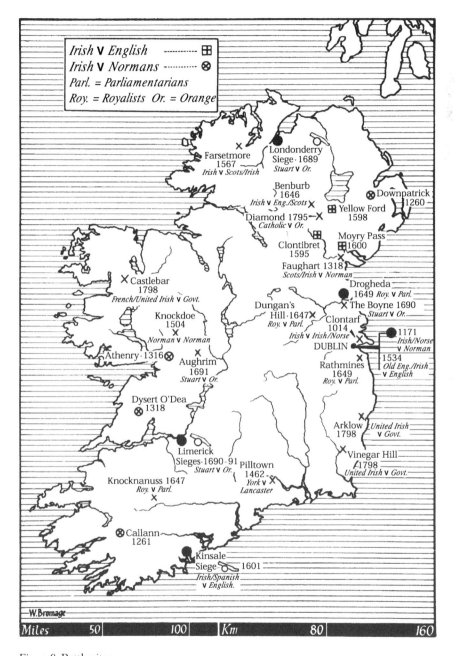

Figure 9 Battle sites.

1260

Downpatrick

As part of the attempt to revive the O'Neill claim to the high kingship, Brian O'Neill of Tirowen led an attack on Norman settlers in Down, and was defeated (13).

1261

Callann

In 1259, a royal grant of Desmond and Decies was made to John FitzThomas. This provoked a rising of the MacCarthys, who at the battle of Callann won a total victory over FitzThomas and the justiciar, and confirmed for a time their control of south-west Ireland (27).

1316

Athenry

On 10 August, the Anglo-Irish of Connacht, under William de Burgh and Richard de Bermingham, crushed a huge Gaelic army, killed over sixty chieftains and ensured Norman supremacy over Connacht (14).

1318

Dysert O'Dea

Contemporaneous with the Bruce invasion were the last stages in the war in Thomond between the native rulers, the O'Briens, and the Norman settlers, the de Clares. In May 1318 came the final confrontation, with a total victory for the O'Briens and a recovery of their kingship, which in 1540 became an earldom (14).

Faughart

Total defeat of Edward Bruce and an army of Scots, native Irish and Norman rebels by a Norman force led by John de Bermingham (14).

1462

Pilltown

Ireland was very largely Yorkist in sympathy during the Wars of the Roses, giving support to Richard, duke of York, when he fled from England. The only notable Lancastrian supporters were the Butlers, whose attempt to prolong the struggle led to their defeat at Pilltown in 1462 by a force led by Thomas, earl of Desmond, and their subsequent exile (27).

1504

Knockdoe

In August 1504 was fought the battle of Knockdoe between the Lord Deputy, the Great Earl of Kildare, and his son-in-law, Ulick Burke of Clanrickard, ostensibly because Burke was challenging the royal authority in Galway, but really because his increasing power was becoming a threat to the Kildare balance of power; Kildare was not prepared to countenance any rival. Kildare's army consisted of his own men (including galloglas) and the forces of his Ulster allies – including O'Neill, O'Donnell, Magennis, MacMahon, O'Hanlon, O'Reilly; of MacDermott, O'Farrell, O'Kelly and the Mayo Burkes from Connacht. He also had the support of the great Pale families, including the Prestons, St Laurences and Plunketts (27). To set against this force, Ulick Burke had the support of the O'Briens of Thomond, the Macnamaras, the O'Carrolls and the O'Kennedys, and his own force of galloglas. The precise numbers cannot be estimated, but they were substantial, with the Great Earl having a numerical advantage and using firearms for the first time in an Irish battle. Kildare's victory was total, and smashed the power of the south-east Connacht/north-west Munster alliance.

1534

Dublin

In February 1534, Kildare was summoned to London and imprisoned in the Tower; his son and deputy, Thomas, Lord Offaly, known as Silken Thomas, on hearing a rumour of his death, led an unsuccessful rebellion in Dublin in which the archbishop of Dublin was killed. Although Offaly took the city he was unable to take Dublin Castle. Under Sir William Skeffington, the new lord deputy, a large army arrived which suppressed the rebellion and in March 1535 took Offaly's Maynooth stronghold by the use of heavy cannon (27).

1567

Farsetmore

Shane O'Neill's attempts at territorial aggrandizement in Ulster continued until 1567, when they were ended by the battle of Farsetmore, brought about by his unsuccessful attack on the O'Donnells. The O'Donnells relied mainly on galloglas, while O'Neill had a force that largely comprised his own people, whom he had militarized over the years to compensate for the shortage of mercenaries (54).

1595

Clontibret

In May 1595, Marshal Sir Henry Bagenal set out to relieve the English outpost of Monaghan, under attack from Hugh O'Neill. He marched with 1,750 men to Monaghan, suffering some harassment on the way. While returning, he encountered several ambushes, culminating in a battle at Clontibret where severe losses were sustained. Only a relief force from Newry prevented total disaster (15).

1598

Yellow Ford

At the Yellow Ford on the Blackwater in August Sir Henry Bagenal marched with about 5,000 men to relieve the Blackwater fort, and was defeated and killed in an ambush by an army led by O'Neill and O'Donnell (15).

1600

Moyry Pass

In September 1600, Lord Mountjoy, attempting to reach Armagh to establish a garrison, found the Moyry Pass barred by a series of trenches. Several attempts to break through resulted in serious losses by the English forces. Until later in the year, when O'Neill chose to cease defending it, the English were unable to penetrate the pass (15).

1601

Kinsale

In September 1601, a Spanish force of fewer than 3,500 landed at Kinsale, which Mountjoy besieged with a force that by December had reached 7,500. By this time O'Neill and O'Donnell were threatening his position with an army of about 6,500. At the ensuing battle, Mountjoy secured a decisive victory which effectively ended the Nine Years War (15).

1646

Benburb

Owen Roe O'Neill, at the head of an army of about 5,000, largely formed of Gaelic Irish, defeated an army led by General Robert Monro, composed of Ulster planters, English and Scots, and numbering about 6,000, at Benburb in June. Monro suffered huge losses, largely as a result of O'Neill's superior tactics (16).

1647

Dungan's Hill

The leader of the Old English Catholic forces, Thomas Preston, besieged Trim in July, and in August his army, which included Catholic Scots, was heavily defeated by the parliamentary commander, Michael Jones, at the nearby Dungan's Hill (16).

Knocknanuss

With Dungan's Hill, Knocknanuss proved to be a deathblow to the Confederation in Munster. In November 1647, Murrough O'Brien, earl of Inchiquin, at the head of a parliamentary force, destroyed Lord Taaffe's Confederate army, which included a large number of Catholic Scots (16).

1649

Rathmines

In an effort to revive the royalist cause, after the execution of Charles I, the marquess of Ormond marched on Dublin with his old enemy and new ally, Lord Inchiquin, who had changed sides. On 2 August they were defeated by the parliamentary leader, Michael Jones, at Rathmines near Dublin, leaving the way clear for Cromwell to land at Dublin thirteen days later, without opposition (16).

Drogheda

Drogheda proved to be Cromwell's first objective in Ireland; with a force of about 8,000 he besieged it on 10 September. When he took it the following day, the soldiers and clergy found within the city were massacred, causing the garrisons of Trim and Dundalk to flee without resistance (16).

1689

Londonderry

In March 1689, James II arrived from his French exile to attempt to establish a base in Ireland from which to regain his kingdom. On 18 April he began the siege of Londonderry, which lasted until 31 July. During this period, despite near starvation, the Protestant inhabitants of the city maintained their defiance until a food ship, the *Mountjoy*, forced its way through a barrier on Lough Foyle and relieved the city (17, XI).

1690

The Boyne

William of Orange, with an army of about 36,000, including English, Scots, Dutch, Danes, Germans and Huguenots, met James II, with an army mainly of Irish and French numbering about 25,000, at the Boyne in July. William's victory opened the way to Dublin, led to James's flight and ultimately won the war (17).

1691

Aughrim

On 12 July a desperate attempt was made at Aughrim to halt William's general, Ginkel. About 20,000 men were on each side. Marquis de St Ruth, the French general, was killed and the Jacobite troops were routed (17).

1690–91

Limerick

A siege of Limerick in August 1690, by William, was repulsed and raised. After Aughrim a siege began, led by Ginkel. On 3 October the treaty of Limerick was signed; Lieutenant-General Sarsfield surrendered the city and the Jacobite army was allowed to go to the Continent (17).

1795

Diamond

From the 1780s there were constant skirmishes between Ulster Catholics and Protestants competing for land. In September 1795, at the Diamond in Armagh, an attack by 300 Catholic 'Defenders' on a meeting-place of the Protestant Peep O'Day Boys was repulsed by armed Protestants; forty Catholics were killed and afterwards a Protestant group founded the Orange Order as a defensive organization (18, XI).

1798

Arklow

On 9 June an army of rebels numbering about 20,000, of whom only about 5,000 were armed, under the leadership of Anthony Perry and later of Father Michael Murphy, attacked Arklow. The town was defended by General Francis

Needham with 1,500 troops, mostly militia. Needham repulsed the insurgents effectively (19).

Vinegar Hill

The Wexford insurgents established their headquarters at Vinegar Hill near Enniscorthy. On 21 June they were heavily defeated there by a large force of militia and yeomanry – effectively ending the rebellion (19).

Castlebar

On 22 August an expedition of 1,000 troops, led by the French General Humbert, landed at Killala. Marching east, Humbert met and defeated a force of yeomanry and militia at Castlebar before finally meeting defeat at Ballinamuck (10, 19).

10   CONTINENTAL INTERVENTIONS

There were two features common to all Continental military interventions in Irish affairs. First, none of them was disinterested: whether launched by France or the papacy, by Spain or Germany, all the expeditions were sent less to aid Ireland against England than to further the military, religious, political or ideological cause of the government that financed them. Second, they were all unsuccessful. Figure 10 shows the more important of these interventions, which are here described briefly.

1579

Dingle Bay

On 18 July Sir James Fitzmaurice, leader of the Munster rebellion, landed at Dingle with a force of about 300 soldiers, mainly Italians and Spaniards, financed by Pope Gregory XIII, who had declared Elizabeth deposed, and also privately by Philip II of Spain. This invasion was announced as a religious crusade, being accompanied by Spanish and English papal commissaries. Its defeat ended in Fitzmaurice's death (54).

1580

Smerwick

In September a papal force of 700 landed at Smerwick, led by Colonel San Joseph. Besieged in the fort of Dún-an-óir, this army was defeated by Lord Grey de Wilton, the earl of Ormond and Sir Walter Ralegh in November, and most of the Italians were massacred.

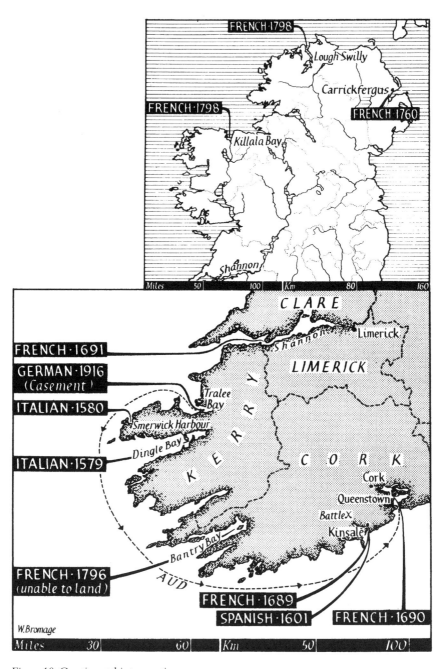

Figure 10 Continental interventions.

1601

Kinsale

On 21 September a Spanish force of fewer than 3,500 landed at Kinsale, led by Don Juan del Aguila. In December, a small force of Spaniards, under Pedro de Zubiar, landed in Castlehaven, 30 miles to the west. They were defeated with the Irish at the battle of Kinsale (15).

1689

Kinsale

On 12 March 1689, James II landed at Kinsale with the Comte D'Avaux and a French fleet of twenty-two ships, ammunition, money and Irish, English and French officers, but no troops, to attempt unsuccessfully to regain his crown (17).

1690

Cork

In March, Louis XIV sent an army of 7,000 French infantry and some gunners under the Count de Lauzun to aid James, in exchange for 5,387 Irish soldiers under Lord Mountcashel, who went to France as part of the Wild Geese and later formed the nucleus of the Irish Brigade. These French troops were with James at the Boyne and were recalled shortly afterwards (17).

1691

Limerick

In May 1691, Marshal St Ruth arrived with arms and money, but no men, to aid the Jacobite army (17).

1760

Carrickfergus

In February a small invading force under the French commander, Thurot, captured Carrickfergus. Meeting only opposition locally, however, he withdrew and was defeated by a British force.

1796

Bantry Bay

Wolfe Tone, with a French fleet of forty-three ships and 15,000 well-armed troops led by Hoche, left Brest on 15 December 1796. Less than half the force ever came within sight of the coast owing to bad weather, and no landing could be attempted even by those ships that had reached Bantry Bay. They returned to France (19).

1798

Killala Bay

On 22 August 1798, three French ships containing 1,100 men led by General Humbert landed in Killala Bay. Despite success at Castlebar, they were forced to surrender at Ballinamuck where they were defeated by Cornwallis (19).

Lough Swilly

In September a French expedition of about 3,000 troops and with Wolfe Tone on board, sailed from Brest. Many of the ships were captured off the Donegal coast, Tone's ship, the *Hoche*, being forced to surrender in Lough Swilly. Tone was captured, condemned to death and, almost certainly, committed suicide (19).

1916

Kerry

On 20 April a German ship, the *Aud*, containing arms and ammunition for the rebels arrived off the Kerry coast. Due to a communications failure there was no one to meet it; when captured by a British ship and brought into Queenstown harbour the following evening, the ship was scuttled by her captain (20).

Tralee Bay

On 21 April Sir Roger Casement arrived in Tralee Bay, on Banna Strand, on a German submarine; he was put ashore and captured (20).

11   THE VIKING INVASIONS

During the ninth and tenth centuries, Europe was threatened militarily on all sides: from the south by Muslims, from the east by Magyars and from the north by the Vikings of Scandinavia.

The name 'Viking' probably comes from the Old Norse word *vikingr*, a sea-rover or pirate, and it is a generic term given to the Danish, Swedish and Norwegian farmers, fishermen and merchant seamen who became raiders during the eighth century. Often called Northmen or Norse, the Vikings were great warriors and seafarers who used the same military tactics wherever they turned their attention. Using brilliantly designed ships suitable for sailing on oceans, lakes or rivers, they launched raids along the coasts of the British Isles

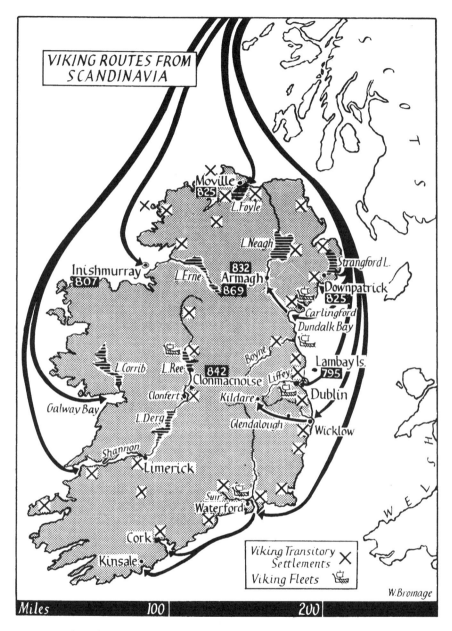

Figure 11 The Viking invasions.

and elsewhere, including the Netherlands, France, Spain, North Africa, Greenland, America and as far east as Moscow and Constantinople. Penetrating the interior of each country by the use of inland waterways, initially they came only to pillage, but ultimately they stayed and were converted to local beliefs and absorbed into the community. Their trading expertise made them valuable members of society.

Vikings are first recorded in Ireland in 795, when they sacked Lambay Island. Sporadic raids continued until 832, when the Vikings began a new phase of systematic and large-scale raids; Figure 11 shows the dates of the first raids. From this period the Vikings began to build fortified settlements throughout the country. Attracted by the wealth of the monasteries and churches, they plundered and ravaged them steadily. Many monks and scholars fled to the Continent, taking with them their most precious possessions.

The invaders established fleets on the main rivers and lakes. In the latter part of the ninth century and the beginning of the tenth, the Viking threat receded for a time, those living in Ireland establishing their settlements and becoming less aggressive, while those outside concentrated their attentions elsewhere. In 914 a new phase of attack and consolidation began with the arrival in Waterford of a great fleet. For much of the century the Vikings ravaged the country and founded new settlements. In the second half of the century, however, the Dál Cais, an east Clare sect, began its rise to power, culminating in Brian Ború's achievement of the high kingship in 1002. Brian benefited from the serious weakening of Viking power that had been brought about by several defeats by Malachy II, his predecessor as high king. In 1014, Brian broke the power of the Vikings permanently at Clontarf (9).

The Vikings continued to develop their role in the Irish community. Although the independent kingdoms they had founded in Dublin, Waterford, Wexford, Cork and Limerick did not survive the Norman invasion, the towns continued to grow and to dominate internal and external trade. As a people, the Vikings quickly became fully absorbed into the religious and political life of Ireland, although their commercial interests kept them centred in their traditional locations in the coastal towns.

12   THE NORMAN INVASION

By 911, the Vikings, or Northmen, had established themselves so powerfully in a large area round the lower Seine that the territory was formally granted to them as the duchy of the Northmen – later to be called Normandy. They achieved a reputation as warriors in their disputes with their neighbours, and in 1016 were invited to southern Italy as mercenaries. By 1030 they had created a principality of their own at Aversa; in 1059 Pope Nicholas II granted them Sicily, Calabria and Apulia. In 1066, William, Duke of Normandy, with only 5,000 men, took the crown of England by force; by 1167, when Dermot MacMurrough, in need of allies to restore him to his kingdom, outlined to

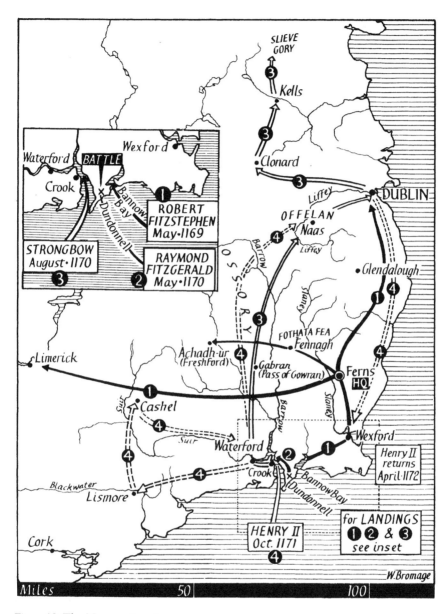

Figure 12 The Norman invasion.

Henry II and his barons the profits to be gained from involving themselves in Irish affairs, the Normans had established a strong kingdom in England and were firmly rooted in Scotland and Wales.

On 1 May 1169, Robert FitzStephen, Meiler FitzHenry and Robert de

Barry, with thirty knights, sixty other horsemen and 300 archers, 'the flower of the youth of Wales', landed at Bannow Bay, in three ships. A contemporary chronicler, Robert Wace, described typical Norman landing tactics. First ashore were the archers, with bow bent and quiver ready, taking up a position on the beach ready for immediate action. Not until a reconnaissance had been completed and the all-clear given would the men-at-arms, all in full equipment, be allowed to disembark with their horses; the cavalry would then ride inland through the screen of archers. Such tactics were typical of the military sophistication of the Normans, which was to bring them to military victory in Ireland despite their inferior numerical strength (13).

On 2 May arrived Maurice de Prendergast, with ten men-at-arms and about 200 archers in two ships. Figure 12 shows the landing places of the main invading armies and traces the more important invasion routes. It should be emphasized that only an indication of direction can be given, not precise itineraries.

The two Norman armies were joined by Dermot MacMurrough, with 500 men, and together they took Wexford. After resting at Ferns, the invading force, now with the addition of a number of Leinstermen and Norse from Wexford – about 3,000 strong – launched an attack on Ossory that met with success despite a spirited defence. Successful expeditions were launched against Offelan and Omurethy (25). Another expedition into Ossory resulted in the defeat of MacGillapatrick at Achadh-ur. At this stage Prendergast seems to have lost enthusiasm for the enterprise and he attempted to return to Wales with his men. When prevented from doing so by MacMurrough, he allied himself with the king of Ossory and caused a great deal of trouble to his erstwhile allies before finally leaving the country.

At this stage the High King, Rory O'Connor, showed unexpected strength in marching into Leinster and forcing MacMurrough to submit to him. He contented himself with taking hostages and exacting from MacMurrough a promise to bring no more foreigners into Ireland and to expel his Norman allies once Leinster was finally subdued. This was a promise that MacMurrough had neither the inclination nor the power to keep.

Late in 1169, two more ships arrived in Wexford, bearing Maurice Fitz-Gerald, FitzStephen's half-brother, with ten knights, thirty mounted retainers and 100 archers. Shortly after this MacMurrough marched towards Dublin and secured the submission of the citizens. Meanwhile FitzStephen led an army to Limerick to attempt an attack on the high king, but was forced back to Leinster.

In May 1170, Raymond FitzGerald (le Gros) arrived with ten knights and seventy archers. Landing at Dundonnell he there defeated the men of Waterford in battle and awaited Strongbow, who arrived in August with 200 knights and 1,000 other troops, accompanied by Maurice de Prendergast, who had been persuaded to return. Until Strongbow's arrival, the invasion had been only partially successful; his intervention was to lead the Norman forces to military triumph. Richard FitzGilbert de Clare, called earl of Striguil and popularly known as Strongbow, was a leading Welsh baron. It had been his original agreement with MacMurrough in 1168 to lend military support in exchange for the succession to the kingship of Leinster that laid the foundations for the Norman invasion and gave it its Welsh character. Landing at Crook, Strongbow joined forces with le Gros to attack and take Waterford. They then joined MacMurrough, who confirmed the alliance by giving his daughter to Strongbow in marriage. Together, they captured Dublin in September and launched attacks on Meath and on O'Rourke's territory, as far as Slieve Gory. MacMurrough then retired to his palace at Ferns, where he died the following year, and Strongbow spent the next year consolidating his military position. After MacMurrough's death the High King besieged Dublin, but was defeated in a surprise attack in September and forced to retire (9).

By the autumn of 1171 Strongbow was master of Dublin, Waterford and Wexford. He was, however, uncomfortably aware that Henry II was intending to intervene to curb his power. Strongbow had already defied an order from Henry to return from Ireland, and had hoped to stave off his wrath by sending a message of loyalty. When Henry arrived in October at Crook with about 4,000 troops in 400 ships, he had two objectives: first to secure the submission of the Irish leaders and second to impose his authority on his own barons. He was successful in both his aims, securing the submission of many of the Irish kings, including MacCarthy, O'Brien and O'Rourke. Although O'Connor and many of the northern kings refused to submit, the High King's resistance was to prove temporary. At a council of Irish bishops in Cashel, fealty was sworn to Henry, and the Irish church was pledged to conform to the practices of the English church (V, 37). Henry restricted Strongbow's power in two ways. Although he granted him Leinster, he removed the towns of Dublin, Wexford and Waterford from his jurisdiction and his pretensions to power were controlled by the appointment as justiciar of Hugh de Lacy, to whom the king granted Meath.

With these grants the conquest became a political reality. Although the military struggle was to continue for centuries, by 1172 the Normans were so strongly entrenched in the east and south-east of the country that there could no longer be any hope of their eventual expulsion. The next century was to prove to be a time of consolidation (13, 26).

13 NORMAN CONSOLIDATION

The contemporary historian, Giraldus Cambrensis, Gerald of Wales, says of the Irish that they 'pay no regard to castles, but use the woods as their strongholds and the marshes as their entrenchments'. The Normans, on the other hand, saw castle-building as a fundamental element in their military strategy. When they took over an area, instead of following the Irish practice of devastating and abandoning the neighbourhood, they consolidated their position by the building of a castle. During the initial stages of the conquest of Ireland, these structures were not castles in the traditional sense, but motes − wooden buildings placed on mounds of earth, surrounded at the base by a ditch. Usually a stockade was constructed beside the mote. Figure 13 shows the distribution of motes, castles and walled towns throughout the country at the end of the thirteenth century. It can be seen that the motes are mainly concentrated in the east and centre of Ireland because they were built during the early stages of the Norman invasion: they were intended as temporary structures only, being easy to erect. Almost all of them were later replaced by stone castles. The Normans appreciated the necessity of ensuring rational distribution of their castles: rather than building isolated castles, they aimed at close intercommunication.

Following the erection of stone castles came the development of surrounding communities. Around the castles were built houses and churches, and from these grew many of the towns of Ireland (73). The Vikings had established the main coastal towns and other towns had developed from major religious centres, but it was the Normans who contributed most to urban development. It is interesting to see the connection between the major castles in Figure 13 and many of the towns that grew around them, for example Carrickfergus, Kildare, Nenagh, Athenry and Athlone. The walled towns marked on Figure 13 all had important castles and were either existing towns fortified by the Normans or new foundations.

The gradual incastellation of Ireland symbolized the steady progress of the Normans in taking over the country. Despite setbacks, they had little difficulty in achieving rapid conquest. Their numerical inferiority was more than compensated for by their military sophistication. In battle they relied on mailed cavalry wielding long swords, skilled Welsh archers armed with the crossbow and experienced Flemish infantry. Against these the Irish could pit only their inadequately clad infantry, who were as inferior in arms as they were in military strategy.

For the first century after the Norman invasion, the Irish fought a losing battle against the conquerors. In 1175 the Treaty of Windsor between Henry II and Rory O'Connor recognized Henry as lord of Ireland and O'Connor as king of Connacht. In 1177 Henry's son John was named 'dominus Hiberniae', lord of Ireland. Simultaneously, Henry granted the kingdom of Desmond to Robert FitzStephen and Milo de Cogan and of Thomond to Philip de Braose, although he reserved the cities of Cork and Limerick for himself. De Braose was unsuccessful in implementing his grant, but FitzStephen and de Cogan captured a considerable area of land in the south, around Cork city.

In 1177 John de Courcy led a small army on Ulster and took a large part of the north-east, having defeated its king, MacDonlevy. He failed at any time, however, to penetrate beyond the Bann. Despite considerable native opposition he quickly built castles in Downpatrick, Dromore, Newry, Coleraine and Carrickfergus. During twenty-seven years as ruler of Ulidia, de Courcy founded monasteries, towns and castles and kept the peace.

In 1185 Prince John arrived in Ireland with an army of over 2,000; with him were Theobald Walter, his butler and founder of the Butler family; William de Burgo, founder of the Burke family; and Bertram de Verdon. To Walter, John granted land in Clare, Offaly, Limerick and Tipperary; to de Burgo, he granted

Figure 13 Norman consolidation: late thirteenth century.

land in Tipperary and Connacht; to de Verdon and Roger Pipard, he granted land in Uriel. Walter failed to conquer Clare, but he built the foundations for the later lordship of Ormond in Tipperary. De Burgo established himself in south Tipperary and his claim to Connacht was not taken up in that generation.

By 1200 the FitzGeralds had received grants of lands in Limerick and Kerry and were building up their Munster possessions at the expense of the MacCarthys.

King John operated on a principle of reducing or diluting the power of his barons in Ireland; he balanced grantees against each other and gave some concessions to the native Irish. In 1205 he confiscated de Courcy's territory and awarded it to the younger Hugh de Lacy as an earldom (though he was later to defeat de Lacy in battle). Throughout his reign he reduced liberties and he also made some grants to the native Irish, like that of Connacht to the O'Connors and Thomond to the O'Briens. He succeeded in altering the purely feudal nature of the Norman occupation by setting up a royal administration.

During the thirteenth century the Normans made continuous attacks on the territories remaining in native Irish hands: in 1235 Connacht was taken by Richard de Burgo, and throughout the country the Normans continued to advance and consolidate. They failed, however, in their attempts on Tirconnell and Tirowen; in Connacht the O'Connors kept the king's cantreds, later called Roscommon. During the second half of the thirteenth century, the native lords began a fight back which flared up in different parts of the country at different times: Connacht was constantly in a state of unrest from about 1280, Leinster from 1283, Meath from 1289. The underlying weakness of the Norman colony was to be strikingly demonstrated by the Bruce invasion in the early fourteenth century (14).

14   THE BRUCE INVASION

One effect of the Norman invasion was to show Irish leaders the necessity for unity in the face of a common enemy. The growing acceptance of this was symbolized in 1263 when a number of Irish chiefs offered the crown of Ireland to King Haakon IV of Norway. Although Haakon's death prevented any follow-up to this, it showed that determination to fight back which from the mid-thirteenth century slowed and even reversed the trend of the Norman advance. The fourteenth century was to see an even more concentrated struggle for control of the country.

In 1314 when the Scots under Robert Bruce decisively defeated the English at Bannockburn, Bruce was in a position to follow up his plan to set up a united Celtic kingdom, by providing a kingdom in Ireland for his restless and ambitious brother Edward. Before Edward's landing in May 1315, Robert had secured the support of Irish chiefs for the venture, so Edward and his 6,000 Scots troops were joined by O'Neill, O'Kane, O'Hanlon, O'Hagan and MacCartan. Marching south, they sacked Dundalk, Ardee and neighbouring

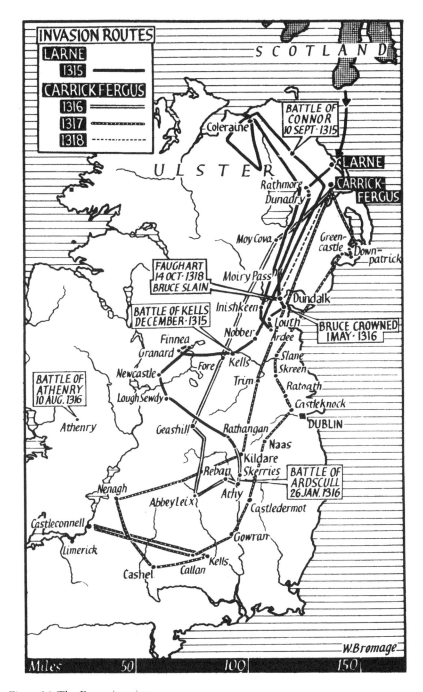

Figure 14 The Bruce invasion.

towns. A gathering of 50,000 opposing forces, led by Richard de Burgo, earl of Ulster, with Felim O'Connor and the justiciar, Edmund Butler, proved abortive, since de Burgo insisted on meeting Bruce independently of Butler, with only 20,000 men. After no more than a brief skirmish, Bruce retreated to Coleraine, where he succeeded in persuading O'Connor to desert de Burgo, whom he defeated shortly afterwards at the battle of Connor.

Bruce now marched south again, taking Nobber and defeating Roger Mortimer, earl of Wigmore and later lord of Meath at Kells; he was joined by many deserting Norman-Irish. Bruce burned Granard, Finnea and Newcastle and advanced to Kildare, where at Ardscull he defeated Butler, FitzThomas and Power.

In Ireland 1316 was a year of famine and disease, exacerbated by the devastation of war. Although the time was propitious for attacking Dublin, Bruce chose instead to return north, taking Athy, Reban, Lea, Geashill, Fore and the castle of Moy Cova on his way, and having himself crowned king of Ireland. He then besieged and took Carrickfergus, which he used from then onwards as his headquarters.

In this same year, Gaelic leaders were making simultaneous attacks on Norman power in Ireland. Aodh O'Donnell and Felim O'Connor had initial success in Connacht, supported by the O'Briens, O'Rourkes and other local chieftains. However, at Athenry in August, the de Burgos won a complete victory that established permanently their pre-eminence in Connacht. The simultaneous attacks of the O'Mores, O'Tooles and O'Byrnes in Laois and Wicklow were inconclusive, but irritating to the Dublin government.

Robert Bruce arrived in Carrickfergus with a large army to aid his brother; in February 1317 they set out to march south. On their route they devastated Downpatrick (where they destroyed the monastery), Greencastle, Slane, Skreen and Ratoath (where they were challenged unsuccessfully by the earl of Ulster). Advancing to Castleknock, the Scots were discouraged from attacking by the defences of Dublin and instead they marched, leaving the usual legacy of destruction, through the south-east as far south as Cashel and as far west as Castleconnell, and back to Carrickfergus, from whence Robert returned to Scotland. Their progress had been virtually without incident, although it had inspired sporadic Gaelic risings in the south. Roger Mortimer, who had been appointed justiciar, had landed at Youghal in April with a large force, but had offered no opposition to the Bruces.

During 1317 Mortimer concentrated on strengthening his position in the south, regaining conquered lands and making peace with Gaelic chiefs. Pope John XXII supported Edward II by excommunicating Bruce's allies. In September 1318, tired of inaction and intending another southern march, Bruce advanced on Dundalk, but at Faughart he was defeated and killed by an army led by John de Bermingham and the primate of Armagh.

With Bruce's death ended the dream of an independent Celtic kingdom – a dream which had brought so much economic and social disaster to Ireland. Nevertheless, his invasion had shown how vulnerable was the Norman colony and had prevented its exploitation by Edward II for the war against Scotland. Tactically, however, Bruce had shown little ability. He failed to consolidate his successes and contented himself with inflicting widespread devastation on the country he hoped to rule. Few, even of his allies, mourned his death.

15 THE NINE YEARS WAR

Queen Elizabeth was determined to Anglicize Ireland and she proceeded steadily throughout her reign towards this objective. By the end of the sixteenth century Leinster, Munster and Connacht had been subdued and the Ulster lords, who had maintained almost total independence over the centuries, began to feel threatened: they were not prepared to see their lands subject to English law and administration and their power reduced. Their anxiety was exacerbated in 1591 by the government's completion of a surrender and re-grant treaty with the neighbouring MacMahons and MacKennas in Monaghan (54) on which, from 1593, Hugh Maguire and Hugh O'Donnell began sporadic raids. In August 1594 they defeated an English army at the 'Ford of the Biscuits' and thereby declared themselves to be in open revolt.

Ulster was uniquely situated for such a rebellion. There were only three ways into the province: the Moyry Pass and the fords of the Erne. Hugh O'Neill, earl of Tyrone, who joined the rebellion openly in 1595, had built up an efficient army with, in addition to his own men, Scottish mercenaries (galloglas) and Irish mercenaries (bonnachta). At Clontibret he defeated an English force under Sir Henry Bagenal (9) and in June he was proclaimed a traitor. Despite this, he made a truce with the government that lasted from October 1595 to April 1596, when peace was declared, all the rebels being pardoned. While paying lip-service to the peace, O'Neill was simultaneously negotiating for Spanish aid and securing the support of several southern chiefs.

In May 1597 the war was renewed, with the Dublin administration suffering such severe defeats on the northern front at Ballyshannon that they agreed to a further truce, which lasted until June 1598.

In August O'Neill and O'Donnell, with Ulster and Connacht troops, defeated Bagenal decisively at the Yellow Ford (9) and thus inspired risings throughout the country. Until April 1599 the English hesitated to make any move against the rebels, but in that month arrived Sir Robert Devereux, earl of Essex and favourite of the queen, with an army of over 17,000. His first action was to march south. On this march his army suffered from guerrilla attacks and disease, a combination that served to reduce his active troops by three-quarters, although it proved uneventful in that it yielded no opportunity for the major engagements he sought. Simultaneously O'Donnell was increasing his power in Connacht, successfully besieging the O'Connor Sligo at Collooney and having a major victory over English forces at the Curlew Hills.

A second brief expedition by Essex had an equal lack of success and in September he marched to the ford of Bellaclinthe where he made a truce with

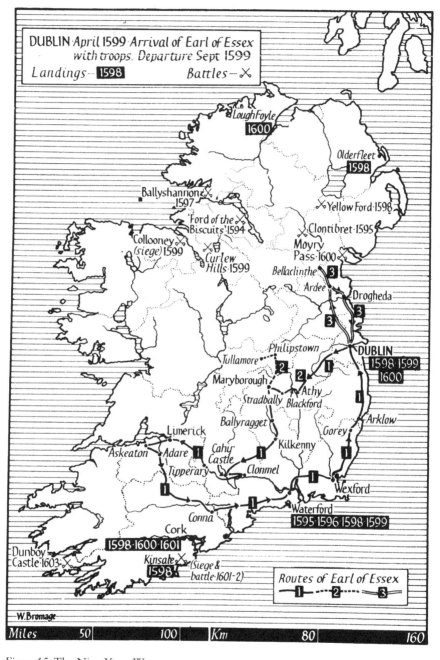

Figure 15 The Nine Years War.

1640

O'Neill that lasted until the end of 1599. Essex returned discredited to England and eventual execution.

By January 1600, having again made use of the period of truce to rearm and strengthen his army, O'Neill ravaged the barony of Delvin in Westmeath. In February 1600 arrived the fateful figure of Charles Blount, Lord Mountjoy, Lord Deputy, with an army of 20,000. With the aid of the new President of Munster, Sir George Carew, the Munster rising was soon crushed and Leinster and Connacht quieted: the English generals could now concentrate on the north. Many of the minor chiefs, scenting defeat, deserted O'Neill's cause and he found himself under severe pressure from new and reinforced garrisons. The English troops were gaining ground in their assaults on Ulster, and at the Moyry Pass they succeeded in forcing the retreat of Irish troops (9). Meanwhile O'Neill anxiously awaited the promised troops from Spain for which he had so long been negotiating.

The Spaniards, when they eventually arrived, landed at Kinsale in September 1601 with a small force (10). O'Neill and O'Donnell marched to join them, securing the help of O'Sullivan Beare and O'Driscoll of Kerry. At the battle of Kinsale, Mountjoy, with inferior numbers, won a decisive victory over the combined Spanish and Irish forces, after which O'Donnell fled to Spain. Some of the Irish made a last stand at Dunboy Castle, not yielding until 1603, and O'Neill, who had returned to Ulster to stand his own ground, eventually submitted to Mountjoy in March 1603.

O'Neill's submission symbolized the end of the Gaelic lordship and a new period of complete English domination of Ireland. Although the Irish had fought with determination and uncharacteristic unity, and although in O'Neill they had a leader of unusual diplomatic cunning and military ability, the English had proved to be indefatigable in warfare. Elizabeth succeeded where her predecessors had failed. Although normally parsimonious in her dealings with Ireland, she was sufficiently pragmatic to see the need in the 1590s for enough money and manpower to ensure its subjugation. Over a seven-year period more than a dozen massive troop landings were made (see Figure 15) and Elizabeth's best generals were sent to lead them. She appreciated the strategic importance of Ireland at a time of Continental warfare (10) and acted accordingly.

16 THE 1640s: THE CONFEDERATION AND CROMWELL

By the 1640s, Ireland was ripe for rebellion. During the reign of James I (1603–25) his plantations (55) had resulted in the dispossession of many Gaelic and Old English families and the introduction to Ulster of a new colonial population. With the accession of Charles I, the Catholic Old English hoped to reach an agreement with the King that would guarantee them secure possession of their lands and a measure of religious freedom. In 1628 an agreement was made by which, in exchange for £120,000, concessions on land and religion known as

1640

the 'Graces' were to be made by the King. Although the money was paid, the Graces were never legally confirmed and this was to prove a serious source of discontent.

In 1633 a new lord deputy, Sir Thomas Wentworth (later Earl of Strafford), arrived in Ireland. His mission was to make Ireland economically viable and this he achieved in considerable measure through his encouragement of industry and mercantile shipping and the virtual eradication of piracy (IX). Despite these successes he succeeded in alienating almost every element in Irish society: his refusal to grant the Graces in their agreed form alienated the Catholic Irish and Old English, as did the threat to their lands posed by his abortive plans for a plantation in Connacht and Clare; members of the Church of Ireland were affronted by his radical ecclesiastical reforms and his importation of Englishmen to fill important ecclesiastical offices; Scots Dissenters suffered considerable harassment, which was all the more resented because of the degree of toleration then being extended unofficially to the Catholics; and, additionally, he imposed heavy fines and confiscations upon colonial settlers who had infringed the terms of the plantation settlement.

When Strafford's enemies finally united to bring about his downfall and execution, Charles attempted to placate the dissident elements in Ireland by a number of conciliatory measures, including the granting of many of the Graces and the abandonment of the proposed plantations. The increasing importance of the Puritan elements in the Irish parliament, however, coupled with the attitude of the two powerful Puritan lords justices, Sir William Parsons and Sir John Borlase, would negate the effect of these measures – most notably in 1641 when the prorogation of parliament by the Lords Justices prevented the legalization of the Graces. Simultaneously, the severe rifts between Charles and his parliament became known in Ireland, and Charles's abortive secret negotiations with the earls of Ormond and Antrim to secure military aid against parliament set the scene for a rebellion designed to take advantage of a confused situation.

In October 1641 Sir Felim O'Neill, Rory O'More and Lord Maguire led a rising of native Irish. Although their plans to take Dublin failed, there was widespread revolt in Leinster and a takeover of the whole province of Ulster. The resulting bloodshed and destruction were considerable, although subsequently exaggerated out of all proportion by the Dublin government for propaganda purposes.

The government responded with panic and incompetence; although it was promised reinforcements by the English parliament, the timescale was too long to enable it to take effective action. By December 1641 many of the Old English, despising the inept administration and conscious of being viewed as disloyal because of their religion, joined with the Irish rebels, from whom they had secured a declaration of loyalty to the crown. The English parliament passed an act known as the 'Adventurers Act', which provided for the repayment in Irish land of money advanced to help quell the Irish rebellion (56).

During the course of 1642 Scottish troops under General Monro arrived to aid the suppression of the rebellion, but for a time the military success of the

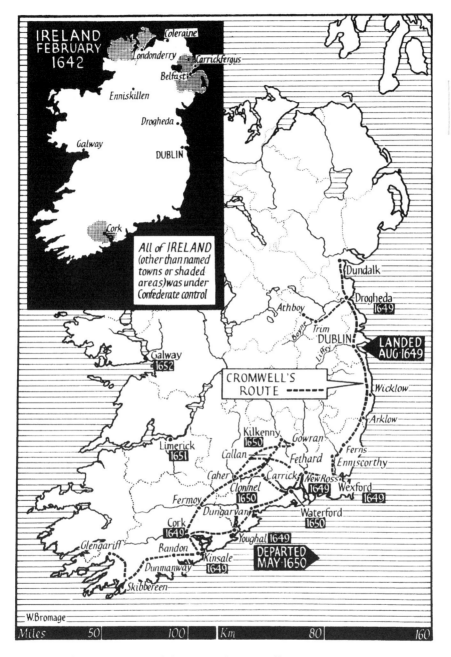

Figure 16 The 1640s: the Confederation and Cromwell.

rebels continued. By February 1642 virtually all of the country was in their hands (see inset map in Figure 16). Later in the year they set up in Kilkenny a provisional government with elected representatives; henceforward they were known as 'the Confederate Catholics of Ireland', their motto being 'Pro Deo, pro rege, pro patria Hibernia unanimis'. Despite this lip-service to unity, there were deep divisions among the Confederates: the Old English were dominated by their loyalty to the King and wished for a quick ending to the war, while the Irish were more concerned to recover lands long since confiscated and wished to see the war through to the bitter end. This disunity was symbolized by the divided command that ensued when Owen Roe O'Neill and Thomas Preston, who had been serving abroad, arrived to aid the rebels. O'Neill commanded a Gaelic-Irish army in Ulster, and Preston an Old English army in Leinster. Their mutual jealousy accentuated the divisions of the Confederates and prevented any real cooperation.

Throughout the rest of the decade the Confederates were never again to equal their earlier successes. Ormond, on behalf of the King, succeeded in 1643 in negotiating with them a truce for one year, which was, however, rejected by the Ulster Protestants and the Munster parliamentarians under Murrough O'Brien, Lord Inchiquin. The disunity among the Confederates was matched by that among their enemies: the war was waged on a provincial rather than a national basis.

In August 1645 a secret treaty between the Confederates and an emissary of King Charles, Lord Glamorgan, promised full religious toleration in exchange for military support against the English parliament. When the treaty became public knowledge, however, Charles repudiated it, and negotiations came to an end, although Ormond continued to negotiate for peace.

In October 1645, the Papal Nuncio, Giovanni Battista Rinuccini, arrived in Ireland; he was to destroy all Ormond's hopes of a peaceful settlement. He maintained an intransigent attitude, insisting that throughout areas under Confederate control the Catholic church should be the only established church, and he gave support to O'Neill and the extremist clerical party. O'Neill's victory at Benburb (9) against Monro gave hope of ultimate victory, but he failed to follow up this success effectively. Under severe pressure in Dublin, Ormond saw that he would have to surrender the city either to the Confederates or to the English parliament. It was to the latter that he transferred his command in June 1647 before leaving Ireland and going into exile.

Subsequently the Confederates had increasing setbacks: Preston was defeated at Dungan's Hill (9) and Inchiquin scored a great victory at Knocknanuss (9). The Confederates agreed to a truce in May 1648 and were excommunicated by Rinuccini, who, however, was discredited and left Ireland early in 1649. A realignment then occurred: Inchiquin adopted the royalist cause and with the Confederates agreed to serve the monarchy under Ormond, who returned from abroad. After some initial successes, Ormond suffered a defeat by Michael Jones at Rathmines (9) that paved the way for the Cromwellian conquest.

In August Cromwell arrived in Ireland, impatient to end the civil war and determined to punish the rebels. His initial expedition was northwards, where after a successful siege of Drogheda his army massacred the garrison, clergy and some of the townspeople; the Dundalk and Trim garrisons fled on hearing the news. Cromwell turned south where he met initial resistance from the Wexford garrison; the slaughter that again followed a successful siege broke the spirit of the resistance. Before the end of 1649 he had taken several towns, including New Ross, Youghal, Cork, Kinsale and Bandon. Cromwell's only check came in Waterford, which, with the help of reinforcements, successfully resisted his siege. In the spring he moved northwards again, taking Kilkenny and Clonmel. By May he felt sufficiently confident of victory to leave the rest of the conquest of Ireland to his lieutenants, Broghill in Munster, Coote in Ulster and Henry Ireton at the head of the main army. By May 1652 the last royalist stronghold, Galway, had surrendered and the whole country was subdued.

This subjugation had been bought at a heavy price; famine and disease were rampant throughout the country. Ormond, Preston and Inchiquin had left Ireland in 1650 and O'Neill was dead. The decade had seen the collapse of the rebellion because of traditional Irish military and political failings: the members of the Confederacy were disunited in their objectives and military strategy; their leadership suffered from personal jealousies; and they overestimated their resources. The intervention of Rinuccini had exacerbated divisions and ruined any chance of an early alliance with Ormond. By the time Cromwell arrived in Ireland the war was already lost and resistance was half-hearted. In the face of a determined and disciplined enemy, defeat was inevitable.

17   STUART AND ORANGE

After the restoration of the monarchy in 1660, Irish Catholics hoped not just for toleration but for preferential treatment; they felt threatened by the fast-expanding Protestant community that was being swelled by a steady influx of Dissenters (40). Under Charles II (1660–85), Catholics had a limited degree of toleration, but with the succession to the throne of James II their position changed dramatically. In 1686, a Catholic, Richard Talbot, Earl of Tyrconnell, became commander of the army in Ireland and later chief governor. By 1688 Roman Catholics were dominant in the army, the administration, the judiciary and the town corporations and by the end of that year Protestant power in Ireland was seriously weakened. When William of Orange landed in England in November 1688 to relieve his father-in-law of his throne, James fled to France but soon left for Ireland, which by now was for him a natural base from which to launch his counter-attack.

By the time of James's arrival in Ireland, in March 1689, only Londonderry and Enniskillen were in Protestant hands. Londonderry had repulsed an attempt of Tyrconnell's to garrison the town with a royal army the previous December, when a group of apprentice boys, in a famous incident much heralded in

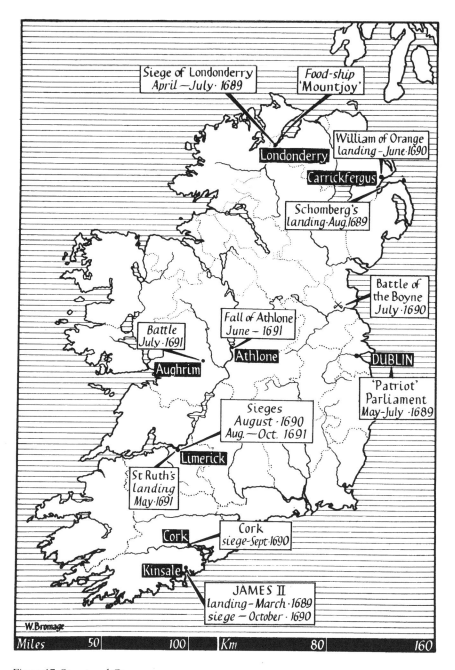

Siege of Londonderry
April — July · 1689

Food-ship
'Mountjoy'

Londonderry

William of Orange
landing — June · 1690

Carrickfergus

Schomberg's
landing · Aug. 1689

Battle of
the Boyne
July · 1690

Fall of Athlone
June — 1691

Battle
July · 1691

Athlone

Aughrim

DUBLIN

'Patriot'
Parliament
May–July · 1689

Sieges
August · 1690
Aug. — Oct. 1691

Limerick

St Ruth's
landing
May · 1691

Cork

Cork
siege — Sept · 1690

Kinsale

JAMES II
landing — March · 1689
siege — October · 1690

W. Bromage

| Miles | 50 | | 100 | Km | | 80 | 160 |

Figure 17 Stuart and Orange.

James — Jacobit
Wm - Stuarts

Orange songs, shut the gates in the face of the troops. The town was James's first objective, and he besieged it in April; militarily unequipped to force the siege, the Jacobites hoped to starve the city into surrender. There were 30,000 inhabitants and food supplies were low, yet despite numerous deaths from starvation during the fifteen weeks of the siege, the besieged proved indomitable in their resistance. On July 28 the food ship *Mountjoy* forced its way through the barriers built across the Foyle; this military and moral victory was of enormous significance in the campaign.

Shortly after this, Marshal Schomberg, William's general, landed near Belfast, besieged and took the Jacobite-held city of Carrickfergus and settled to await reinforcements. He concentrated on consolidating his position in Ulster and avoided any direct confrontation with James. Apart from holding a parliament in Dublin which repealed the Penal Laws against Catholics and in effect transferred almost all the land of Ireland back to Catholic ownership (30), James was inactive during this period. He remained in Dublin until William's arrival at Carrickfergus in June 1690, when he decided to confront him at the Boyne (9). William's triumph in this battle was a result of his military superiority, which was based both on strategy and on numbers.

James left Ireland at maximum speed, leaving Tyrconnell in command of the army. The Jacobite forces had to retreat westwards to Limerick, where they were unsuccessfully besieged by William, who returned to England leaving General Ginkel in command. Ginkel took little action until June 1691, during which time the Williamite commander Marlborough had captured Cork and Kinsale, and the Jacobite commander St Ruth had landed with arms and supplies at Limerick. Ginkel took the town of Athlone and won the battle of Aughrim in June and July, after two military engagements in which famous stories of courage on the Jacobite side have provided inspiration to Irish nationalist poets and musicians. The second siege of Limerick resulted in an early Jacobite surrender and the signing of the Treaty of Limerick (57).

An important military result of the defeat was the mass exodus of Jacobite officers and men: 11,000 sailed to France and joined the army, in which they formed the famous Irish Brigade. This Brigade and others formed in European armies were reinforced throughout the next century by thousands of Irishmen, known in song and legend as the Wild Geese.

The Stuart–Orange war is of particular contemporary interest in Ireland: the siege of Londonderry and the battle of the Boyne have a present-day significance enjoyed by no other Irish military encounters. They have been re-fought in the streets of Belfast and Derry in every clash between Catholic and Protestant; they are symbolized in every Orange parade.

18   THE IRISH MILITIA

After the defeat of the Jacobites in 1691, there was little appetite in Ireland for active resistance. The military-minded left the country to fight in foreign armies: it is estimated that at least half a million Irishmen joined the French army alone between 1691 and 1791.

During the eighteenth century, however, there were aggressive incidents perpetrated by secret societies formed by peasants throughout the country. Their origin was resentment at the loss of common pasturage for raising cattle, which was encouraged by the lifting in 1759 of restrictions on the export of Irish cattle to England (68). The Whiteboys were the most widespread of these groups, although the Hearts of Oak and the Hearts of Steel were also important. All were concerned with local agrarian problems, and were swift and brutal in meting out their particular notions of justice. In Ulster, peasant movements were dominated by sectarian land disputes. The Defenders were the main Catholic society: their Protestant equivalents were the Peep O'Day Boys (XI).

Despite the lack of any other signs of military activity in the country, fears of invasion by France and Spain, coupled with agrarian crime and the absence of any militia, led to the formation of a number of volunteer forces throughout the country. By 1780 the Volunteers had reached an estimated strength of 40,000 and were still growing; they were unpaid and equipped themselves with arms and uniforms. After the lapsing of the Continental military threats of the 1770s and 1780s, they turned their attention to political reform (30). By the mid–1780s, however, their influence was on the wane and they ceased to be a significant force in Irish politics.

In the early 1790s, alarmed by the French Revolution, fearing foreign invasion but unwilling to risk a resurgence of Volunteer activity, the government determined to set up a proper militia. The force had a proposed complement of 16,000, and was virtually full-time, being composed mainly of Irish peasants and artisans, although there was a significant number of English non-commissioned officers. Officers were usually Protestant, although overall Catholics were in a majority of about three to one.

As an aid to discipline, units were quartered away from the county of their origin, and these quarters were changed frequently. Figure 18 shows the distribution of militia companies in 1794 and the number raised in each county. It is interesting to see, for example, that although Dublin contributed fourteen companies, it quartered only one, while Cork, which contributed twenty-four, quartered seventy-one. The disruption caused by such companies in many rural communities was considerable.

In 1796, responding to doubts about the loyalty of the militia, the government set up a part-time yeomanry force, which within two years had reached about 40,000. Being mainly made up of landlords and their own tenants, it was largely Protestant.

When, in 1798, the rising put both the yeomanry and the militia to the loyalty test, there appears to have been little difference in their performance. Allegations of brutality were made against both forces, and it is clear that the rebels received no mercy from their co–religionists (19).

Despite its loyalty, the militia did not survive long. In 1801 recruitment and re-enlistment were stopped, and in 1802 the force was disembodied. Although

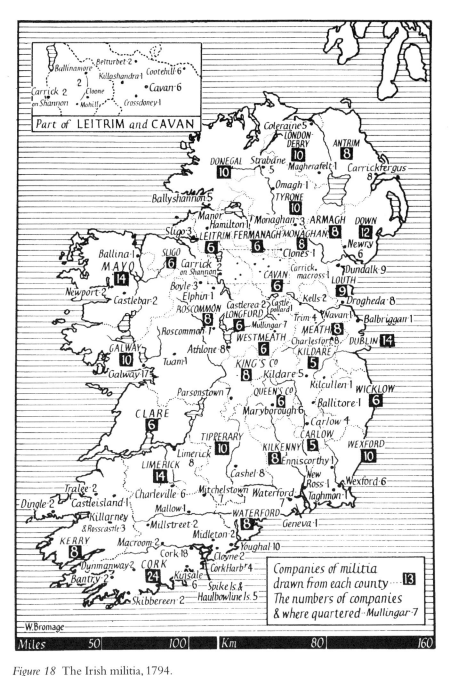

Figure 18 The Irish militia, 1794.

it was later re-embodied and survived until its eventual dissolution in 1816, the changes in policy caused a great deal of hardship to members of the militia. Many of them joined the British army, which had about 150,000 Irish recruits from 1793 to 1815. The army, like the yeomanry and the militia, was a useful source of employment for landless peasants (49).

19   THE 1798 RISING

The virtual disbandment of the Volunteers (18) and the consequent political frustrations felt by many of its members provided inspiration for the formation of the United Irishmen. The French Revolution had had a considerable influence on Irish popular opinion, many elements of which wanted religious equality and radical extension of the franchise. Under the leadership of Theobald Wolfe Tone, the Society of United Irishmen was founded in Belfast in 1791 to pursue these policies. The society contained the rump of the Volunteers, who were mainly middle class; other societies were founded throughout the country. The leadership included Lord Edward Fitzgerald, Thomas Addis Emmet, James Napper Tandy and Henry Joy McCracken.

Various government attempts at conciliation were ineffectual. The outbreak of war between France and England and the suppression of the Volunteers in 1793 led to a hardening of attitude among the United Irishmen, many of whom favoured an alliance with France; by 1795 the society was pledged to republicanism. In 1796, in an attempt to prevent rebellion or invasion, the government introduced repressive measures that included the suspension of *habeas corpus*. As Defenders flocked to join the United Irishmen and the rank and file became largely Catholic peasants, its anti-sectarian nature was undermined. Tone had been exerting pressure on the French Directory to mount an invasion of Ireland and in December the unsuccessful *Hoche* expedition (10) was launched. Increasingly brutal attempts were made by militia and yeomanry alike to stamp out sedition. In Ulster, under General Lake, successful efforts were made to set Orangemen against the United Irishmen; many joined the yeomanry, although a few Presbyterians were sympathetic to the rebels. Martial law was declared in March 1797 and the brutality of the troops increased; several Presbyterian ministers were among those executed.

The continual pressure forced the society to plan for an early rebellion. However, government spies were effective and two months before the proposed date, many of the leaders, including Addis Emmet, were arrested; Fitzgerald was captured later and died in prison.

On 23 May 1798 the rebellion broke out. The United Irishmen leaders had believed they could count on an army of over a quarter of a million, of whom over 100,000 would be from Ulster. In the event, in the absence of the leadership and a central plan, risings broke out locally without coherence. The first revolts were in Leinster, in Meath, Dublin, Kildare, Carlow and Wicklow; many

GENERAL
HARDY
Lough Swilly

ANTRIM
Glenarm
Larne
Ballymena•
Randalstown•
Antrim
Bangor
New-
townards
Comber
Ballynahinch•
DOWN

GENERAL
HUMBERT
Killala Bay

Killala•
Crossmolina
Colloney•
Lough
Allen
Foxford•
Drumshanbo•
Cloone
Ballina-
muck
Castlebar

MEATH
Navan
Tara

DUBLIN

KILDARE
Naas
Rathangan
Kildare•
Kilcullen
Narraghmore•
Dunlavin
Ballitore•
Stratford
WICKLOW
Baltinglass
Arklow

CARLOW
Carnew•
Gorey
Ferns•
Camolin
Enniscorthy
WEXFORD
×Vinegar
Hill
New Ross•
Wexford

Navan
Tara•
Naul
Dunshaughlin
Dunboyne
Kilcock
Leixlip•
Lucan
DUBLIN
Clane
Rathcoole
Rathfarnham
Prosperous
Tallaght
Dalkey
•Naas
Kilcullen
Curragh

Abortive
risings } Italic underlined

W. Bromage

Miles   50   100   Km   80   160

Figure 19 The 1798 rising.

of these proved abortive, but even those that achieved some success were quickly crushed. The most significant outbreak was in Wexford, where the insurgency lasted from 25 May to early July. The most notable incidents were the capture by insurgents of Enniscorthy and all of county Wexford except New Ross. The worst atrocity was the burning to death of more than 100 government supporters including women and children in a barn at Scullabogue. The beginning of the end came with the battle of Vinegar Hill, where the rebels were defeated (9).

In Ulster there were two main risings, neither of which lasted more than a week; in Antrim about 6,000 men were led by McCracken, but they were quickly defeated; in Down Henry Munro led an army of about 7,000 in another unsuccessful action. Both McCracken and Munro were executed.

On 22 August the French landed at Killala Bay and had some short-lived success (10). In late September another unsuccessful French expedition with Tone on board entered Lough Swilly (10).

Roy Foster described the 1798 rising as 'probably the most concentrated episode of violence in Irish history'. There were mass atrocities perpetrated by both sides, about 30,000 people died and over £1 million worth of property was destroyed. After this rebellion and that of Robert Emmet in 1803 (III), the government extended its military precautions. Among defensive measures taken was the building of military roads, including one across the Dublin and Wicklow mountains. During the Napoleonic wars, increased fears of foreign invasion led to the widespread construction of Martello towers along the Irish coastline.

Apart from the destruction of the United Irishmen and the consequent discrediting of the ideals of fraternity and religious equality that had been at the base of its thinking, an immediate consequence of the rising was to increase pressure for union between Ireland and Britain. As the final irony, the main result of the 1798 rising was to bind Ireland closer to Britain for more than another century.

20   THE 1916 RISING

In 1912 Prime Minister Asquith introduced the third Home Rule Bill for Ireland; this eventually received the royal assent in September 1914, although it was suspended for the duration of the First World War. By this time, however, the Ulster Unionists had established the Ulster Volunteers with the aim of using 'all means which may be found necessary to defeat the present conspiracy to set up a Home Rule Parliament in Ireland'. In 1913 Eoin MacNeill had founded the Irish Volunteers as a counter-force and John Redmond and his political party (32) had become closely involved with it. Both forces were armed with smuggled weapons. There was also the tiny Irish Citizen Army, formed in November 1913 during the Dublin lockout and controlled by the Marxist labour leader James Connolly.

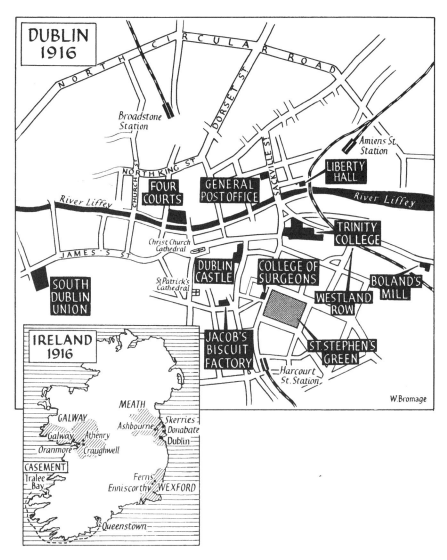

Figure 20 The 1916 rising.

With the outbreak of war, Redmond urged the Irish Volunteers to join the British army. MacNeill left the organization, taking between 3,000 and 10,000 men with him, and retained the name. The 150,000 or so who remained became the National Volunteers (49). Fears of conscription led to increased support for the radical nationalist Sinn Féin ('Ourselves') movement – founded in 1905 by Arthur Griffith and committed to cultural, economic and political self-sufficiency – and gave a fresh impetus to the activities of the Irish

Sinn
Fein
1905

Republican Brotherhood (IRB), a secret society with about 2,000 members, many of whom were in key positions in the Irish Volunteers. IRB leaders began talks with German leaders and Sir Roger Casement and Joseph Plunkett visited Berlin. Expecting a German breakthrough in the European war, the IRB Military Council, without the knowledge of many of the executive but with the cooperation of Connolly, who allowed his nationalism to transcend his Marxism, planned an Easter 1916 rising, for which German arms were promised. In April Casement left Germany in a submarine that was to rendezvous with the German arms ship, the *Aud*. The plan failed and when Casement landed on Banna Strand on 21 April with two companions, they were captured; on the same day, the *Aud*'s captain scuttled the ship to avoid capture.

MacNeill, only now made aware of the plot, then banned the Volunteer parade scheduled for Easter Sunday that had been intended to provide the opportunity for the rising. However, the Military Council of the IRB – Eamon Ceannt, Thomas Clarke, James Connolly, Sean MacDermott, Thomas MacDonagh, Patrick Pearse and Joseph Plunkett – decided to go ahead; on Monday, 24 April at midday the rising began. There were five battalions in Dublin, MacDonagh being brigade commandant.

1st Battalion: Commandant Edward Daly, at the head of about 120 men, occupied the Four Courts and set up barricades to the north and west.

2nd Battalion: Commandant MacDonagh occupied Jacob's Biscuit Factory, while some of his men joined the force in the General Post Office (GPO). They failed to follow the plan that required them to place barricades to the north-east.

3rd Battalion: Commandant Eamon de Valera, at the head of about 130 men, occupied Boland's Mill and Westland Row Railway Station, and set up barricades and outposts to the south, one being at Mount Street Bridge.

4th Battalion: Commandant Ceannt, at the head of about 130 men, occupied the South Dublin Union Workhouse and set up outposts to the east and south-east.

5th Battalion: Commandant Thomas Ashe led a force drawn from north county Dublin, which operated outside the city. They took Skerries and Donabate and attacked Ashbourne.

The Irish Citizen Army split into three sections.

Section 1:   Commandant Michael Mallin and Countess (Constance) Markievicz, at the head of about 100 men, occupied the College of Surgeons and set up outposts in Harcourt Street Station and at Portobello Canal Bridge.

Section 2:   Under Commandant Sean Connolly, about fifty men took up key positions near the entrance to Dublin Castle.

Section 3:   About seventy men joined with some sixty Volunteers and – under the leadership of Connolly, Pearse and Plunkett – occupied the GPO.

When Pearse proclaimed an Irish Republic from the GPO, he styled himself President of the Provisional Government and Commandant-in-Chief of the Army, with Connolly becoming Commandant-General of the Dublin Districts.

Throughout the course of the insurrection, fewer than 2,000 insurgents were involved at any time in Dublin. There was little action elsewhere. In Leinster there were only Ashe's skirmishes outside the city and some activity in Wexford, led by Paul Galligan. In Galway, there were some unsuccessful skirmishes initiated by the force of about 500–600 led by Liam Mellows.

From the start the rebellion had no chance of success. The insurgents were underarmed, and poor communications and contradictory orders had virtually restricted the action to Dublin and drastically reduced the numbers taking part.

Although at the outbreak of the rebellion there were only 2,500 troops in Dublin, reinforcements arriving from other parts of Ireland and from England brought a speedy conclusion to the insurrection by shelling most of the city centre to ruins. Pearse ordered a surrender on 29 April.

The casualties of the rising were 450 deaths (116 soldiers, sixteen policemen, seventy-six insurgents and 242 civilians) and over 2,600 injured, mostly civilians.

Sixteen of the rebels were executed:

3 May: Thomas J. Clarke, Thomas MacDonagh, Patrick Pearse
4 May: Edward Daly, Michael O'Hanrahan, William Pearse, Joseph Plunkett
5 May: John MacBride
8 May: Eamonn Ceannt, Cornelius Colbert, Sean J. Heuston, Michael Mallin
9 May: Thomas Kent
12 May: James Connolly, Sean MacDermott
3 August: Sir Roger Casement

The British response to an insurrection in time of war was harsh enough to alienate Irish public opinion but too mild to smash violent nationalism. The executions were to rebound on the British government in the 1918 election, since they swung the sympathy of the electorate behind the revolutionaries rather than the constitutionalists. Another action that was to secure sympathy for the rebels was the arrest of around 3,400 men and women following the insurrection. Most of them were released within a month and by the end of 1916 only a small hard core – regarded as heroes – were still interned in prison camps in Britain. The appointment of the uncompromising Lord French as viceroy in May 1918 alienated public opinion still further. He placed a number of revolutionary leaders under arrest, including de Valera, Arthur Griffith and

Countess Markievicz, many of whom had been in prison from May 1916 until their release a year later; their reimprisonment was extremely unpopular with the country as a whole. However, the major reason why nationalism became radicalized was the British government's threat in April 1918 that conscription would be imposed on Ireland; the massive anti-conscription campaign that followed culminated in the sweeping victory of Sinn Féin (32) in the election of December 1918.

21 THE WAR OF INDEPENDENCE (ANGLO-IRISH WAR)

In 1918 the Irish Volunteers, reorganized since the 1916 rebellion (20), were about 100,000 strong. There were divisions within the movement between those who – though prepared to resist conscription by the use of force – hoped for a negotiated settlement of the claim to independence, and those who believed that only physical force could bring about separation from Britain.

The threat of conscription disappeared with the conclusion of the armistice in November 1918 and, coupled with the political success of Sinn Féin in the December election (32), led to a dwindling in the ranks of Irish Volunteers. Some of the believers in physical force took matters into their own hands: on 21 January 1919, under the leadership of Sean Treacy and Dan Breen, a handful of Tipperary Volunteers killed two Royal Irish Constabulary (RIC) men in an ammunition raid at Soloheadbeg. Others followed suit and during 1919 sporadic arms raids and murders of policemen were carried out.

By the end of 1919 morale in the RIC was low and numerical weakness was forcing the evacuation of outlying barracks. The British government encouraged the recruitment of ex-servicemen into the RIC and by March 1920 these were beginning to arrive in Ireland. Inadequately trained and badly disciplined, these British recruits in the early days had not even a proper uniform; their mixture of khaki and black outfits earned them the nickname of Black and Tans. They were joined in August by a force of ex-officers known as the Auxiliary Division, RIC. They met terror with counter-terror, raids with reprisals; during 1920 and 1921 the violence and brutality escalated on both sides.

By June 1921 the Volunteers – who had come to be known as the Irish Republican Army (Óglaigh na hÉireann) – had about 4,500 members interned and around 2,000 on active service. They were matched against almost 40,000 troops, and just over 14,200 RIC and 2,200 Auxiliaries. While they could not hope to win a military victory, the IRA's pertinacity, combined with international criticism, had finally convinced Lloyd George of the need to compromise. In July 1921 a truce was declared: treaty negotiations began in October (34).

During the two years of the war some popular heroes had emerged. Terence MacSwiney, Lord Mayor of Cork, had died on hunger strike in an English jail.

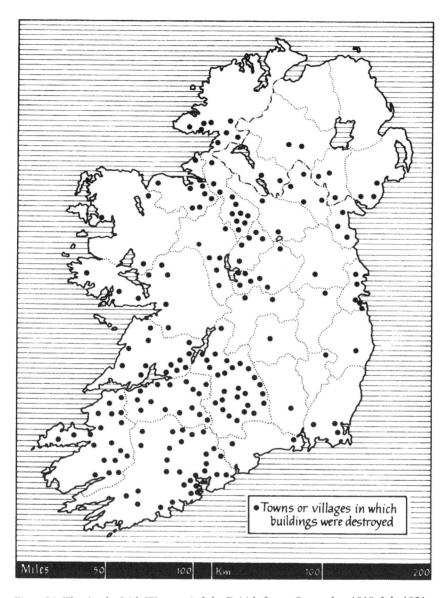

Figure 21 The Anglo-Irish War: reprisals by British forces, September 1919–July 1921.
Source E. Rumpf and A. C. Hepburn (1977) *Nationalism and Socialism in Twentieth-Century Ireland.*

Kevin Barry, an eighteen-year-old medical student, had been hanged for his part in a raid in which six soldiers were killed. As director of intelligence of the Volunteers/IRA, with the aid of his network of spies, informers and assassins, Michael Collins had waged a vicious war but had shown fine leadership and great personal courage. About 1,400 people (624 British security forces and around 550 IRA) had been killed and both sides had committed atrocities (on 'Bloody Sunday', 21 November 1920, Collins's 'squad' assassinated fourteen intelligence agents, in retaliation, the Black and Tans killed twelve and wounded sixty at Croke Park) and engaged in gratuitous destruction, for instance the burning of a large part of the centre of Cork city by the Black and Tans and the burning by the IRA of the Customs House in Dublin and numerous fine private houses. Still, the number of Irish people who died amounted to fewer than 5 per cent of the Irish soldiers killed in the First World War.

22   THE CIVIL WAR

As the Dáil split over the treaty (33), so did the IRA. To men like Liam Mellows, Rory O'Connor and Liam Lynch, the treaty was a denial of the Irish republic they had fought for. On 7 January 1922, the final vote in the Dáil brought acceptance of the treaty and over the next two months there was a struggle for control of the IRA; the Free State Provisional Government, under Collins, was building up a separate army and police force (the Garda Síochána – 'Guardians of the Peace' – were established in 1923 to replace the RIC) while IRA men were staging arms raids. On 26 March a general army convention assembled which was attended solely by anti-treaty men and banned by the government. It chose its own executive and declared the IRA independent of the Dáil. On 14 April the Four Courts and other buildings were seized by a group of armed Republicans. They remained unchallenged by Collins, who feared a disastrous confrontation.

All attempts at compromise failed and when the general election of 16 June showed that the country was behind the treaty, the Republicans (or 'Irregulars', as the anti-treatyites were later called) refused to accept the democratic verdict. Civil war became inevitable. On 22 June, Sir Henry Wilson, who had accepted the post of military adviser to the Northern Irish government, was assassinated in London; believing this (probably erroneously) to be the work of the IRA the British government put pressure on Collins to take action. Four days later the Four Courts garrison, under the leadership of O'Connor, seized General J. J. O'Connell of the Free State army and on 28 June – O'Connor having ignored an ultimatum to leave the Four Courts – the Republicans were besieged by Free State forces armed with British artillery. Before the Republicans surrendered, the Public Record Office, part of the Four Courts complex, was destroyed. Simultaneous fighting was going on in O'Connell Street, where Cathal Brugha and sixty-three others were killed, and over £5 million worth of damage was caused. Fighting broke out in the country. Figure 22 shows how the IRA divisions split, most Republican strength being in the south and west.

Within a month the 'Irregulars' had been forced back into what was known as the Republic of Munster, behind a line running from Limerick to Waterford. The Free State forces, led by Collins, showed initiative, skill and determination in their assault on their opponents and their large stock of British artillery gave

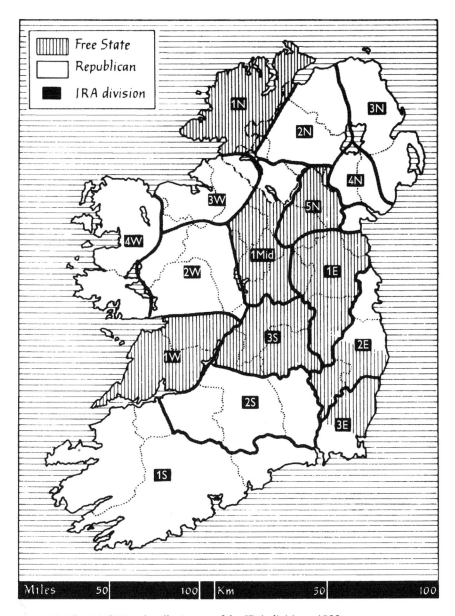

Figure 22 The Civil War: the allegiances of the IRA divisions, 1922.
Source F. O'Donoghue (1954) *No Other Law.*

them a tremendous advantage. By 11 August the Free State forces were in control of Munster and the Republicans had to fall back on the guerrilla tactics of the Anglo-Irish war.

The Civil War was viciously and ruthlessly conducted by both sides;

assassinations, beatings, arms raids and arson were common. In August, Collins was shot dead in a Cork ambush. In October the Dáil gave the Free State army the emergency powers to hold military courts and order the death penalty: seventy-seven Republicans, including Erskine Childers, O'Connor and Mellows, were executed over the next few months. By April it was clear that the Republicans were beaten; many of their leaders and 10,000 of their supporters were jailed or interned. Having tried and failed to secure a ceasefire on favourable terms, de Valera, whose military role had been very minor but who had been the Republicans' political leader, ordered them on 24 May 1923 to give up the struggle.

The most likely estimate of those killed is between 1,500 and 2,000, of damage to property and the state's infrastructure around £30 million and of the cost of financing the war another £17 million. Among the uglier aspects was the continuation by Republicans of the sectarian campaign against Cork Protestants: seventy out of 200 civilians shot in that county by the IRA between 1920 and 1923 were Protestant – five times the proportion of Protestants in the civilian population; 85 per cent of houses burned were Protestant-owned. There were terrible atrocities on both sides and the extent of the psychological damage to the young state was beyond calculation.

23   IRELAND AND THE SECOND WORLD WAR

Under Articles 6 and 7 of the Anglo-Irish treaty of 1921, the British government retained certain military and naval privileges in southern Ireland. However, in April 1938, under an agreement between the Chamberlain and de Valera governments, Britain renounced all these privileges, including its rights to the use of the Irish ports of Cobh, Berehaven and Lough Swilly.

This development made it practicable for Ireland to adopt a position of neutrality on the outbreak of the war between Britain and Germany. However, in regaining control of the ports, Ireland had also lost its rights to the defence of its coastline by Britain. Despite strong political differences, their ties were too strong to make it desirable to have Ireland used as a base for enemy attacks on Britain. With a well-concealed slight bias towards the Allies, de Valera maintained Ireland's precarious neutrality successfully throughout the war (which was termed 'The Emergency'), although the country was divided. A number of Fine Gael politicians and supporters, notably James Dillon, were unhappy about neutrality and pressed for Irish involvement in support of Britain. Right-wing Republican elements favoured an alliance with Germany, and although most members of the Blue Shirt quasi-fascist movement (34) were pro-British, some believed that Ireland should become part of an alliance of Germany, Italy, Spain and Vichy France. In the event, many southern Irishmen joined the British army, while only a handful joined the German army, although Irishman William Joyce, who had been active in Oswald Mosley's fascist movement for four years, was to secure widespread notoriety as 'Lord Haw Haw'.

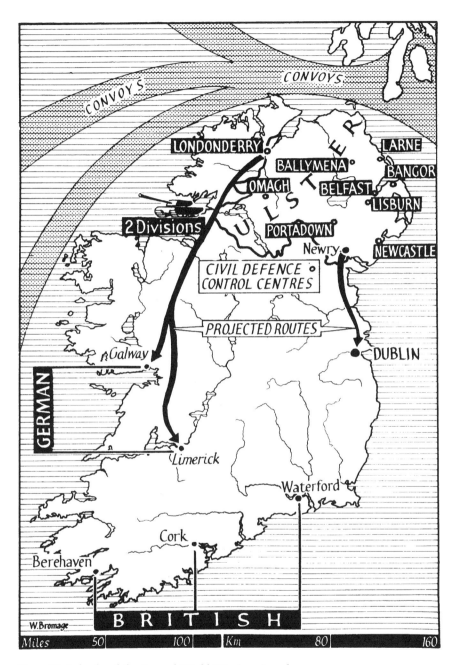

Figure 23 Ireland and the Second World War: invasion plans.

After the fall of France fears of a German invasion of Ireland became very real, both to the Irish and British governments, since the latter could not afford to allow such an occurrence. Figure 23 shows the German invasion plans which were under consideration at the time, and the British counter-plans. While the only realistic German plan involved invasion from the west, the British already controlled the north, and could take the east and west from its northern base and the south from the sea. While no invasion ever materialized, the existence of detailed plans indicates how precarious was Ireland's neutrality.

De Valera handled the diplomacy of the situation skilfully. There were some embarrassments caused by German support for the IRA (24) and IRA bombs in England (24), and also, later in the war, by American pressure on Ireland to abandon its neutrality. Additionally, without British defence forces to rely on, Ireland was obliged to attempt to provide an adequate defence against invasion. From an establishment of 26,000 men in 1940, including regular and reserve forces, by 1941 the figure had increased to almost 250,000 men serving in various defence organizations.

Northern Ireland, on the other hand, was actively involved in the war. Although, mainly because of resistance from the Catholic community, conscription was not introduced, the province was of great economic and military importance. Its ports were crucially placed. With France in German hands from 1940 onwards the Northern Ireland coastal waters were essential for ocean convoys, and the ports for repairs and supplies; there were also aircraft bases. During the war Belfast built 10 per cent of all British shipping, including 140 warships, and it also manufactured tanks and weapons. Additionally, from 1942, Northern Ireland became host to thousands of American troops. Civil Defence forces were strong throughout the province and had to face serious problems from air raids. In two raids in 1941, 850 people were killed and 10,000 made homeless. Despite the importance of Belfast shipyards and factories to the war effort, military defences such as anti-aircraft guns were totally inadequate.

24   PARAMILITARY ACTIVITY: 1926–2004

In November 1925, the IRA, which had not handed in its arms, regrouped and adopted an amended constitution. By claiming to be the true government of the 'Irish Republic' and insisting on its right to achieve a united Ireland through the use of physical force, the organization made clear its refusal to accept the legitimacy of the Irish Free State. Still, the IRA was fading fast: between August 1924 and December 1926, its membership fell from around 14,500 to 5,000. It still indulged in sporadic violence and ruthless jury- and witness-intimidation. In July 1927 three IRA men murdered the hated Kevin O'Higgins who as Minister for Home Affairs and Minister for Justice had been an implacable defender of the state. The following month de Valera took his Fianna Fáil party into the Dáil and gradually eased anti-treatyites into constitutional politics.

When de Valera took power in 1932 (34), though IRA prisoners were released, he began weaning most of its members away from violence and undermining its popular support by granting any requests he thought reasonable. The organization was banned in 1936. However, in 1939, on the age-old principle that England's difficulty was Ireland's opportunity, the hard core made overtures to the Nazis. A bombing campaign in England resulted in seven dead and 137 injured; a botched attempt killed another five civilians in Coventry. At the same time a raid on the Irish army's weapons in Dublin enabled de Valera, then Taoiseach, to seek emergency powers. Many hundreds of activists were interrogated, 500 interned and 600 imprisoned, three allowed to die on hunger strike and six hanged; Sean Russell, the Chief of Staff, died in 1940 on a German U-boat; the campaign petered out and the IRA virtually went out of business.

Post-war, a few ex-members re-established the IRA, which made a gesture towards the southern state with a commitment not to attack gardaí or members of the Irish army. Although there were unplanned killings (most recently, in 1996, Garda Jerry McCabe), the IRA abided by this commitment in all subsequent campaigns: Northern Ireland was the war zone and the South the logistical base. In the 'Border campaign' of 1956–62, there were eighteen deaths, including eight IRA men. Public support was lacking and de Valera again introduced internment, as did the Stormont government, effectively closing the organization down militarily, though during the 1960s it drifted into left-wing agitation.

When what became euphemistically known as the 'Troubles' first broke out in Northern Ireland in 1969, it was spearheaded by the civil rights movement. In the midst of sectarian turmoil, the IRA was at first so inactive that a famous Falls Road piece of graffiti spelled out: 'IRA – I Ran Away'. Republicans soon remedied this. The movement split in 1969. The Official IRA (OIRA), embracing a Marxist ideology and seeking to spearhead a national liberation front engaged in political as well as military activity, suspended offensive military operations in 1972 on the grounds that violence would increase sectarianism; a splinter group of about 100 in 1974 formed the hard-left Irish National Liberation Army (INLA). Some OIRA members became involved in vicious feuds with INLA and the Provisional IRA (PIRA) which peaked in 1975 – but OIRA gradually went out of the paramilitary – although not entirely the criminal – business. Although in the minority at the time of the split, the militaristic Provisionals ('Provos'), who had the sectarian instincts of their Defender forebears, recruited rapidly in republican ghettoes and were soon in the majority; they remained abstentionist and opposed to all constitutional activity. Their stated aim was British withdrawal from Northern Ireland and they were committed to a military campaign of bombing and killing members of the security forces until this was achieved. In practice, civilians were frequently the victims, so, gradually, the IRA extended its definition of legitimate targets to include anyone providing any services whatsoever to the security forces or the state: most Protestants and many Catholics qualified.

Loyalist paramilitary activity developed in tandem: like their republican

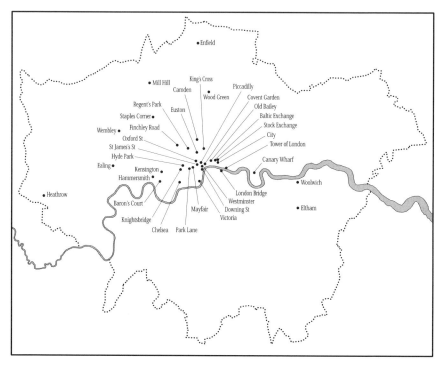

London

	Date	Place	Dead	Injured
1	1973	Old Bailey	1	230
2	1973	King's Cross	–	5
3	1973	Euston	–	8
4	1974	Westminster	–	11
5	1974	Tower of London	1	41
6	1974	St James's St	–	3
7	1974	Woolwich	2	26
8	1975	Baron's Court	1	–
9	1975	Kensington	1	–
10	1975	Park Lane	2	63
11	1975	Piccadilly	1	20
12	1975	Kensington	1	–
13	1975	Mayfair	1	15
14	1975	Chelsea	2	23
15	1975	Enfield	1	–
16	1979	Westminster	1	–
17	1980	Hammersmith	–	5
18	1981	Chelsea	2	39
19	1981	Oxford Street	1	–
20	1982	Hyde Park	4	28
21	1982	Regent's Park	7	31
22	1983	Knightsbridge	6	91

	Date	Place	Dead	Injured
23	1988	Mill Hill	1	8
24	1990	Eltham	–	5
25	1990	Wembley	1	4
26	1990	City	–	19
27	1990	St James's St	–	20
28	1990	Stock Exchange	–	–
29	1991	Downing St (3 mortar bombs)	–	–
30	1991	Victoria	1	38
31	1992	London Bridge	–	29
32	1992	Baltic Exchange	3	91
33	1992	Staples Corner	–	–
34	1992	Covent Garden	1	4
35	1992	Wood Green	–	11
36	1993	Camden	–	18
37	1993	City	1	44
38	1993	Finchley Road	–	5
39	1994	Heathrow (3 separate mortar bomb attacks)	–	–
40	1996	Canary Wharf	2	40
41	1996	Covent Garden	1	8
42	2001	Ealing (RIRA)	–	7

Figure 24 Republican bombing/shooting campaign in London and England: 1972–2001.

England

	Date	Place	Dead	Injured			Date	Place	Dead	Injured
A	1972	Aldershot (OIRA)	7	17		J	1989	Deal, Kent	11	21
B	1973	Birmingham	1	–		K	1990	Litchfield	1	2
C	1974	M62, near Chain Bar				L	1990	Stafford	–	1
		junction, Cleckheaton	12	8		M	1990	Pevensey	1	–
D	1974	Latimer, Bucks	–	10		N	1991	St Albans	2	1
E	1974	Guildford	5	57		O	1992	Derby (INLA)	1	–
F	1974	Coventry	1	–		P	1992	Tadcaster	1	1
G	1974	Birmingham	21	160		Q	1992	Manchester	–	64
H	1975	Manchester	–	26		R	1993	Warrington	2	54
I	1984	Brighton	5	30		S	1996	Manchester	–	200

Notes:

Unless otherwise stated the perpetrators were the Provisional IRA

ORIA = Official IRA; RIRA = Real IRA; INLA = Irish National Liberation Army counterparts, loyalist paramilitaries would gradually descend into criminality. Violent loyalism splintered into numerous groups (including the Ulster Defence Association (UDA), Ulster Volunteer Force (UVF), the Ulster Freedom Fighters (UFF) and the Loyalist Volunteer Force (LVF)), all of whom shared the primary objective of keeping the province British. Since the only 'legitimate' targets of loyalism were in the IRA, many loyalist organizations simply targeted Catholics; members of the security forces sometimes colluded in pointing them towards IRA members. Reflecting the Dissenting tradition of Northern Irish Protestantism, loyalist paramilitaries lacked the discipline and obedience to authority of their Provisional IRA counterparts. Fuelled by drugs and drink, some of them – particularly the Shankill Butchers – exhibited what, even by the vicious standards of all the paramilitaries, was psychopathic cruelty (87).

On 30 January 1972, on what became known as 'Bloody Sunday', British paratroopers killed thirteen civilians on an illegal civil rights march in Derry, massively boosting IRA recruitment (as the deaths of hunger strikers would do in 1981). The death toll in that worst of years was 497, of whom 259 were civilians, 134 soldiers and seventeen police. In what would be typical, while republican and loyalist paramilitaries were respectively responsible for 280 and 121 deaths, they suffered only seventy-four and eleven fatalities respectively.

What the IRA called a war and latterly a conflict but the British insisted was insurgency continued over the next twenty-five years: republicans often sought to make England and sometimes the Continent a battlefield (murders included the British Ambassador to The Hague and several British military personnel and civilians in Germany and the Netherlands) and obtained arms from abroad, notably from Libya and the USA. In 1971 PIRA bombed the Post Office Tower in London; in 1972 OIRA devastated Aldershot barracks; and the following year PIRA began a sustained campaign in Britain with four car bombs (planted by, among others, Gerry Kelly, later the Sinn Féin spokesman on Justice, and Dolores and Marian Price, later a spokeswoman for the political wing of the Real IRA). The campaign reached its height in 1974 and 1975 with the Guildford, Woolwich and Birmingham bombs and the reign of terror in London of the Balcombe Street gang, who with guns and bombs murdered at least sixteen people. They were responsible for the Guildford and Woolwich bombs, for which the Guildford Four and Maguire Seven were wrongly convicted. The perpetrators of the Birmingham bomb, for which six men were wrongly convicted, are unknown.

There were many other notorious attacks: in March 1979, the INLA murdered Margaret Thatcher's close colleague, Airey Neave, MP, at Westminster with a booby-trap bomb; in July 1982, four cavalrymen and several horses were blown up by a bomb in Hyde Park, and seven bandsmen when playing in Regent's Park; in October 1984, in an attempt to murder Prime Minister Thatcher and the British cabinet, the IRA placed a bomb in a Brighton hotel during the Conservative Party conference and killed five; in September 1989, ten bandsmen were killed in the Royal Marines School of

Music in Deal in Kent; in July 1990 the IRA blew up Thatcher's friend Ian Gow, MP, in Sussex; in February 1991, the IRA fired mortars at Number 10 Downing Street during a cabinet meeting; a bomb in Canary Wharf on 9 February 1996 signalled the end of the IRA ceasefire (86); in 1997, before the ceasefire of 20 July, the IRA caused massive disruption to the rail network and motorways and caused the postponement of the Grand National. From 2001 the Real IRA, a new splinter group, began a campaign in England, which included bombing the BBC and mortaring MI6.

Loyalists rarely attacked the Republic of Ireland, although UVF bombs killed two men in Dublin in December 1972, one in February 1973, in May 1974 thirteen other civilians in Dublin and Monaghan (87) and two men in Dundalk in 1975.

The British government followed its time-honoured tradition of veering between coercion and conciliation. Internment had been botched in 1971 (86) – not least because it did not include loyalists – so was never tried again, but often ineffectual anti-terrorist laws were rushed through parliament in response to various atrocities. The 1985 Anglo-Irish agreement that recognized the right of the Dublin government to be consulted on affairs in the North was intended to address republican and nationalist alienation, but led instead to an upsurge in loyalist violence.

After the embarrassment of the 1970 arms trial, when Irish government ministers were accused (but acquitted) of smuggling arms north of the border, every major Irish political party was careful to condemn paramilitary activity and dissociate itself from the IRA, while paying lip-service to a united Ireland. Members of paramilitary organizations were prevented from broadcasting, but there was foot-dragging over extradition of suspects to Britain.

If the governments were unsuccessful in containing the paramilitaries, IRA/Sinn Féin, after twenty-five years of violence, were no closer to their aim of a united Ireland, and being militarily, electorally and financially in trouble embarked on what became known as the 'peace process' (86); on 31 August 1994 the IRA called a 'cessation'. On 13 October, loyalists declared a ceasefire, conditional on that of the IRA. In 1995, deaths were down to nine, the first single figure since 1969, but the following year the IRA, claiming they had nothing to show for their commitment, bombed Canary Wharf in London's Docklands on 9 February, killing two newsagents and causing millions of pounds worth of damage. The cessation was restored on 20 July 1997 and has largely held since.

In the thirty-five years from 1969 to 2004, deaths caused by the conflict were 3,702, of whom 56 per cent were civilians. Perpetrators have been brought to book for only about a third of the killings. Contrary to popular perception, the statistics demonstrate the disproportionate suffering of the security forces compared to their paramilitary opponents: republican paramilitaries killed 2,157 and lost 397 and loyalists killed 1,100 and lost 171, while the British army killed 301 and lost 503, local defence forces (Ulster Defence Regiment/Royal Irish Regiment) killed eight and lost 206 and the Royal Ulster Constabulary killed fifty and lost 303. In the Republic, the Irish army and police killed five and lost seven to republicans; police in England killed one and lost five (see figure 87 for killings in Ireland).

Paramilitary violence has continued, but on a much smaller scale and primarily from republican and loyalist splinter groups. Yet, on 15 August 1998, a Real IRA bomb caused the greatest single atrocity of the Troubles, when twenty-nine people and unborn twins were murdered in Omagh: RIRA and CIRA (Continuity IRA) remain dedicated to murdering their way into a united Ireland. Like its loyalist counterparts, the IRA and other republican paramilitaries maintain a vigilante presence in their own ghettos, beating, shooting and occasionally murdering those members of their community of whom they disapprove. Sectarian rioting and ethnic cleansing continue on a smaller scale than previously, as do spates of loyalist pipe-bombing of vulnerable Catholics as well as internecine republican and loyalist feuding. All paramilitary organizations are involved in crime: activities include smuggling, forgery, counterfeiting, robbery, money laundering, vehicle theft, benefit fraud, people-trafficking and protection rackets. Loyalist paramilitaries are heavily dependent on drug-trafficking and dealing, while republicans – whose elected representatives have a high-profile anti-drug position – generally confine themselves to exacting money from approved dealers. Republican gangs operate south of the border while loyalists are strong in Scotland. Both sometimes operate in England and all major paramilitary organizations have close links with English and Continental criminals.

The IRA, who are estimated to make tens of millions annually from crime, are increasingly buying into legitimate businesses north and south, of which the pubs, clubs, bureaux de change, taxi companies, security and construction firms are particularly convenient for laundering stolen money. After a robbery in December 2004 of £26.5 million from the Northern Bank in Belfast was attributed to the IRA, and police raids in the Republic revealed evidence of widespread money-laundering, it became clear that the IRA (by now nicknamed the Rafia) had become probably the largest criminal gang in Europe.

IV Politics

[handwritten annotations: "Anglo Saxons — when?", "Scots first then Celts then Vikings Normans throughout — trib against trib"]

Until after 13,000 BC, Ireland, like the rest of Europe, was in the grip of the Ice Age. With Britain, Ireland was physically joined to the Continent – not becoming a separate entity until about 6000 BC. It was at about this period that the first immigrants – the Mesolithic people – arrived in Ireland. Primarily fishermen who spread from Scotland into the north of Ireland in search of flint, they travelled by water as far south as Carlow. Some traces of the Mesolithic people remain, but our first extensive knowledge of Ireland's early ancestry comes with the advent of the New Stone Age and Neolithic man, who arrived about 3000 BC.

Neolithic people did not have their predecessors' predilection for water. Where the Mesolithic had used the seas, lakes and rivers of Ireland for food and transport, and had dwelt beside the waters, the Neolithic were farmers. They made effective tools from stone, learned to till the soil and raise domestic animals, and began to clear the forests which covered most of the country and had discouraged the earlier inhabitants, with their primitive flint tools, from venturing away from the water. During this period, the whole country was gradually inhabited by successive waves of settlers, some of whom brought with them a rich and mature culture. Their most spectacular legacies were megalithic ('built of great stones') tombs that are spread throughout Ireland in their thousands; the largest are the massive passage-graves, many of which are ornately carved. Newgrange, the most famous of these, is over 40 feet high and covers nearly an acre of ground.

By the Bronze Age, about 2000 BC, yet another race had made its mark on Ireland; these were miners and metalworkers. Following them, between the third and first century BC, came the Celts, who brought to Ireland an expertise in the use of iron, a well-defined religion, complex tribal laws, a warlike tradition and a Celtic language. Although by this date the Celts had established their dominance throughout central and western Europe, it was in Britain and Ireland that their influence was to prove most lasting. By the first century BC they were fully established in Ireland and until the Norman invasion their pre-eminence was not seriously challenged.

The Brehon law of the Celts, like their culture, was highly developed and was transmitted orally by professionals. Jurists interpreted and adjudicated on a most complex and rigid legal code that affected every aspect of life. Basically protective in character, it put the rights of individuals – both male and female – ahead of property. In modified form, it functioned for as long as Gaelic Ireland maintained its identity – right up to the Elizabethan conquest (15). The other professionals, the poets, historians, druids and musicians, travelled between tribes and were greatly honoured – a practice which also continued as an integral part of Gaelic society. It was not until the ruin of the Gaelic landed proprietors in the seventeenth century that the itinerant poets lost their position of privilege and prosperity (88).

The political divisions of Ireland at this time have been described elsewhere (1). Basically it was divided into 150 little kingdoms called *tuatha*. There were three classes within each kingdom, the professionals (*aos dána*), the free (*saor aicme*) and the unfree (*daor aicme*). The free owned land and cattle and were warriors, while the unfree were slaves. Many of the unfree were prisoners or descendants of prisoners, many of them having been captured from Roman Britain. During the fourth and fifth centuries, at the height of Irish raids on Britain (43), many prisoners were captured during raids abroad, including the boy who was later to become St Patrick.

From an early stage, about 800 AD, the *tuatha* were grouped into larger tribal organizations: in the north-west the main tribe was that of the Northern Uí Néill; in the north-east were the Dál Riata, who had earlier been founders of a Scottish kingdom (43); a large part of the centre of Ulster was occupied by the Airgialla; in Meath the southern Uí Néill were the chief family; throughout Leinster the various branches of the Laigin alternated as overlords of the province; in Munster the Eóganacht dynasty was divided into a number of groups throughout the province and dominated all other tribes; in the west the Connachta were the chief tribe, among whom the Uí Fiachrach, Uí Briúin and Uí Maine were important; and the Uí Briúin were powerful in Breffny. (See Figure 25a for the position in the ninth century.)

The chief family of Ireland for over a thousand years were the Uí Néill, who were named after their fifth-century ancestor, Niall of the Nine Hostages, whose legendary exploits at home and abroad gave his family a status exaggerated in poetic and genealogical tracts. The Uí Néill spread from Connacht over most of Ulster, Meath and Westmeath and launched continuous attacks on southern families; in doing so they destroyed the tribal structure of the country. Ultimately they claimed to be high kings of Ireland, although at no time did they succeed in achieving recognition from all the other ruling families. Nevertheless, their claim to the high kingship was not seriously challenged until the tenth century, when Brian Ború of the east Clare Dál Cais tribe overthrew the established order.

25   IRELAND BEFORE THE NORMANS

Brian Ború's struggle for the high kingship of Ireland was symbolic of the political violence of the centuries before the Norman invasion, although it was typical of an age of centralization. Devastating as had been the attacks of the Viking invaders, the internecine warfare of the Irish provincial kings proved equally disastrous. Brian overthrew the traditional Uí Néill high kings; he spent almost thirty years justifying his claim to the title, and most of his fourteen years as high king was spent resisting successive attempts to overthrow him. Nevertheless, he remained strong enough to destroy the power of the Vikings permanently at Clontarf (9, 11). The only high king to reign unchallenged after Brian was the man he had deposed, Malachy II, who died in 1022. After him, the annalists use the term *co fresabra*, 'with opposition', to describe the high kings.

By this period there were five discernible major divisions of the country: Leinster, Meath, Munster, Connacht and a group of northern kingdoms. Munster was now ruled chiefly by the O'Briens (who had displaced the Eóganachta), at different times from Kincora, Killaloe and Limerick; the Eóganachta's traditional royal seat, Cashel, went to the church in 1101. The O'Brien supremacy was frequently challenged by the MacCarthys, who had several virtually independent lordships within the province.

Leinster was ruled from Ferns by the MacMurroughs and Connacht from Tuam and later from Galway by the O'Connors; the O'Rourkes ruled the subkingdom of Breffny. There were four main northern kingdoms: Tirowen was ruled from Aileach until its destruction, when the MacLochlainn kings moved to Tullahoge, Tirconnell was ruled mainly by the O'Donnells, Ulaidh by the MacDonlevys, and Uriel by the O'Carrolls, who had displaced the Uí Briúin. Meath was still the territory of the southern Uí Néill, of whom the high king Malachy II was a member; after his death they played no positive part in subsequent struggles for supremacy.

The high kings with opposition during this period included Turloch O'Brien of Munster, who died in 1086, acknowledged as high king in Leinster, Meath and Connacht. He was succeeded as king of Munster in 1093 by his son Murcertach, who secured recognition as high king from all the kingdoms of Ireland, although the O'Connors and MacLochlainns fought bitterly against him, and the latter ultimately defeated him in 1103. Despite this, O'Brien was still able to preside in 1101 as High King at the first reforming synod (V) of the Irish church.

Turloch O'Connor, King of Connacht, operating on the principle of 'divide and rule', conquered and politically divided Munster, Meath and Leinster, and in 1119 succeeded O'Brien as High King, holding the position until his death in 1156. Murcertach MacLochlainn (King of Ailech, 1136–43, 1145–66), however, proved to be an indefatigable enemy, who resisted O'Connor pretensions throughout Turloch's reign, and after his death won the high kingship from Turloch's son Rory. In 1166, however, MacLochlainn was killed after a rebellion of the sub-kings of the north in alliance with Rory O'Connor, and his ally Dermot MacMurrough was expelled from Leinster – with far-reaching consequences (12). O'Connor remained high king in practice until the Norman invasion, and in theory until 1175, when he recognized Henry II as overlord of Ireland.

Figure 25(a) Ireland before the Normans: ninth century.

Figure 25(b) Ireland before the Normans: twelfth century.

26   FOURTEENTH-CENTURY IRELAND

No map can properly indicate the changing territorial divisions of Ireland during the later Middle Ages. The history of Ireland throughout the whole of this period is a story of changes in political power, a shifting kaleidoscope of Norman advance, Gaelic defeat, Gaelic resurgence and Norman retreat. Figure 26 is intended to show very generally the most important political divisions of the country at this period.

Broadly speaking, in pre-Tudor Ireland, although the country was theoretically organized according to English law and governed by a royal administration centred in Dublin, in fact the king's writ ran fully effectively only throughout a small portion of the country – the Pale – which varied dramatically in extent at different periods (28). In the territories surrounding the Pale, in Kilkenny, Carlow, Wexford and also in Waterford, Tipperary, Cork, Kerry and Limerick, which were administered by feudal lords, theoretically according to established law, the royal law was of varying effectiveness. In Galway and in the earldom of Ulster, sporadic and usually ineffectual efforts were made to impose the law and in the rest of the country the immutable Brehon law held undisputed sway.

Figure 26 shows that part of Ireland had been shired (1) and that there were a number of liberties in existence. The concept of the liberty was borrowed from English law: during the Anglo-Saxon period many great landowners had been awarded royal dues from shire courts. The Normans extended this right by permitting feudal lords in their liberties to hold feudal courts and maintain considerable freedom from royal officialdom.

The same system pertained in Ireland. Within a liberty, the law was administered by officials of the lord and it was his writ, rather than the king's, which ran throughout his territory. Government in liberties was modelled on royal government, with seneschals acting as representatives of the lords, chancellors running the household and treasurers in charge of the exchequers. The law which was administered within the liberty was the law of the country as the lord chose to interpret it: legal uniformity was later to be increased by the use of charters and parliamentary statutes.

By the fourteenth century the Normans had established in Ireland basic political divisions that at least were to form the theoretical basis of those now existing. The situation shown in Figure 26 was to change, in minor ways, very rapidly. By 1350 changes included Kerry becoming a liberty under the Desmonds and Tipperary a liberty under the Ormonds (27), while Louth had been briefly a liberty under John de Bermingham. It was to take another 150 years to finish shaping the permanent political divisions of the country.

27   THE GREAT FAMILIES OF IRELAND

Despite the Normans' desire for territorial aggrandizement, they did not attempt to eradicate the native population: they were content to take over the

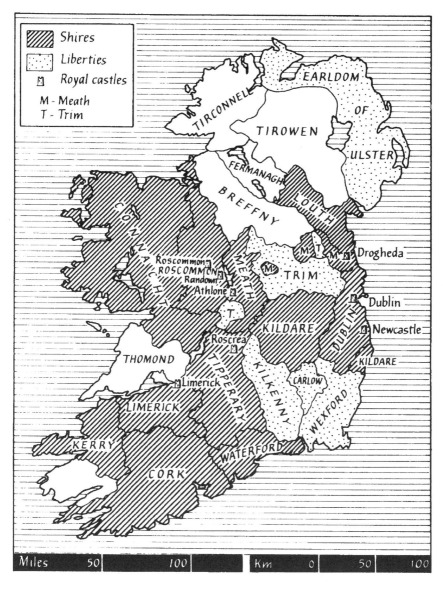

Figure 26 Ireland *c.* 1300.

good land, permitting the dispossessed Irish to remain in, or move to, poor land. Many Gaelic families therefore remained in their old territories, although keeping part of them only, while many others moved to neighbouring areas, often in turn driving out the indigenous native inhabitants.

The family names in Figure 27 are those which were most numerous or most powerful by the end of the Middle Ages. Despite the instability of life

Figure 27 The great families of Ireland: late Middle Ages.

throughout Irish history, despite the invasions, wars, rebellions, famines, emigrations and plagues, many of these names have dominated the same areas for 500 or even 1,000 years. The O'Neills, O'Donnells, O'Connors, O'Briens and MacCarthys, for example, although their territories were progressively reduced, and although they gradually lost their political power, nevertheless appear in the histories of their various provinces throughout the whole of recorded Irish history.

By the sixteenth century, the Normans had made little progress in Ulster. The names dominating the province are those of Gaelic chiefs; only the small territory of the earldom of Ulster remained even nominally in Norman hands, and that had been steadily pushed back by the growing territories of O'Neill Clanaboy and the O'Cahans and MacDonnells. In Connacht, mainly because of the tenacity and courage of the de Burgos, the Norman influence remained strong. Although theoretically more and more integrated with Gaelic society, the Connacht Normans maintained many of the qualities of their race. They intermarried with the Irish, adopted their customs and Gaelicized their names, but they continued to consolidate their military achievements, secure their territories and capitalize on any opportunity for increasing their prosperity, whether by obtaining ecclesiastical appointments, of which they had locally a near monopoly, or acquiring commercial wealth; the Burkes of the fifteenth century still had much in common with their de Burgo forebears.

In Munster there were two great Norman families, the Fitzgeralds and the Butlers. The Fitzgeralds had built up the great palatine liberty of Desmond over most of the counties of Kerry, Limerick, Cork and Waterford. The Desmond earls were virtually independent of the Dublin administration, although they were defenders of the Yorkist cause. When in 1468 Thomas, Earl of Desmond, was executed as a traitor for flouting the laws condemning fraternizing with the Irish, by order of the lieutenant, Sir John Tiptoft, the earls of Desmond cut themselves off completely and ruled what became virtually an independent state in the south until their downfall in 1583 (54). The great Irish families of Munster offered little resistance to the Fitzgeralds, but carved new territories for themselves from the lands of lesser chieftains. The MacCarthys and O'Sullivans moved south-west and established themselves in new territories.

In Leinster, where the Normans secured a lasting success, the great Irish families, the O'Tooles, O'Byrnes and MacMurroughs, took over territory in Wicklow and Wexford, leaving Dublin and Kildare to the Normans. The liberty of Kildare was a late creation of Garret More Fitzgerald, eighth Earl of Kildare, who brought his family to pre-eminence among all the families of Ireland: the territory covered land in Kildare, Meath and Wicklow. Effectively taking over the administration of the country with the virtual abdication of the Butlers and the alienation of the Desmonds, the house of Kildare maintained its importance for sixty years, until its fall in 1534 after the rebellion of Silken Thomas (9).

The Butlers of Ormond had land extending across Tipperary and Kilkenny. Although they had been supreme among Norman lords during the thirteenth century, they were usually absentees during the fifteenth: they made notable appearances only in aid of the fateful Lancastrian cause. The senior line died out in 1515, and the head of a cadet branch of the family, Sir Piers Butler, became ninth Earl of Ormond. Throughout Irish history, the Ormonds were to show a devotion to the English monarchy that was rarely adequately appreciated. During the fifteenth century they suffered for their loyalty to the Lancastrians and during the seventeenth and eighteenth centuries for their loyalty to the Stuarts, although ultimately that loyalty was rewarded when after the Restoration the earldom was elevated to a dukedom. Their devotion persisted despite numerous slights from monarchs who failed to see the importance of a loyalty remarkable in Britain and unique in Ireland.

28   THE PALE: 1300–1596

Until the final subjugation of Ireland in the sixteenth and seventeenth centuries, the extent of the Pale symbolized the state of English fortunes in Ireland. The limits of the Pale represented the limits of effective royal jurisdiction: outside was at best sporadic recognition of the royal authority, at worst anarchy or rebellion.

By the beginning of the fourteenth century, the limits of effective rule, in so far as they can be decisively delineated, stretched from Dundalk westwards to the Shannon, south to Athlone, east to Kildare and south to Waterford. Within that area, apart from the Leinster plateau from which it never proved possible to dislodge the main Irish families, the king's writ ran. Throughout the succeeding centuries attempts were constantly made to maintain, consolidate and even extend the specifically English territory of the Pale. For example, one of Richard II's objectives in Ireland was to create a wholly English land east of a line drawn from Dundalk to the Boyne and south to Waterford – a territory much smaller than that of the English marches of 1300, to be granted to wholly English colonists. In this he was, of course, unsuccessful. Seventy years later, in an unhappy recognition of the status quo, an Irish parliament of 1465, admitting that the only portion of true English land remaining consisted of the counties of Meath, Louth, Dublin and Kildare, ordered the Irish living therein 'to take English surnames, to go as English, and be sworn as lieges within a year'.

An Act of 1494 provided for the construction of a ditch (never completed) around the whole area of the Pale to prevent cattle raids; the precise area involved (28) was delineated in the Act.

By 1537 the Pale had shrunk to its minimum size and was described by Richard Stanihurst as 'cramperned and crouched into an odd corner of the country named Fingal, with a parcel of the King's land of Meath and the counties of Kildare and Louth'.

Despite occasional expressions of concern for the success of the Dublin administration, the interest of English monarchs in Ireland diminished throughout the late Middle Ages. From the time of the last personal visit by an English

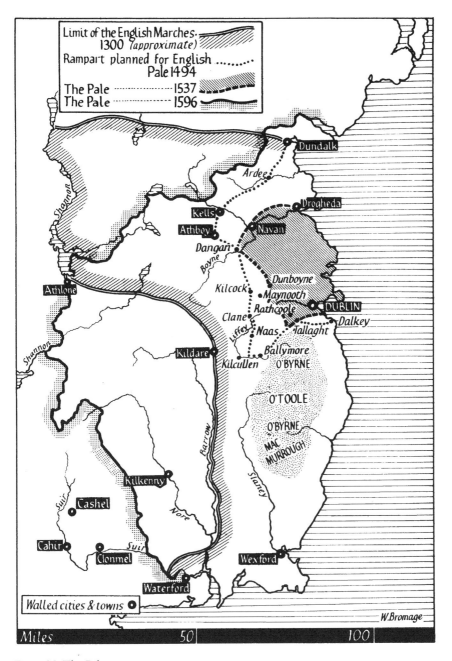

Figure 28 The Pale.

king – the ill-fated Richard II in 1399 – royal interest in Ireland was for the next century to be indirect. Ireland was to English kings at best a source of troops for the war with France or at worst a source of danger to the crown, as, for example, when Richard of York found a secure base and widespread support in Ireland shortly after being attainted by the English parliament. During the reign of Henry VII this same adherence to the Yorkist cause showed itself in Irish support for the pretenders to the English throne, Lambert Simnel (1487) and Perkin Warbeck (1491).

The lack of English knowledge or understanding of Ireland is symbolized in the preamble of an Irish address to the English Council in 1537: 'Because the country called Leinster and the situation thereof is unknown to the King and his Council, it is to be understood that Leinster is the fifth part of Ireland.'

It is, however, from that period that the reassertion of English authority in Ireland began with the adoption of the policy of 'surrender and re-grant': by the end of the century, confiscations had extended the boundary of the Pale to include Dublin, Wicklow, Wexford, Kilkenny, Carlow, Kildare, Laois, Offaly and Louth.

29   THE DEVELOPMENT OF THE IRISH PARLIAMENT

Parliaments were a thirteenth-century development throughout much of western Europe. Originally the name *parliamentum* was applied to formal sessions of courts, and probably parliament had a judicial purpose before its later financial preoccupation with taxation.

The first recorded parliament in Ireland was in 1264: it initially consisted of the council and lay and ecclesiastical magnates. By the second half of the thirteenth century, however, the pressure for representation before taxation was growing, and regularizing of representation was introduced.

By the mid-fourteenth century a parliament always contained the following elements: the council, peers, bishops, clerical proctors and the commons, who were representatives of shires, liberties and towns.

A number of important acts of Irish parliaments of the Middle Ages included the following:

1366:   The Statutes of Kilkenny were passed in 1366 to attempt to prevent any closer integration of the Norman colonists and the native Irish by forbidding the Normans to intermarry with the Irish or adopt their customs, speech and laws. These statutes were largely unsuccessful.

1460:   A parliament held at Drogheda in 1460 was summoned by Richard, Duke of York, then attempting to gain the English crown from an Irish base. It declared Ireland independent of English laws, being subject only to its own parliament and disloyalty to York to be treason, and it ordered the striking of Ireland's own coinage.

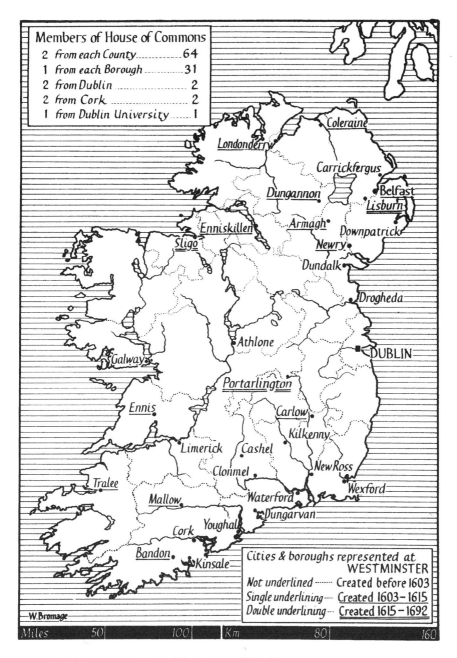

Members of House of Commons

2	*from each County*	64
1	*from each Borough*	31
2	*from Dublin*	2
2	*from Cork*	2
1	*from Dublin University*	1

Coleraine
Londonderry
Carrickfergus
Dungannon
Belfast
Lisburn
Armagh
Downpatrick
Enniskillen
Newry
Sligo
Dundalk
Drogheda
Athlone
DUBLIN
Galway
Portarlington
Ennis
Carlow
Kilkenny
Limerick
Cashel
New Ross
Clonmel
Tralee
Wexford
Mallow
Waterford
Dungarvan
Youghal
Cork
Bandon
Kinsale

Cities & boroughs represented at WESTMINSTER

Not underlined ------ Created before 1603
Single underlining --- Created 1603–1615
Double underlining --- Created 1615–1692

W.Bromage

| Miles | 50 | 100 | Km | 80 | 160 |

Figure 29 Irish representation at Westminster: 1801–32.

1494: Poynings's parliament in 1494 attainted Garret More for treason, reduced the power of the Irish lords in the administration and passed Poynings's Law, which stated that the Irish parliament could meet only with the permission of the King and his English council and their prior approval of the acts to be passed.

The parliaments of the Tudor period showed some signs of independence and after the Reformation opposition from recusants became an increasingly important element. In 1536 the Reformation Parliament, with some disorganized opposition, passed the act that severed the relationship between the Irish church and the papacy; the 1541 parliament recognized Henry VIII as king of Ireland. During the sixteenth century few parliaments were held in Ireland; in the seventy years before 1613 there were only four.

From 1613–15 a parliament sat which in composition was different from its predecessors. Before 1536 no native Irish had sat in parliament. In 1613, eighteen of the 232 members of the commons were Irish and 100 of them Catholic; in the lords, twelve of the thirty-six were Catholic. This parliament demonstrated the resentment of the Old English, mostly Catholic, against the Dublin administration's handling of land titles and religious matters.

Figure 29 shows the cities and boroughs that sent representatives to Westminster after the Act of Union of 1800 and indicates their parliamentary history. Of the thirty-three shown, eighteen sent representatives to the Irish parliament during the Tudor period and twelve more during the reign of James I. Only three were later creations and even they were created during the seventeenth century. There was therefore a strong element of continuity of parliamentary representation.

Tudor – up to James I' who was Stuart

30   THE IRISH PARLIAMENT: 1613–1800

Before the Stuart accession, thirty-four boroughs were in existence. Forty new boroughs were created to send representatives to the 1613 parliament, many totally unimportant and chosen solely to ensure Protestant representatives. This parliament achieved little other than the fomentation of ill will between Catholics and Protestants.

During the Wentworth administration (16) clever use was made of the Irish parliament of 1634; many concessions were exacted without the representatives securing any compensatory measures. In the parliament of 1640, however, an alliance between the Catholics and Puritans was sufficient to contribute to the political destruction of Wentworth.

Parliament had little relevance again until after the Restoration, when it was reconvened from 1661 to 1666; in 1662 the Act of Settlement was passed and in 1665 the Act of Explanation.

Probably the most controversial parliament of the seventeenth century was the 'patriot parliament' of 1689. The Earl of Tyrconnel had succeeded in

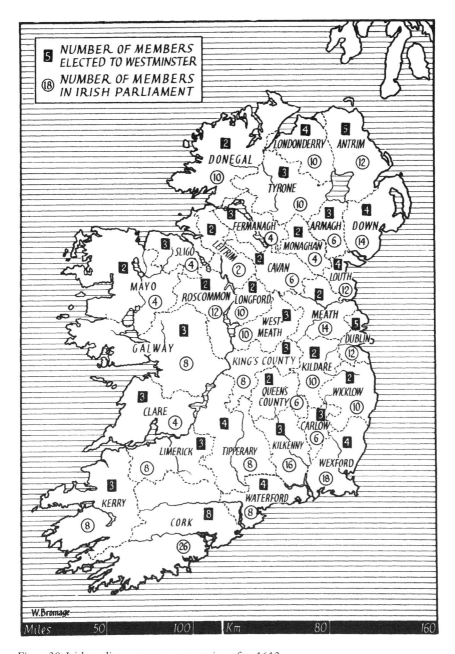

Figure 30 Irish parliamentary representation after 1613.

changing the representation from the boroughs so that there was now a Catholic majority of 212 (17). This parliament, by means of the Bill of Attainder, confiscated the estates of over 2,000 people, although its acts were later nullified.

In 1692 King William convened an exclusively Protestant parliament. Although scarcely enlightened in religious matters, the members showed a new independence of attitude that was a forerunner of things to come and they made serious attempts to secure constitutional concessions.

In 1698 William Molyneux in his pamphlet, *The Case of Ireland's Being Bound by Acts of Parliament in England Stated*, argued that the English parliament had no right to make laws for Ireland. Simultaneously, parliament was showing its resentment at English commercial pressures, culminating in the 1699 act on the export of woollen goods (67). These were the two grievances that were to inspire the move of Irish Protestants to press for an independent parliament.

The power of the Irish parliament was even further curtailed in 1720 when the 'Sixth of George I' was passed as a consequence of a constitutional dispute; this law affirmed the right of the English parliament to make laws binding on Ireland. Bitter resentment at this was evident in the writings of Swift (88), and his attacks on Ireland's inferior constitutional position were seminal in framing the political thought of later generations.

Pressure for electoral and constitutional reform continued to develop during the eighteenth century, and in the 1770s obtained political expression through Henry Flood and his followers, who were known as the 'patriots'. The 'patriots' were not a new phenomenon; constitutional resistance from the Protestant ascendancy had manifested itself early in the eighteenth century. The setback that the patriot party experienced with the acceptance by Flood of government office was offset by Henry Grattan's swift assumption of the leadership.

The outbreak of the American War of Independence in 1775 and fear of foreign invasion from America's allies, France and Spain, led to the formation of the Volunteers (18). Although their armed might was valuable to the government, they were resented when they began securing commercial and constitutional reforms. The trading concessions secured during 1779 and 1780 (68) were followed by a strong agitation for the repeal of Poynings's Law and the Sixth of George I, a demand that was met by the new Whig government of 1782 which repealed the latter and considerably modified the former. This legislation, often known as 'the constitution of 1782', established the formal independence of the Irish parliament.

This independence lasted only eighteen years. It was a period of greater economic prosperity; some religious restrictions were lifted and some half-hearted steps were taken towards parliamentary reform. But there was too much strife within parliament itself to enable it to present a united front towards those British political forces that were finally to undermine its independence. Fears that Ireland might eventually sever the connection with Britain altogether, coupled with the 1798 rising, stiffened the resolve of the British parliament to secure a union of the two countries. In 1800, largely due to the exertions of

Lord Castlereagh, the Irish Chief Secretary, in persuading, bribing and intimidating, the Irish parliament voted for amalgamation.

Figure 30 shows the distribution of Irish representatives to the Irish parliament and, after the Act of Union, to Westminster. As can be seen, the Irish parliament had an enormous and uneven distribution; there were 300 members of the Irish House of Commons and only 100 Irish members at Westminster. Irish seats were most unrepresentative: a large majority of the boroughs were either rotten (virtually uninhabited) or pocket (landlord controlled).

31   O'CONNELL AND YOUNG IRELAND

Despite the modification of most of the Penal Laws during the 1780s and 1790s, at the beginning of the nineteenth century there were still restrictions on Catholics: they could not sit in parliament, hold important state offices or obtain senior judicial, military or civil-service posts. Hopes that Catholic emancipation would follow the Act of Union proved to be misplaced.

Between the union and 1823 all attempts to make the granting of Catholic emancipation a political issue proved unsuccessful. It remained a middle-class preoccupation until, in 1823, Daniel O'Connell, an Irish lawyer, determined to make it a popular issue and with Richard Lalor Sheil democratized the Catholic Association. This organization did not limit its aims to the securing of Catholic emancipation, but also sought to represent the interests of the tenant farmers.

O'Connell set out to obtain a broadly based support, securing the active co-operation of the clergy and of Catholics of all classes. He introduced a Catholic rent of a penny a month which – being paid by all members – encouraged the active participation in the movement of even his poorest supporters; it also supplied the necessary financial backing for his organization, at one stage bringing in several hundred pounds a week.

In 1826 the Catholic Association gave a practical demonstration of its political strength when it intervened in the general election. In four constituencies, Monaghan, Louth, Westmeath and Waterford, the sitting members were defeated by candidates who supported Catholic emancipation. Even though voting was public and reprisals from landlords not uncommon, the backing of the association coupled with the local leadership of the clergy gave the tenant farmers the backing to flout their landlords' wishes and vote for the association's candidates.

An even more dramatic victory was achieved in 1828 when, at a by-election in Clare, O'Connell stood for parliament and secured twice as many votes as the sitting member. Although an anti-Catholic Test Act prevented him from taking his seat, his success precipitated government action. The Prime Minister, Wellington, and the Home Secretary, Sir Robert Peel, were sufficiently pragmatic to see the necessity for yielding on this issue; on 13 April 1829 the Catholic Relief Bill was passed. Although the simultaneous raising of the franchise qualification from 40 shillings to £10 was a disappointment, and although the act really benefited only the middle and upper classes, it was nevertheless seen as a great popular victory.

For twelve years after the granting of emancipation, O'Connell and his parliamentary followers supported the Whigs, who were in government for much of the period. A number of reforming measures were passed, including a reduction in tithes (V), extension of the franchise, the establishment of national education (78) and improvements in municipal government and the police force. With the return of a Conservative government in 1841, O'Connell decided to launch another popular agitation, this time for repeal of the union between Ireland and Britain. He followed much the same strategy as that of the 1820s: he founded a National Repeal Association, collected a repeal rent and again obtained the support of local clergy. During the emancipation campaign he had held many mass meetings, but these he now vastly increased in number and scale. At the peak of the campaign in 1843 he held about forty of these meetings; Figure 31 shows the location of all those attended by over 100,000 people. It is significant that none of these was held in the area which is now Northern Ireland, and only one in the rest of Ulster.

O'Connell hoped to secure repeal by emphasizing his massive popular support but this was unrealistic. Catholic emancipation had had the backing of many influential British politicians to whom repeal was totally unacceptable: Peel's government and the Whig opposition were united in implacable opposition to the demand. When in October 1843 the government banned a monster meeting at Clontarf, O'Connell, who was totally opposed to any risk of bloodshed, cancelled the meeting. For many supporters of the Repeal Association this was a sign of weakness and the movement gradually declined in effectiveness from then onwards, although it continued to do well in elections to parliament. Although there were thirty-six repeal supporters in the 1847 parliament (32) – more than ever before – popular support was fast diminishing. In 1847, with O'Connell's death, the constitutional movement collapsed.

One element in the National Repeal Association which had early provided a fillip to its popularity, but was later to contribute to its destruction, was the Young Ireland movement. In 1842 a group of young men, Thomas Davis (88), Charles Gavan Duffy and John Blake Dillon, founded the *Nation* newspaper to assist the repeal movement. They became disenchanted with O'Connell at an early stage, mainly due to differences over tactics, personal jealousies and their absolutist exaltation of nationalism, which O'Connell saw would inexorably lead them towards revolution: by 1844 they had split from him completely. With John Mitchel, Thomas Francis Meagher and William Smith O'Brien they became known as the Young Irelanders and many of them made valuable contributions to Irish political thought. Davis wrote more articulately about the concept of non-sectarian Irish nationality than any of his predecessors; as a Protestant nationalist he occupied an important place in the tradition that stretched from Tone to Parnell. Gavan Duffy, who was later in his career prime minister of Victoria in Australia, produced valuable ideas on the tactics of

Figure 31 O'Connell and Young Ireland: the 1843 repeal meetings; the 1848 uprising.

parliamentary opposition, and a fringe member of the group, James Fintan Lalor, wrote trenchantly on the land question.

In practical politics, however, the Young Irelanders were incompetent. Frustration with the collapse of the repeal movement and with the wretched condition of the country after the famine led them to decide on rebellion in 1848; this was to prove more farcical even than Emmet's rising. The inset map in Figure 31 shows the locations of a rebellion that petered out ineffectually due to poor leadership and non-existent planning.

The Young Irelanders' rebellion was opposed by the backbone of the repeal movement, the clergy and the middle classes and it effectively discredited the whole repeal movement. Not until Isaac Butt began the Home Rule campaign in 1870 did repeal of the union again become a respectable constitutional issue.

32   IRISH REPRESENTATION AT WESTMINSTER: 1800–1918

Until the passing of the Catholic Relief Bill in 1829 (31) there was no organized Irish party at Westminster: most Irish members were an integral part of one of the two main parties. With O'Connell's entry into the House of Commons the nucleus of a distinctively Irish party was formed, although the drastic cut in the electorate (from over 100,000 to 16,000) resulting from the disenfranchising of the 40-shilling freeholders severely restricted its support.

In his first decade in parliament, O'Connell supported the Whigs, whole-heartedly allying himself with them between 1835 and 1841. Although their Irish reforms fell short of those promised, he made allowances for their weakness; his support had been sufficiently valuable to them to secure certain concessions that otherwise might not have been granted.

With the return of a Conservative government in 1841, O'Connell espoused the cause of repeal much more actively. In 1847, of the Irish members returned, a third were identifiable as being supporters of repeal, but with O'Connell's death and the collapse of the movement, the organization of a united Irish party ceased.

The next significant development for the Irish at Westminster came with the tenant right movement, which had as its aim the legalizing throughout Ireland of the Ulster Custom (VII). In the general election of 1852, with an electorate increased in 1850 from 61,000 to 165,000, over forty of the Irish members elected subscribed to these principles; in alliance with the Whigs, Peelites and radicals, they defeated the Derby government. In the next ministry, Aberdeen's, two leading members of the party, Sadleir and Keogh, accepted office, and thus compromised the independence of the party and destroyed its unity: by the end of the decade the party was barely in existence.

There was little coherence among the Irish members at Westminster from then onwards. With improved economic circumstances, and with the Catholic clergy supporting the political status quo, popular enthusiasm for any movements towards independence was conspicuously lacking: it was necessary to find the

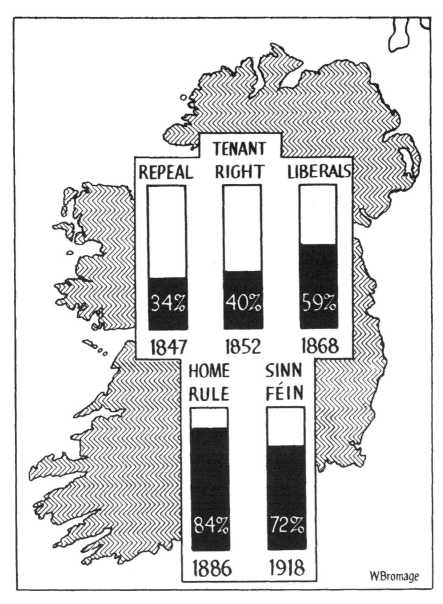

Figure 32 Irish representation at Westminster: 1800–1918.
Note Sinn Féin did not take their seats.

right issue and the right leader. The Fenian movement (III, 51) did not believe in the virtues of constitutional agitation and operated outside parliament.

In 1870 a Protestant barrister, Isaac Butt, a Conservative who nevertheless believed that Ireland was being misgoverned, founded a Home Government

Association; he saw Ireland's salvation in self-government by the middle and upper classes. This association was non-sectarian and initially had only one aim: the establishment of an Irish parliament. When it extended its aims to include land and educational reform it began to score some successes in by-elections. In 1874 the Home Rule League, as it was now called, won fifty-nine seats: significantly it won only two in Ulster – both in Cavan. There was still a need to gain popular support and the need for charismatic leadership was obvious. It was met by the emergence of Charles Stewart Parnell, who became leader in 1880. In 1879 Parnell had become president of the Land League (51) and this gave him a solid base of popular support with which to ally his parliamentary party.

In 1885, Liberals won 335 seats, Conservatives 249, and Parnell's party – which had benefited from an electoral increase of 700,000 under the 1884–5 reform acts – won eighty-six (every Irish seat outside north-east Ulster and Dublin University). Parnell had supported the Conservatives in that election, but while he now had the votes to keep them in power he could not give them a majority. However, with Gladstone's conversion to home rule, Parnell combined with the Liberals to defeat the Conservative government and allow Gladstone to form a government in 1886. Gladstone's first Home Rule Bill was narrowly defeated in 1886 and at the ensuing general election the Liberals lost power. Though Parnell could command eighty-five votes, British Liberal Unionists, who had won seventy-eight seats, supported the Conservatives.

The alliance between the Home Rule party and the Gladstonian Liberals continued until 1890, when the O'Shea divorce action, in which Parnell was named as co-respondent, split the disciplined and effective party he had built up over a decade. Parnell died in 1891. Although the party continued to be a major force in Irish politics for the next twenty-seven years, it never recovered its former importance, although it continued to win an impressive number of seats. In the 1892 election the Irish party lent its support to Gladstone to enable him to form a ministry and in 1893 he introduced the second Home Rule Bill; it passed the Commons but was defeated in the Lords. With Gladstone's resignation in 1894 and Rosebery's assumption of the office of prime minister, the alliance began to falter. In 1895 the government resigned and the ensuing election proved a triumph for the Conservative Unionists who remained in office until 1906.

The split that had occurred over Parnell's leadership after the divorce case did not end with his death. During the 1890s the Irish party was concerned with its own battles and many of its supporters turned from party politics to cultural movements like the Gaelic League (79) or more extreme movements like the Irish Republican Brotherhood. When the Liberals returned to power in 1906 the prospects for home rule looked brighter, and after the 1910 election the Irish party under John Redmond held the balance of power. In 1911 the Irish party combined with Asquith's Liberals to pass the Parliament Act, which provided a mechanism to override a Lords veto; it was therefore possible in 1914 to pass the Home Rule Bill, although it was suspended for the duration of the First World War.

Parnell's party had been the focal point of Irish political action, but though Redmond's Irish Parliamentary Party still represented the mainstream of political activity until 1917–18, it was gradually losing ground, especially among the young, to more radically nationalist and separatist movements and extra-constitutional political activity. The IRB, which had developed from the Fenian movement, was gaining strength and the Gaelic Athletic Association, founded in 1884, came more and more under IRB influence in the late nineteenth and early twentieth centuries. The Gaelic League, although solely committed to cultural nationalism, was also to prove to be an influence on revolutionary separatist movements. Political expression was given by Arthur Griffith's Sinn Féin ('Ourselves'), committed to abstention from Westminster (20). Although Griffith did not support revolution he capitalized on the public sympathy arising from the 1916 rebellion as well as on the anti-conscription movement and, in the 1918 general election, the reconstructed Sinn Féin party under Eamon de Valera crushed the Irish Parliamentary Party.

Although Ireland did not secure independence officially until 1922, since the Sinn Féin members refused to take their seats, 1918 saw the end of effective Irish representation at Westminster.

33   LABOUR IN IRELAND: 1907–23

Ireland remains unusual in Europe in that the late-nineteenth- and early twentieth-century industrial agitations did not lead to the polarization of politics along a left/right divide. There is an Irish Labour Party, but from 1932 to 2004 it averaged only 11 per cent of the vote, although at the first post-treaty elections in 1922 Labour performed spectacularly, returning seventeen of its eighteen candidates and winning 21.4 per cent of the vote (34). In Waterford it came out well ahead of all other parties, taking almost a third, compared to 24 per cent for the pro-treatyites and 16 per cent for the anti-treatyites. This result came after fourteen years of urban and rural upheaval.

The history of labour in Ireland has tended to be subsumed into the history of what is termed 'the national struggle', but as Roy Foster writes: 'For a considerable time it appeared that the critical confrontation in early twentieth-century Ireland would take place not between the British government and Irish nationalism, but between Irish capital and Irish labour.' In this alternative history of early twentieth-century Ireland, the key date is not 1916 but 1913, the year of the lockout.

Irish labour was a part of British labour but did not begin to organize until relatively late, as in the late nineteenth century it was hampered by the easy availability of non-union labour. An exception to this rule was Belfast, which was highly industrialized and had huge gaps between skilled and unskilled wage rates. An Independent Labour Party branch was set up in Belfast in 1892, and Thomas Sloan's and Lindsay Crawford's Independent Orange Order, established in 1903, emphasized the working-class roots of Orangeism, and even

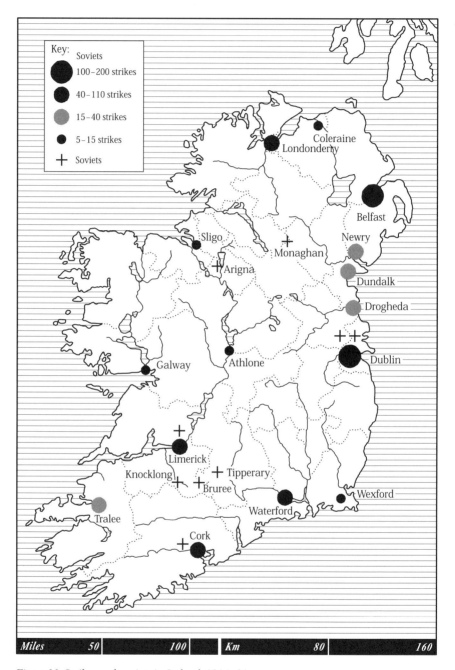

Figure 33 Strikes and soviets in Ireland: 1914–21.

Source David Fitzpatrick, 'Strikes in Ireland, 1914–21', *Soathair* 6.

made overtures across the sectarian divide. In 1907 the socialist James Larkin capitalized on these beginnings with the great Belfast dock strike, an all-out confrontation involving Protestant and Catholic workers which developed into a police mutiny and had to be put down with military intervention. It looked briefly as if labour might transcend sectarianism, but by 1908 conflicts were again polarized along nationalist/unionist lines and the Independent Labour Party performed badly in the council elections.

In 1908 Larkin founded the Irish Transport and General Workers' Union (ITGWU), the most influential Irish union (in 1990 it would amalgamate with the Federated Workers' Union of Ireland under the name of SIPTU – the Services Industrial Professional Technical Union), and moved to Dublin, where he introduced militant European-style syndicalism, which culminated in the labour disputes of 1913–14. These involved at least thirty different sectors (painters, bricklayers, carpenters, barbers, seamen, firemen, dockers, etc.) and involved 20,000 strikers and the loss of 1.7 million workdays in 1913. When in August 1913 Larkin hubristically extended the strike action to William Martin Murphy's Dublin United Tramways Company, Murphy persuaded the Employers' Federation to lock out all members of the ITGWU; by the beginning of 1914 the strikers were effectively defeated and the eve of the First World War saw the syndicalist movement subdued, with little to show in industrial terms for its costly actions of the previous few years. Larkin went to America and James Connolly became acting ITGWU general secretary.

War reduced unemployment throughout the United Kingdom, since the unskilled were recruited into the army and there was increased demand for workers in engineering, chemicals, agriculture, etc. However, this trend was less marked in Ireland, where recruitment was much lower and fewer munitions factories were established. Also, Irish labour (outside the north-east) felt less constrained to put its battle with capital on hold for the greater good of the war effort (indeed Connolly's anti-war sentiments would lead him to participate in the 1916 insurrection (20)). After a brief lull there was a steady increase in industrial action from mid-1915 to the end of the war.

Most pre-war action had taken place in Dublin and Belfast, but while between 1914 and 1918 two-fifths of strikes and two-thirds of strikers were still located in these two cities, action was spreading to other areas, mostly south Munster and the north-east. After the war there was an immediate economic slump, unemployment in the United Kingdom in 1919 exceeded the pre-war level and strike activity was intensified. There were more strikes across Ireland in the two post-war years, 1919–21, than throughout the entire war and they were more evenly spread across the country, though the Belfast engineering and shipbuilding strike of 1919 affected 40,000 people and caused the loss of 750,000 workdays.

Much of the post-war success of Irish labour was attributable to the ITGWU, which trebled in size during 1918, grew by a further two-thirds over the next eighteen months and crucially helped to radicalize farm workers, 40,000 of whom enrolled between 1918 and 1920, particularly in the south-east. In July

1919 a strike of farm labourers in Meath and Kildare saw 2,500 ITGWU members striking against 1,100 employers; tactics included sabotage of crops, livestock, auctions and fairs; the celebrated 'battle of Fenor' in Co. Waterford in November 1919 saw 300 labourers rioting against 120 RIC men. Industrial and agricultural action was backed up by workers' cooperatives, and from November 1918, even by soviets (workers' councils). In response to the Russian Revolution, and to the alarm of the authorities, eight soviets, flying red flags, were declared from 1918 to 1921; in which workplaces were seized, management expelled, and the workplaces operated by a soviet. The name was also adopted famously by the Limerick soviet of April 1919, when the local trades council effectively governed the city during a two-week general strike.

It is this background that explains the exceptionally strong Labour performance in the 1922 election, where it won more votes than the anti-treatyites and seemed poised to become a major political player. That it did not is attributed variously to the hostility of the Free State government, which bore down strongly on labour action (a farm strike in Waterford in 1923 was won by the farmers with military backing from the state); to the essentially conservative bourgeois nature of Irish politics and society; to the power of the Roman Catholic church; and to the weakness and failure of the Labour Party itself. Its two key figures, Larkin and James Connolly, were gone: Connolly had been executed in 1916; Larkin was famously expelled for extremism by the ITGWU in 1923 and the surviving leaders were more cautious parliamentarians. Then, too, the horrors and bitterness of the War of Independence (21) and the Civil War (22) helped knock the fight out of the Left; during the 1927 election campaign Labour leader Thomas Johnson declared: 'We have had one revolution and one revolution in a generation is enough.'

34   POLITICAL AFFILIATIONS IN DÁIL ÉIREANN: 1918–2002

Sinn Féin won seventy-three seats in the December 1918 Westminster elections, the Irish Parliamentary Party six and the Unionists twenty-six; all 105 were invited to take their seats in an independent national assembly, Dáil Éireann, on 21 January 1919. Only Sinn Féin members accepted, and of them only twenty-eight were free to attend: this group declared a republic, agreed a constitution and a programme of social and economic reform and appointed delegates to the Paris Peace Conference (they were never allowed to participate). Coincidentally, on the same day, the Anglo-Irish War began (21).

In April 1919 Eamon de Valera, on the run from prison, was elected president, with Arthur Griffith his deputy and minister for home affairs and Michael Collins at finance. The new executive set out to establish a republican infrastructure throughout the country, with alternative courts, police and other institutions – a task that was carried out with considerable success. The British hold over Irish institutions was further weakened by Sinn Féin's success in the 1920 local elections. Lloyd George's Government of Ireland Act (1920), which gave very limited powers to parliaments representing the six north-eastern and twenty-six other counties, was rejected by Sinn Féin and accepted by the Unionists. Elections under this act were held in May 1921; Sinn Féin was returned unopposed throughout the South and formed the second Dáil. In July 1921 de Valera agreed to a truce.

From October to December 1921 treaty negotiations were held in London. The leading members of the British delegation were Lloyd George, Lord Birkenhead, Austen Chamberlain and Winston Churchill. Arthur Griffith led the Irish delegation, among whom were Michael Collins and Erskine Childers. The treaty was signed on 6 December: it approved the setting up of an Irish Free State with dominion status, but stipulated that an oath of allegiance to the crown should remain obligatory on Irish legislators. It was mainly this that led to the split which led to civil war (22).

The Dáil debated the treaty until 7 January 1922, when it was approved by only sixty-four votes to fifty-seven. Those in favour of it argued that it offered, in Collins's words, the 'freedom to achieve freedom'. De Valera led the anti-treaty side and when he lost the deciding vote he resigned as president of the Dáil and was succeeded by Griffith. Collins was appointed chairman of the provisional government, which – although appointed by and responsible to the parliament of southern Ireland that had been set up under the Government of Ireland Act of 1920 – was mandated by the terms of the 1921 treaty. The provisional government went to the electorate in the twenty-six counties of southern Ireland and won a decisive victory over the anti-treaty section, then known as the Republicans. Concurrently with the split in the Dáil had come a split in the IRA, the anti-treaty party of which broke away from Dáil control.

The general election of 16 June 1922 showed a clear majority for the treaty; twelve days later the Civil War broke out. Within two months the Free State government had lost two outstanding leaders, with the death of Griffith from a cerebral haemorrhage on 12 August and of Collins in an ambush ten days later. The new head of government was W. T. Cosgrave, with Kevin O'Higgins at home affairs and Richard Mulcahy at defence; they proved to be as effective and ruthless as their predecessors in crushing their opponents. By April 1923 the Republicans were defeated. De Valera, who had not taken an active role in the war, although he had supported and encouraged the Republicans, ordered a ceasefire in May. The bitterness engendered by the Civil War would dominate Irish politics right into the twenty-first century.

The Free Staters first set up a political party called Cumann na nGaedheal ('Party of the Irish') in 1923, which in 1933 merged with two smaller parties to form Fine Gael ('Irish race'). The Republicans were not represented in the Dáil until 1927; Sinn Féin, dormant in 1922, was revived in 1923 and won forty-four seats, which were not taken because of continued opposition to the oath of allegiance and a belief in the illegitimacy of the Free State and its institutions. Unable to convert the party from abstentionism, in 1926 de Valera abandoned it to impotence and founded Fianna Fáil ('Soldiers of Destiny'), which won forty-four seats in the fifth Dáil; the members took the oath of allegiance. In 1932

Fianna Fáil formed a government and took over from Cumann na nGaedheal, which had ruled for a decade and had established the new state as an independent country under a responsible government.

De Valera came to power pledged to economic self-sufficiency. During the early 1930s he waged an economic war with Britain, which was initiated by the Irish government's refusal to pay the land annuities still owing from the Land Acts (59). Although the trade war protected infant industries and perhaps reduced emigration, it proved very expensive for Ireland, being especially disastrous for agriculture; in 1938 de Valera was obliged to make a trade agreement with Britain. Still, anti-Britishness remained a defining aspect of Irish politics and culture, those with British or unionist sympathies kept quiet and, in de Valera's words, Ireland was 'a Catholic nation' which strove to be Gaelic as well.

A feature of Irish politics during the 1930s was the problem the two big parties had with extremist groups. Fine Gael was formed from Cumann na nGaedheal, the Farmers' Party and General Eoin O'Duffy's quasi-fascist Blue Shirt movement. O'Duffy was actually elected President of Fine Gael but was afterwards asked to resign and was succeeded by Cosgrave. The Blue Shirts had a brief period of notoriety before O'Duffy disappeared to Spain with about 700 men to help Franco win the civil war. Unlike the 150 or so socialist republicans (some from the IRA) who under Frank Ryan formed the Connolly Column of the anti-Franco International Brigade, they saw little action and soon came home.

Simultaneously Fianna Fáil was being embarrassed by its erstwhile allies in the IRA. After an increase in IRA activity in the early 1930s under the Cosgrave government, there was a hiatus for a time after de Valera took power. When it increased again in the mid–1930s, de Valera, with characteristic pragmatism, cracked down; in 1936 he declared the IRA illegal.

Cumann na nGaedheal / Fine Gael was traditionally the party of the middle classes and large farmers and Fianna Fáil that of the smaller farmers and the lower middle classes. However, de Valera's magnetism enabled him to poach many traditional Fine Gael voters and win six consecutive elections. From 1932 until 1973 Fianna Fáil was out of office for only six years (1948–51 and 1954–7), when multi-party coalitions took power, yet after 1973 the Irish electorate changed government at every election until 2002, when it finally voted for a Fianna Fáil-dominated coalition to continue for a second term. Fianna Fáil's traditional rejection of coalition had been abandoned in 1989 so opening the door to smaller parties. This volte-face caused difficulties for Fine Gael, which has never had an overall majority and has counted on other parties to form its anti-Fianna Fáil coalitions. Labour, traditionally the natural ally of Fine Gael, went into government with Fianna Fáil in 1992 – switching back to Fine Gael two years later without precipitating an election.

Fianna Fáil's new approach to coalition helps account for the more stable position of small parties in Irish politics from the late 1980s on. The Progressive Democrats (PDs), an economically right-wing party, formed in 1985 in a breakaway from Fianna Fáil (mainly over the leadership of Charles Haughey), carved out a comfortable niche, taking between four and twelve seats at every election and – between 1987 and 2004 – spending more years in government than either Fine Gael or Labour.

In the history of the Dáil the normal trajectory for even the most successful small parties has been to disappear after a few elections: this was the case with Clann na Talmhan ('Party of the Land'), the populist farmers' party (1939–54), the republican economically left-wing and socially right-wing Clann na Poblachta ('Party of the Republic') (1946–65) and, most recently, the Democratic Left – the successor of the majority of the Workers' Party and its predecessor, Official Sinn Féin – which merged with the Labour Party in 1999. As well as the PDs, two other parties – the Green Party and Sinn Féin – have a good chance of survival. The Green Party, which has benefited from the rising concern for environmental issues and the growth of Green parties across Europe, attracts a largely middle-class support; its share of the vote increased nationally from 0.4 per cent in 1987 to 3.8 per cent in 2002, and its seats from one in 1989 to six in 2002 – five of which were in Dublin.

Sinn Féin's is a more complicated history. After de Valera left, the rump of Sinn Féin remained abstentionist, and took neither its five seats in 1927 nor its four in 1957. In October 1986, it dropped its abstentionist policy in the Republic (leading to a split and the creation of Republican Sinn Féin) but won no seats until it secured one in 1997 in the favourable climate of the peace process; in 2002, it doubled its vote and took five. Young, hard-working, well-financed and cross-border, and under the direction of household names from Northern Ireland like Gerry Adams and Martin McGuinness, it polls well in deprived areas as well as in traditionally republican areas like Kerry and border counties. To date political parties in the Republic insist Sinn Féin should not be in government until the IRA goes out of business.

The recent success of small parties notwithstanding, the Dáil has largely maintained, throughout its history, the pattern set during its formative years: two main parties, which are not, as in almost every other European country, divided along left/right ideological grounds, but on the traditional perception of Fianna Fáil as the greener (i.e. more nationalist), and Fine Gael the more law-and-order party; a relatively marginalized Labour Party (33), and an assortment of usually short-lived smaller parties and independents. At certain moments in the history of the Dáil (the late 1920s, the late 1940s and the early 2000s), small parties have been prominent and have collectively taken almost a third of the vote, but as Figure 34 shows, the two main parties have always maintained solid support bases. For Fianna Fáil average support since 1932 has hovered at 42–50 per cent; for Fine Gael it has been around 30 per cent. The persistence of 'Civil War politics' is evident in the dynastic nature of Irish politics. (In 2004 over a fifth of TDs (35) – members of parliament – were related to other TDs, past and present: father to son or, increasingly, father to daughter is the most common manifestation of this tradition; it is estimated that being related to a TD is worth 1,300 votes.) This persistence is also evident in

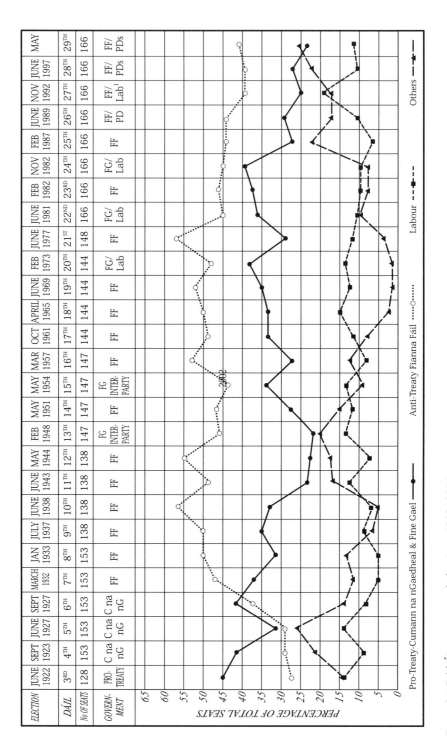

The table embedded in the figure:

ELECTION	JUNE 1922	SEPT 1923	JUNE 1927	SEPT 1927	MARCH 1932	JAN 1933	JULY 1937	JUNE 1938	JUNE 1943	MAY 1944	FEB 1948	MAY 1951	MAY 1954	MAR 1957	OCT 1961	APRIL 1965	JUNE 1969	FEB 1973	JUNE 1977	JUNE 1981	FEB 1982	NOV 1982	FEB 1987	JUNE 1989	NOV 1992	JUNE 1997	MAY 1997
DÁIL	3RD	4TH	5TH	6TH	7TH	8TH	9TH	10TH	11TH	12TH	13TH	14TH	15TH	16TH	17TH	18TH	19TH	20TH	21ST	22ND	23RD	24TH	25TH	26TH	27TH	28TH	29TH
No OF SEATS	128	153	153	153	153	153	138	138	138	138	147	147	147	147	144	144	144	144	148	166	166	166	166	166	166	166	166
GOVERN-MENT	PRO-TREATY	C na nG	C na nG	C na nG	FF	FF	FF	FF	FF	FF	FG INTER-PARTY	FF	FG INTER-PARTY	FF	FF	FF	FF	FG/Lab	FF	FG/Lab	FF	FG/Lab	FF	FF/PD	FF/Lab[1]	FF/PDs	FF/PDs

Figure 34 Dáil Éireann general elections: 1922–2002.

Note: 1 In December 1994, without an election, a new government was formed, made up of FG, Labour and Democratic Left.

Legend: Pro-Treaty–Cumann na nGaedheal & Fine Gael ——•——   Anti-Treaty Fianna Fáil ·····○·····   Labour – –■– –   Others – –▲– –

the European parliament, where Fianna Fáil and Fine Gael have no obvious homes in any of the main blocs, and their links are made haphazardly rather than ideologically; Fine Gael is not obviously more 'Christian Democrat' than Fianna Fáil.

Corruption has also been an important feature of modern Irish politics. Initially small scale and usually local, it reached the highest echelons of government under Charles Haughey, aided by public indifference and a culture of secrecy and intimidation, as well as repressive libel laws that inhibited investigative journalism. Since the early 1990s myriad well-founded and publicly aired allegations prompted the establishment by the Dáil of tribunals of inquiry under various judges into specific matters of public importance – which have been lengthy, hugely costly in lawyers' fees and frequently inconclusive. The Hamilton inquiry into the beef-processing industry (1991–4) and the provision of massive export credit assurance for a $134 million contract with Iraq found that the beef baron Larry Goodman had profited from his intimacy with government; however, Albert Reynolds, as Minister for Industry and Commerce, was found to be legally entitled to ignore the advice of senior civil servants in making decisions on credit insurance. Following the McCracken inquiry of 1997 into payments to politicians – which uncovered payments from Ben Dunne of Dunnes Stores to various politicians, but had insufficient evidence supporting claims that payments were made in exchange for political action – the Moriarty tribunal was set up to investigate claims of payments made to ex-Taoiseach Haughey and to former Fine Gael minister Michael Lowry.

The Irish electorate seemed relatively unconcerned about political sleaze. While Haughey's reputation was certainly sullied by revelations about an immensely extravagant lifestyle funded by indulgent businessmen and the taxpayers, Fianna Fáil – senior members of which had colluded and worse – did not suffer at the poll, while Lowry, expelled from his party for massive tax evasion, topped the polls in Tipperary as an independent. After sensational revelations to the Flood (now Mahon) inquiry (1997– ongoing) into corrupt payments in the planning context, one public servant was imprisoned, both a senior Fianna Fáil minister and a long-serving TD were disgraced and other party members implicated, yet Fianna Fáil still went on to take the 2002 election with ease. A growing cynicism among the electorate has been capitalized on by Sinn Féin, which campaigns against financial corruption in spite of being partly financed by IRA racketeering. In the 2004 local elections, the Fianna Fáil share of first preferences went down to 31.9 per cent from the 1999 figure of 38.9 per cent, while Sinn Féin went up from 3.5 per cent to 8.0 per cent. (For the European elections, see 53.)

35   GOVERNMENT IN IRELAND

The Irish Republic, de facto since 1937, has a president as head of state, elected for seven years by the whole electorate. The president is supreme commander of the armed forces and is empowered (on the recommendation of the house of representatives, the Dáil) to appoint the prime minister (taoiseach), sign laws, and invoke the judgement of the supreme court on the constitutionality of bills. The presidents have been: Douglas Hyde (1938–45), Sean T. Ó Ceallaigh (1945–59), Eamon de Valera (1959–73), Erskine Childers (1973–4), Cearbhall Ó Dálaigh (1974–6), Patrick Hillery (1976–90), Mary Robinson (1990–97) and Mary McAleese (1997–). Heads of government have been: William T. Cosgrave (1922–32) and Eamon de Valera (1932–7) who were known as Presidents of the Executive Council, a title then changed to Taoiseach (leader); Taoisigh (plural) have been de Valera (1937–48, 1951–4, 1957–9), John A. Costello (1948–51), Costello (1954–7), Seán Lemass (1959–66), Jack Lynch (1966–73), Liam Cosgrave (1973–7), Lynch (1977–9), Charles Haughey (1979–81, 1982, 1987–92), Garret FitzGerald (1981–2, 1982–7), Albert Reynolds (1992–4), John Bruton (1994–7) and Bertie Ahern (1997–).

The Irish parliament (*oireachtas*) consists of the president and two houses, the Dáil, now comprising 166 members (Teachtaí Dála – TDs, known as deputies) representing forty-three multi-seat constituencies elected by adult suffrage according to a system of proportional representation, and the Senate (Seanad Éireann) comprising sixty members, eleven nominated by the Taoiseach, six elected by specified universities and forty-three elected to represent five panels: culture and education, agriculture, labour, industry and commerce, and public administration. TDs, outgoing senators and the members of every county or city council elect representatives of each panel. Although some independent members have raised the quality of debate, the Senate has little influence and less power, can block no legislation passed by the Dáil and can delay it at most for ninety days. The constitution can be amended only by referenda, of which twenty-seven have been held since its ratification in 1937; *inter alia*, they have permitted entry to the European Community (now the EU), have ratified the Single European Act, the Maastricht and Amsterdam treaties and the Treaty of Nice (the second time around) and have abolished capital punishment.

Since the foundation of the Irish Free State electoral acts have increased the number of constituencies but decreased the number of members per con-stituency: in 1923 the majority of constituencies had between five and nine members, but under the Electoral Amendment Acts of 1969 and 1974, the majority had only three, each representing about 14,000 electors. A further Electoral Amendment Act (1980) increased the number of constituencies with four or five members, but that of 2004 reduced them; the majority have only three or four. Electoral changes have been introduced largely because smaller parties have tended to be more successful in constituencies with more members and, under the present system of proportional representation, using the single transferable vote, it is difficult for any party to secure an absolute majority; governments have usually had to rely on the support of smaller parties or independents. For this reason Fianna Fáil attempted unsuccessfully in a referendum in 1959 to replace proportional representation by the simple

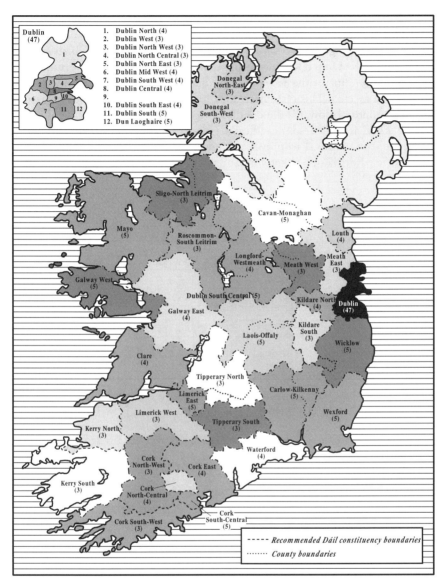

Figure 35 Government in Ireland: electoral boundaries 2004. Government in Ireland: Dublin electoral boundaries, 2004.

majority vote. A similar attempt, partly supported by Fine Gael, was made in 1968, again unsuccessfully.

As a percentage of the total population, electors have increased from 1 per cent in 1832 to 14 per cent in 1885, 58 per cent in 1923, 63 per cent in 1977 and 76 per cent in 2002. From 1932–81, turnout in Dáil elections averaged

75 per cent; during the 1990s it fell to 67 per cent and in 2002 to 62 per cent, the lowest turnout since 1923 and well below the European average.

Although a general election must be held within five years of the previous election, the average term of an Irish government is three years, which is comparable with the United Kingdom, suggesting that the failure of governments to obtain absolute majorities is less of a hindrance to effective government than might be expected. This insecurity does, however, appear to encourage a conservative approach towards the conduct of government, although membership of the EU has forced some radical legislative changes. However, multi-seat constituencies continue to provoke intense competition between TDs and to encourage parochialism, clientelism and pork-barrel politics.

V Religion

There is little precise information about the pre-Christian religions in Ireland, although such massive passage tombs as Newgrange, Knowth and Dowth at Brú na Bóinne on the Boyne, built by the Neolithic inhabitants in around 3200 BC, almost certainly testify to a widespread devotion to their gods (IV).

When the Celts came to Ireland they brought with them their own gods, many of whom survive by name in Irish mythology. The Tuatha Dé Danann were Celtic gods who were later recorded in the oral tradition as one of a series of prehistoric invaders. The Celtic priests, the druids, had a privileged place in the Irish community, and they put up a stout resistance to Christianity, which was nevertheless successfully introduced to Ireland, with the missionaries showing considerable skill in reconciling pagan traditions with Christian ritual.

With Christianity writing was introduced to Ireland, which hitherto had relied almost entirely on oral communication, the only exception being ogam writing (43). Irish monasteries educated the people, and gradually the druids adapted to the new religion and became either professional men of learning or monks.

The early Irish Christians were zealous and took to the monastic life with tremendous dedication. They were less enthusiastic about the introduction of an episcopal structure along the lines of the Roman model. Ireland was politically too diversified to conform to a centralized administration, and it was not for several centuries that bishops became really powerful in the Irish church. The expansion of monasticism within the country continued until the seventh century, when the impetus slackened somewhat. The monastic life was strict by Continental standards, and there was a tendency towards extreme austerity in many individual monasteries, particularly in those following the rule of Columbanus. From the sixth century onwards, much of the missionary spirit of the Irish monks was directed outwards to the Continent (44) and for several centuries they had a widespread reputation for sanctity and scholarship. Even abroad, however, the Irish were slow to accept the Roman system of episcopal jurisdiction.

The Viking wars (11) brought disruption to the Irish church; by the early eleventh century there was less spiritual fervour, and most monasteries had become more Hibernicized and worldly. The Irish church took little effective action against infringements of some aspects of reformed Christianity, including concubinage, and from late in the century Rome began to take an active interest in the moral and jurisdictional well-being of Ireland. During this period a series of reforming popes were successfully tightening up discipline throughout the Christian church, and it was only a matter of time before Ireland came under close scrutiny. At the same time Lanfranc, the reforming Norman archbishop of Canterbury, began to take an interest in Ireland and wrote to the High King urging him to summon a reforming synod. Three important synods were held during the twelfth century: Cashel in 1101, Rathbreasail in 1111 and Kells in 1152. Their purpose was to reconcile Irish law and Roman canon law, restrict the power of the great monastic foundations by orienting the country towards episcopal authority, and set up an episcopal if not a diocesan organization; all this was largely accomplished within the century. In its legislation on Christian marriage, the synod of Kells conformed to Roman church law, and it set up an ecclesiastical structure that has changed little. Ireland was divided into four ecclesiastical provinces: Armagh, Dublin, Cashel and Tuam.

The most important names in the Irish reform movement are those of Celsus and Malachy, two prelates of Armagh; Gilbert, bishop of Limerick; and St Laurence O'Toole, archbishop of Dublin. As a result of the work of these and many other reforming clergy and laymen, and particularly the achievement of St Malachy in bringing the Cistercians to Ireland, the church in Ireland at the time of the Norman invasion was spiritually and administratively very healthy. Nonetheless, in his bull *Laudabiliter*, Pope Adrian IV authorized the invasion of Ireland in the interests of ecclesiastical and moral reform, and the Irish church quickly accepted Norman rule.

The Normans were enthusiastic patrons of the church, gave financial aid to old and new religious orders and throughout Ireland built many magnificent monasteries and churches (37). Many of them joined the church; Archbishop Richard FitzRalph of Armagh was the most distinguished theologian and churchman of medieval Ireland.

During the later Middle Ages the Irish church once again entered a period of spiritual decline, although reformed orders of friars during the fifteenth century had considerable success in restoring some moral prestige to the clergy. Paradoxically it was the Reformation that was to rekindle the spiritual imagination of the people, and by the end of the Counter-Reformation (39), despite the poverty of the church and the persecution to which it was exposed, it commanded great devotion from the Irish people. The Reformation, however, established episcopalian Protestantism as the officially recognized form of Christianity, though most of the people continued to be Roman Catholic.

By 1829 most anti-Catholic legislation was removed from the statute book but Catholics were still required to pay tithes to the established church. This cause of resentment was not removed until Gladstone's disestablishment of the Church of Ireland in 1869. Throughout the modern period the history of the Irish church was mainly concerned with the Catholic church's emergence from a state of persecution to that of being not only tolerated but given special privileges under the law. Under Article 44 of the constitution of the Irish Republic the Catholic church was recognized as having a special position, and it was not until 1972 that as a result of constitutional change it was placed on a footing of equality with, not superiority to, other religions.

Throughout the past 400 years, religion in Ireland has been both a unifying and a divisive force. It served to unite the Irish and Old English against a common enemy, and to give all social classes a common bond. On the other hand, religious divisions have served to polarize attitudes in Northern Ireland where a Presbyterian colonization in the seventeenth century led to a situation where a man's religion normally determined his social and financial status and his political and moral attitudes (XI).

36   THE COMING OF CHRISTIANITY

'Ad Scottos in Christum credentes ordinatus a papa Caelestino Palladius primus episcopus mittitur.' Thus Prosper of Aquitaine tells of Pope Celestine's consecration of Palladius in 431 as the first bishop of the Irish who believed in Christ; this and other evidence shows that there were Christian settlements in Ireland before the arrival of St Patrick. Little information is, however, available on the widespread conversion of the Irish; the efforts of Palladius and other missionaries were ignored by contemporary and later chroniclers, who chose to attribute to Patrick credit for the conversion of the whole island. This belief persisted perhaps because Patrick seems to have been concerned with the pagan Irish while other contemporary missionaries were more involved with the believing Irish. Nevertheless, conversion was not fully complete even by the sixth century.

As a result of popular legend and Patrick's own writings, especially *The Confession*, his reputation as the Apostle of Ireland has obscured those of his contemporaries. It is still not clear whether he worked in Ireland from the 430s to the 460s or from the 460s to the 490s. However, even if exaggerated, his impact was considerable. His main achievement seems to have been to inspire a great many fervent disciples, who with their successors were to complete the conversion of Ireland and extend their influence throughout Britain and Europe (44).

The Irish church was theoretically episcopal, and dioceses were formed to correspond with the petty kingdoms (1), but monastic ideals quickly took root, and by the end of the sixth century abbots were more powerful than bishops, and over 800 monasteries had been founded. Some of the more important of these are shown in Figure 36. The monasteries had an international reputation for piety and many of them also for learning. The copying of manuscripts became an important part of the monastic traditions, producing such masterpieces of illuminated manuscripts as the *Book of Kells* and the *Book of Durrow*. Irish monastic scholarship was characterized more by dedication to the highest

Figure 36 The coming of Christianity: ecclesiastical foundations *c.* fifth–eighth centuries.

artistic standards in the transcription of manuscripts than by originality, but above all it displayed a deep veneration of learning.

Over fifty large churches were also founded during this period, many of them allegedly by St Patrick. Some of the more famous Irish saints of the period were St Colmcille (Derry, Durrow), St Finnian (Clonard, Moville), St Ciaran (Clonmacnois), St Kevin (Glendalough), St Brigid (Kildare), St Brendan (Clonfert) and St Enda of Aran.

37   MEDIEVAL ECCLESIASTICAL IRELAND

After the early fervour of the monastic movement in Ireland the church began to decline, fewer monasteries were founded and, as a result of Viking attacks, many existing monasteries were destroyed or abandoned.

By the time of the Norman invasion, the few monasteries still surviving operated along early Celtic lines and showed little sign of foreign influence. The reform movement of the twelfth century set up a territorial diocesan hierarchy similar to what was common in the Western Church and which with minor modifications, such as Tuam's absorption of Mayo and Annaghdown, has remained in existence until now. The 1152 synod of Kells determined this hierarchy, setting up four metropolitan archbishoprics – Armagh, Dublin, Cashel and Tuam – with Armagh retaining the primacy of Ireland.

Following on the revival of religious enthusiasm manifested in the reform movement came a monastic revival. This was inspired first by Malachy of Armagh, who introduced Augustinians of Arrouaise and Cistercian monks to Ireland, and then by the Normans, who were responsible for many foundations, especially of Knights Hospitallers and Templars. As a result of a policy of strict segregation, Celtic and Norman monks mixed less and less.

Religious fervour was reignited in the thirteenth century with the arrival of the mendicant orders, but the economic and social disasters of the Black Death (1348–9) and other famines and pestilences of the fourteenth century had a serious effect on existing foundations. Between the mid-fourteenth century and the Reformation no more monasteries of monks or regular canons were founded, although there were over 100 new houses of friars.

Monastic life degenerated considerably during the fifteenth century, succumbing through poverty and paucity of recruits to indiscipline and spiritual decline.

It is not possible to give precise figures for the number of monastic foundations existing in Ireland during the medieval period. Figure 37 notes the major foundations and indicates their distribution. An estimate is given below of the number of foundations of the major religious orders during this period.

Canons regular: Augustinians of Arrouaise – 181 foundations, mostly twelfth century; Crutched Friars – nineteen foundations, mostly thirteenth century; Premonstratensians – nineteen, mostly thirteenth century.

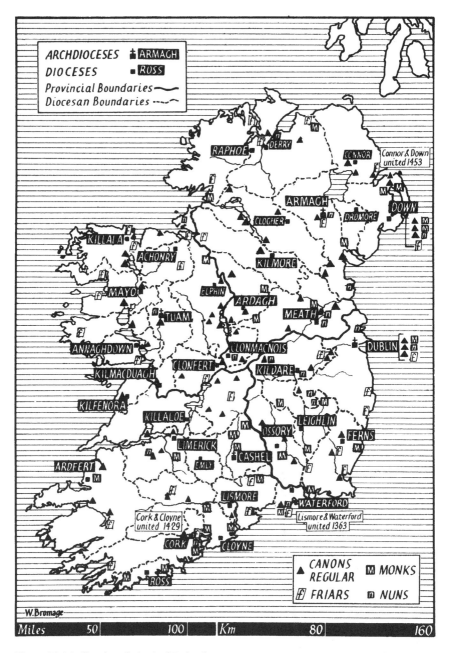

Figure 37 Medieval ecclesiastical Ireland.

Monks:	Benedictines – sixteen foundations, mostly twelfth century; Cistercians – fifty-two, mostly twelfth century.
Friars:	Dominicans – forty-one foundations, mostly thirteenth century; Franciscans – sixty-two foundations, mostly thirteenth century; Carmelites – sixty-five foundations, mostly thirteenth and fourteenth centuries; Augustinians – twenty-two foundations, mostly fourteenth century; Franciscan Third Order Regular – forty-eight foundations, mostly fifteenth century.
Military orders:	Knights Templars – sixteen foundations, mostly twelfth century; Knights Hospitallers – twenty-one foundations, mostly thirteenth century.
Nuns:	Records for many convents are often poor or non-existent, so figures are uncertain. There were about ninety recorded, of which over forty were under the rule of Augustinians of Arrouaise.
Hospitals and hospices:	During most of this period these were maintained by the regular orders, notably the Crutched Friars, Augustinian canons and Benedictines. They numbered over 200.

The other important foundations of this period were the thirty-five or so secular colleges, which were founded mainly in the thirteenth century.

38 POST-REFORMATION IRELAND

In 1534 King Henry VIII became 'Supreme Head on Earth of the Church of England' and in 1536 'Supreme Head on Earth of the Church of Ireland'. He set out to reform the Irish church at a time when it was temporally prosperous and spiritually poor. Despite the efforts of the friars, and especially the Franciscan Third Order Regular, to bring about a spiritual revival in the early sixteenth century, the need for reform was still very obvious. Consequently, there was less opposition to Henry's proposed reforms than might have been expected, there being in his favour the positive need for reform and some anti-clericalism.

Outside the monasteries, in the rest of the Irish church, the position was no better. In the Gaelic areas parishes and dioceses went to scions of the powerful local families: within the English areas, royal support was a necessary prerequisite for ecclesiastical office. The clergy were often poor, greedy and uneducated.

The main responsibility for introducing the Reformation to Ireland was given to George Browne, archbishop of Dublin from 1536 to 1554, who began by participating in a parliament in 1536, which unwillingly declared Henry 'Supreme Head on Earth of the Church of Ireland'. It passed a number of other acts: the Act of Slander declared that the penalty for calling Henry a heretic,

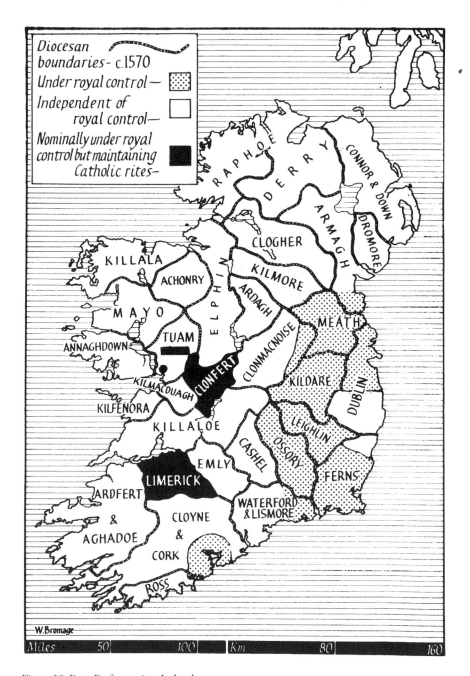

Figure 38 Post-Reformation Ireland.

schismatic or usurper would be conviction of high treason; the Act against the Authority of the Bishop of Rome provided for the effective outlawry of any person supporting 'the advancement and continuance of the [pope's] . . . famed and pretended authority'; under the Act declaring the king, his heirs and successors to be Supreme Head of the Church of Ireland, it was laid down that any subject could be required to take an oath of allegiance to Henry as head of the church; anyone refusing was guilty of high treason. Contemporaneously, provision was made for the suppression of the monasteries (39).

The Reformation had little success initially, except in the Pale and in the towns: the Gaelic areas offered passive resistance. The attempts of Edward VI (1547–53) to introduce doctrinal innovations were strongly resisted in Ireland. Mary (1553–8), although she theoretically restored Roman Catholicism, did little in practice and failed to restore more than a few monasteries.

Elizabeth (1558–1603) set out to extend the Reformation throughout Ireland. A parliament of 1560 reaffirmed the provisions of the 1536 parliament and added the Act of Uniformity, which enforced, on pain of a fine, attendance on Sundays at a service performed according to the Book of Common Prayer. Ultimately, her religious policy was no more successful in Ireland than that of her predecessors. The Jesuits had considerable success in countering attempts at proselytizing, and by the end of Elizabeth's reign – despite persecution and deprivation – Roman Catholicism was as strong as it had been for generations. Additionally, opposition to the new religion had proved to be a force for unity between the Gaelic Irish and Old English.

39   THE DISSOLUTION OF THE MONASTERIES

Over 400 monasteries were suppressed during the reigns of Henry VIII and Elizabeth, the majority during the reign of Henry VIII in areas where the king's writ ran. In many cases, however, suppression was more apparent than real. Local officials often reported the suppression of a monastery while in fact allowing it to remain in existence. It was not easy for monasteries to survive for long, since they relied on endowments which could not continue after confiscation, but the friars, who traditionally relied on the generosity of the local people, could continue in many areas indefinitely.

During Elizabeth's reign she tried to ensure the suppression of religious houses in practice by granting them to towns, Anglo-Irish or Gaelic lords, or English settlers. However, some of these grantees were themselves Catholic in sympathy and did not expel the monks. Despite this occasional tolerance, the persecution of religious became increasingly severe, resulting in the imprisonment and execution of many. Between 1570 and 1603, seventy-six identifiable individuals were put to death in reality on religious grounds, and twenty died in prison: of these, seven were prelates, eighteen secular priests, seven Cistercians, two Dominicans, thirty-six Franciscans, two Jesuits,

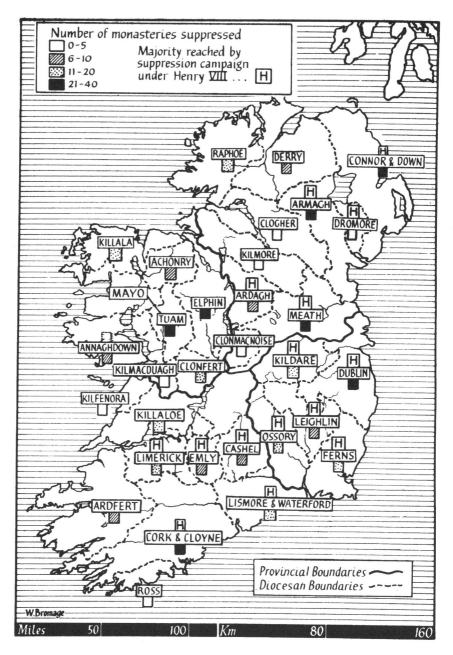

Figure 39 The dissolution of the monasteries.

twenty-three laymen and one a laywoman. Persecution was at its height during the early 1580s: forty-six of the deaths occurred between 1579 and 1584.

During Elizabeth's reign few Catholic bishops remained in Ireland, most of the dioceses were ruled by absentees, and few parochial clergy remained; only the friars performed services. Still, the courage of the Catholic clergy remaining in Ireland during the period of persecution proved a fine example to the people for whom they were working, and helped to keep Catholicism strong throughout the country. By the end of the century, although few religious houses remained in existence, even the Pale and the towns were still Catholic.

Early in the seventeenth century there was a religious revival. The Jesuits, who had been working in Ireland with a number of isolated friars from the middle of the sixteenth century, were joined by new recruits and by members of the mendicant orders who had trained abroad at Continental colleges (45). In 1615 large numbers of Capuchin Franciscans arrived and in 1625 many Discalced Carmelites. Gradually many of the old foundations were rebuilt and reoccupied, and new ones built. It is estimated that during this period the number of religious in Ireland equalled the number in the country at the zenith of the medieval period.

40   DISSENTERS IN IRELAND

Although Ireland was always numerically dominated by Roman Catholics it had a large and varied Protestant population. Like the Catholics, those Protestant groups that refused to conform to the Church of Ireland suffered at various times from discriminatory laws and the requirement to pay tithes to the established church. This discrimination persisted until disestablishment of the Church of Ireland in 1869.

A brief summary of the history of the main groups of Dissenters follows. Figure 40 shows the distribution of some relatively small groups whose location by the early eighteenth century can be demonstrated with some certainty.

Huguenots

French Protestants were known as Huguenots; they became disciples of Calvin and were essentially Presbyterian. Their intensive persecution began in France during the sixteenth century. Many emigrated to England, and there were some small and unsuccessful settlements in Ireland, in Cork and Swords. After the Edict of Nantes in 1598 gave them protection, most returned to France. The recommencing of persecution in the seventeenth century led to mass emigration to England, Scotland and Ireland. The main exodus to Ireland happened from the 1620s to 1641; in 1649 with Cromwell; from 1662, when the Duke of Ormond introduced into parliament 'An Act for Encouraging Protestant Strangers and Others to Inhabit Ireland' and established a number of colonies

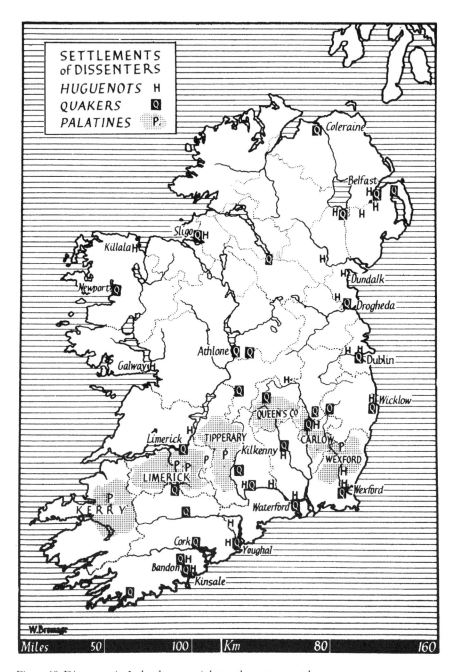

Figure 40 Dissenters in Ireland: some eighteenth–century settlements.

throughout the country; and when some of those arriving with William of Orange from Holland and Switzerland established new settlements in Lisburn, Kilkenny, Dundalk and Lurgan. Easily absorbed through intermarriage, Huguenots were celebrated for their textile expertise, specializing in weaving, lace-making, glove-making and the manufacture of linen and cloth.

Presbyterians

By far the most numerous group of Dissenters, most Presbyterians who settled in Ireland were Scots followers of John Knox who suffered persecution from James VI and I, who persuaded them to emigrate. The vast majority settled in Ulster during the seventeenth century, whence during the eighteenth century large numbers emigrated to America to avoid the Penal Laws (46). Some English Calvinists settled in Dublin and the south of Ireland; a less severe sect than other Calvinists, they united with the Presbyterians in 1696.

Quakers

Quakers were an extreme section of the Puritan movement of the mid-seventeenth century. Their first Irish group was established in Lurgan in 1654 and they spread throughout Ulster, Leinster and Munster before the Restoration. They also specialized in textiles, but were additionally merchants and farmers.

Palatines

To escape persecution, about 3,000 German-speaking Protestants from the Palatinate of the Rhine fled to Ireland, arriving in Dublin in 1709. They settled in substantial numbers throughout Limerick, and scattered throughout several counties. Many of them became Methodists at a later date.

Baptists

Baptists, Congregationalists and Independents came to Ireland during the Commonwealth and Protectorate, formed a large part of the Cromwellian army and were very powerful politically; after the Restoration many of them emigrated to America. In the eighteenth century Congregationalists and Independents ceased to be distinct sects. Most of those who did not emigrate after the Restoration suffered persecution and became absorbed into other churches.

Methodists

John Wesley founded Methodism to encourage a more personal religion; he did not intend the break from the established church, which happened later.

1 million in 1672

Methodism in Ireland originated in the 1740s and by the early nineteenth century had over 30,000 followers.

By 1834 Dissenters were down to below 9 per cent of the population, a decline that continued until the end of the twentieth century.

41   RELIGIOUS AFFILIATIONS

When in 1672 Sir William Petty estimated the population of Ireland as 1.1 million, he judged that more than 72 per cent of these were Catholic. By 1834 when a Royal Commission looked at religion in Ireland it established the figures shown in Table 1.

The 1861 Census found that Roman Catholics had an absolute majority over all other religions except in counties Antrim, Armagh, Down and Londonderry and in the towns of Carrickfergus and Belfast. This census examined religious affiliations in detail and produced the figures shown in Table 2.

These figures are easy to interpret. The fundamental problem of Ulster is shown in the evenness of the division between Catholic and Protestant, while throughout the rest of Ireland, only in Leinster – with over 20,000 – were there any significant number of Protestants.

The trend continued steadily towards an increasing Roman Catholic majority in southern Ireland (the twenty-six counties that became the Republic) – from 89.5 per cent in 1881 to 93.1 per cent a century later (between 1911 and 1926, at a period of political upheaval, many Protestants left the country –

Table 1 Religious affiliations, 1834

Religion	Number of members	Percentage of the population
Roman Catholic	6,436,060	81
Established Church	853,160	11
Presbyterians	643,058	8
Other Protestant Dissenters	21,822	0.3

Table 2 Religious affiliations in percentages; 1861

Province	R.C.	Total Prots.	C. of I.	Pres.	Meth.	Ind.	Bap.	Jews	Quakers	Others
Ulster	50.50	49.47	20.4	26.30	1.70	0.10	0.20	–	0.10	0.67
Leinster	85.90	14.01	12.4	0.85	0.40	0.10	0.03	0.02	0.10	0.13
Munster	93.80	6.07	5.30	3.00	0.30	0.03	0.02	–	0.05	0.07
Connacht	94.84	5.13	4.45	0.34	0.29	0.03	0.01	–	–	0.01

voluntarily and involuntarily – and the Catholic majority in the South went from 89.6 per cent to 92.6 per cent). In the same period the Church of Ireland dropped from 8.2 per cent of the population to 2.8 per cent, Presbyterians from 1.5 to 0.4 per cent, Methodists from 0.5 to 0.2 per cent, and Jews, who had barely featured before the census of 1901, when they numbered 0.09 per cent, were down to 0.06 per cent. The only growing non-Catholic sector was people of no religion: 0.32 per cent in 1881 and 1.15 per cent a hundred years later.

Those southern Irish Protestants remaining in the south accepted that they were living in a confessional state (the 1937 constitution acknowledged 'the special position of the Holy Catholic Apostolic and Roman Church'; it would not be amended until 1972) and resignedly saw their numbers shrink as a result of intermarriage with Catholics; under the terms of the *Ne temere* papal decree of 1907 their children had to be brought up Catholic. Although there were Protestant TDs, and indeed a Protestant president, until the 1960s Irish legislation was almost unquestioningly infused with Catholic morality: repressive censorship, no divorce, no contraception (let alone abortion), exclusively Catholic theology in the National University of Ireland (which was theoretically non-denominational) and a preoccupation with keeping the people sexually pure and well away from what were thought to be corrupting influences. John Charles McQuaid, Archbishop of Dublin from 1940 to 1971, was the symbol of an age of Catholic power – not so much the 'Rome Rule' feared by Northern Protestants as the harsher Irish Catholic version; in 1944 to attend Trinity College Dublin – which he considered 'a danger to faith and morals' – without a dispensation was decreed to be a mortal sin; in 1951, episcopal pressure over what the church regarded as a morally unacceptable health plan known as the 'Mother and Child Scheme', helped to bring down the government.

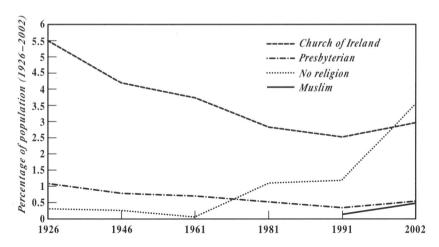

Figure 41 Minority religions in the Republic of Ireland as percentage of population: 1926–2002.

The decade between 1991 and 2001, however, saw some significant changes in religious affiliations in the Republic. The percentage of Catholics fell from 91.6 per cent in 1991 to 88.4 per cent in 2002 (the lowest percentage for more than 150 years) and there were sizeable increases recorded in Protestant denominations: the Church of Ireland rose from 2.53 per cent to 2.95 per cent, Presbyterians from 0.37 per cent to 0.53 per cent and Methodists from 0.14 per cent to 0.25 per cent. The biggest change, however, was in the growth of non-Christian religions. In 1991 there were 3,900 Muslims in the state (0.1 per cent of the population); by 2001 their numbers had quadrupled to 19,100 (0.49 per cent); Russian or Greek Orthodox adherents were up from 400 to 10,000; and other religions from 0.56 per cent to 1.02 per cent. A sudden rise in immigration is the principal cause of these rises, but it is likely that the sharp rise in atheists or agnostics, from 1.88 per cent to 3.53 per cent, can also be attributed to disillusionment with the Catholic church (42).

In Northern Ireland the trend is different, although the figures need to be viewed with caution, as in 2001 9 per cent of the population refused to state their religion. Since 1926 the percentage of those declaring themselves Catholic has increased from 33.5 per cent to 40.3 per cent, while the Church of Ireland has dropped from 27 per cent to 15.3 per cent and Presbyterians from 31.3 per cent to 20.7 per cent. The immigrant community (mainly Chinese and Indian) is too small to be statistically significant, but, as in the Republic, there is a steady rise in atheists and agnostics from 3.8 per cent in 1991 to 5 per cent.

42   CATHOLICISM IN CRISIS

When Pope John Paul II visited Ireland in 1979, an estimated 1 million people turned out to see him in the Phoenix Park – the same as had come out for the Eucharistic Congress of 1932. It was a massive endorsement of a church that was just beginning to experience difficulties which would become manifest in the 1990s. The 1980s saw more overt public support of Catholicism. Abortion was outlawed in the constitution (A referendum on 7 September 1983 resulted in 67 per cent in favour), and three years later the referendum to legalize divorce failed (26 June 1986; 63 per cent against). In both polls, the advice of the Fine Gael government was ignored and the results were seen as victories for conservative Catholics against the liberalizing trend of Irish society that dated from the late 1960s. Yet in reality both results reflected a deep urban/rural divide (see Figure 42a). In Dublin, five out of eleven constituencies opposed the abortion amendment, and the overall majority in favour was slim (51.7 per cent) and far below the national average. Still, Ireland remained the most Catholic country in Europe.

By the mid-1990s the position of the church was more grim. Following the controversial 'X' case in 1992, arising from the efforts of a fourteen-year-old rape victim to travel to Britain for an abortion, the electorate voted

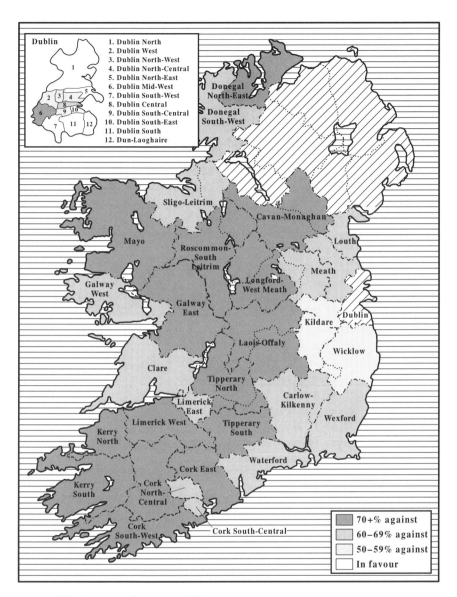

Figure 42(a) Divorce referendum: 1986.
Adapted from M. A. Busteed, *Voting behaviour in the Republic of Ireland* (1992).

(25 November 1992) in favour of the right to travel (62 per cent) and the right to information on abortion services abroad (60 per cent). That year also saw further liberalization of family-planning laws so that contraception became freely available; the following year homosexuality was made legal following a directive from the European Court of Human Rights. Three years later

(24 November 1995), divorce was legalized, although by the slimmest of margins: 50.3 per cent in favour. The urban/rural divide was again significant.

The bishops' reaction to these developments was muted; they emphasized that they would accept the people's will and merely pointed out that 'no change in State law can change the moral law'. This was in stark contrast to their trenchant and uncompromising remarks on social issues in earlier decades, but they had been humbled by a series of scandals: in May 1992 had come the news that the popular Bishop Eamon Casey of Galway, while Bishop of Kerry, had had an affair with an American divorcée, had fathered a son and had used diocesan funds to extricate himself; in 1994 the story of the paedophile priest Brendan Smith made headline news and opened a floodgate of similar allegations. The revelation that some priests were not practising what they preached did the church incalculable damage. Weekly Mass attendance began to decline dramatically: still running at 85 per cent in 1990, in 2003 adult attendance was down to 60 per cent in rural and 43 per cent in urban areas, while pilgrimages to Lough Derg halved between 1990 and 2000.

The church's response to the crises was revealing. In 1994 the Bishop of Meath was still blaming everyone but the church for its problems – the Labour Party, Dublin 4 liberalism (a reference to the smartest part of the city), the media and so on. However, in 1997 the Bishop of Killaloe admitted that the 'strong' church of the 1920s to the 1960s had been at times oppressive. In 2000, following myriad allegations, lawsuits and charges, the church advanced a sum to compensate victims abused in its care (though the state will bear the brunt); cases of alleged abuse are being reviewed by an independent commission expected to run till about 2015. The clergy in general became the scapegoat for a society that from independence had consigned orphans, children in trouble and single mothers to the clergy to look after and educate, and had then ignored them.

The scandals were not responsible for initiating the church's decline, but they accelerated it. Social changes revealing an increasingly liberal society can be dated from the late 1960s: in 1970, 2.7 per cent of births were outside marriage, rising to 5 per cent in 1980, 14.6 per cent in 1990 and almost 30 per cent in 2000 (81). However, the real and possibly irreversible crisis in the church was one of personnel: vocations to a clerical life began a steady decline in the mid-1960s and substantial numbers of clergy began to leave. In 1995, 134 students preparing for the religious life left before completing their training and ninety-five left when they were fully ordained or professed – twice as many as the new recruits. The decline in the number of clerical teachers was contemporaneous: in 1966 they accounted for 50 per cent of all teachers; six years later this had fallen to 34 per cent.

The church in Ireland seems to be in terminal decline, as it continues to contract and Irish Catholics become more like their European counterparts – liable to reserve the church for 'big events' like Christmas, baptisms, first communions, weddings and funerals, while ignoring its social teachings. Disillusionment with the institution of the church should not, however, be confused with a decline in popular piety, which remains intense in Catholic Ireland: an

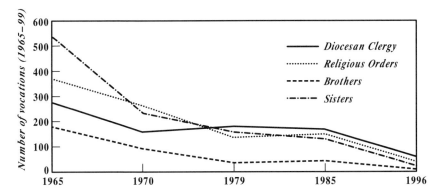

Figure 42(b) Vocations: 1965–96.
Source Louise Fuller, *Irish Catholicism since 1950* (2002).

estimated 3 million turned out to venerate the relics of St Thérèse of Lisieux, the Little Flower, as they were moved from diocese to diocese between Easter Sunday and 1 July 2001; during that period the *Glenstal Book of Prayer* entered the best-seller list. The challenge for the Catholic church is to harness popular piety and spiritual hunger.

VI   The Irish abroad

Over a period of 1,500 years the Irish have left Ireland for two main reasons: to evangelize or to escape poverty or persecution at home. Not since the fifth century has territorial aggrandizement been a reason for emigration. Ireland produced few explorers. The Antarctic explorers, Ernest Shackleton (1874–1922) from Kildare and Tom Crean (1877–1938) from Kerry, are outstanding exceptions.

There are obvious reasons why such warlike and predatory people as the Irish of the fourth and fifth centuries should have given up external military aggression. With the advent of Christianity in the fifth century their main drive became religious in character, and many of the military aristocracy became noted monastic or episcopal leaders.

The Irish monks who went abroad from the sixth century to the early part of the ninth left in a spirit of self-sacrifice and mortification, seeking exile. Wherever they settled they became missionaries. From the mid-ninth century onwards the emigration of religious was for self-preservation, to escape the depredations of the Viking invaders.

Throughout the medieval period the Irish church was inward- rather than outward-looking. Although many Irishmen, both religious and lay, went on pilgrimages, especially to Italy and Spain, and although many of them went to Rome in search of jobs or benefices at home, contact with the Continent was essentially one-way and involved the importation into Ireland of Roman ideas on church uniformity and of foreign religious orders.

From the ninth century onwards there was never to be an opportunity again for Irish military activity abroad, except as members of foreign armies, since Irish political leaders were to be preoccupied with warfare either against each other or against the Vikings and, later, the Normans. The main foreign contacts came through Irish and foreign traders (IX).

Emigration did not again become a significant element in Irish life until after the Reformation, when many religious sought sanctuary on the Continent (45). From the early seventeenth century also began the phenomenon of large-scale emigration of Irish soldiers ('the Wild Geese'), who were to serve in large numbers in Continental armies throughout the seventeenth and eighteenth centuries. This exodus reached its height between 1690 and 1745, during which time the military and the religious were joined on the Continent by students, farmers, merchants and others whose way of life in Ireland was being seriously affected by persecution.

Simultaneously, persecution of the Dissenters was initiating emigration to North America. Mass emigration – which began after the Napoleonic wars and increased to enormous proportions during the mid-nineteenth century – was to be the most important element in the social history of Ireland: famine and emigration together were to reduce the population by 29 per cent between 1841 and 1861. Those Irish who went abroad were to have an important influence on the development of a number of countries: although many through their labour made a very positive contribution, their sheer numbers, poverty and religious convictions caused serious social problems in Britain, especially in Scotland, where historical Catholic/Protestant hostility can still be observed in Old Firm (Celtic and Rangers) football matches today (83). In America, many were also a disruptive force – especially in gangland New York – for a considerable period, until the majority of immigrants began to identify more with American than Irish values.

This question of identification has been the crucial problem of the Catholic Irish abroad. There was often great resentment that so many Irish considered themselves Irish first and put the interests of their homeland and compatriots before those of the country in which they had chosen to make their permanent home. This self-conscious 'Irishness' was to be a divisive force in Australian religion and politics until very recently (47). And although the insistence of the Catholic church on sectarian education could create a bond with some other ethnic groups, it was an isolating force in countries like Australia, New Zealand and America where the majority of Catholics were Irish.

Until quite recently, the Irish in America succeeded in integrating far more thoroughly than those in Britain. A major reason was that emigrants to America had no historical antipathy to the country, and their isolation from their home-land forced them to accept the permanence of the move and consequently to make the best of it. Irish political success in America has also been a major reconciling factor. It is significant how quickly the majority of Irish Americans involved in Clan-na-Gael (51) began to see themselves as Americans first and Irish second: indeed de Valera's refusal to realize and accept the commitment of successful Irish-Americans to the country that had given them social and financial security and status was the main reason for his split with Clan–na–Gael.

Ultimately the Irishman abroad retains an interest in his native country, but commitment to his new country eventually comes with acceptance by the indigenous community. These days, in Britain, the Irish are largely successful, popular and content.

Where emigration used to mean permanent exile, in the past few decades there have been enormous changes. With membership of the European Union, preferential treatment for work visas in America, portable skills, confidence and cheap flights, most young people leave home now to gain experience that will be useful to them when they go home to take up the jobs created by the

Celtic Tiger (a phrase coined in the early 1990s when Ireland's high economic growth rate drew comparison with such successful Asian economies – nicknamed 'tiger economies' – as Hong King, Singapore, South Korea and Taiwan (72)).

43   FOURTH-CENTURY EXPANSION

By the end of the third century AD, the Goidels of Ireland (or *Scotti* as they are generally described) had begun to carry out sporadic raids on the western coasts of Britain. During the course of the fourth century they established a number of settlements in Britain, and became politically powerful, especially in south-western Wales and western Scotland.

Evidence for the extent of Irish expansion is largely archaeological, although some literary evidence exists in Welsh sagas and Irish legend. Some remains of Roman forts suggest that they were built to hinder Irish attacks across the Pennines.

The main evidence is, however, in the distribution of ogam stones, which were stone monuments with ogam inscriptions – ogam writing being a method of representing Latin letters by groups of lines set at different angles. With the exception of a few ogam stones of Pictish origin, all those found in the British Isles are of Irish origin, and testify to the spread of the Irish settlers. As Figure 43 shows, the vast majority of ogam stones are found in Ireland; there are over 200 in Cork and Kerry alone. However, as indicated, others have been found in north and south Wales, in Cornwall, Devon, Hampshire, and some in Scotland, as far north as Orkney and Shetland. The absence of these stones from Brittany suggests that the traditional stories about attacks on Brittany by Niall of the Nine Hostages may not be founded in fact, or at least that no settlement occurred.

The decline of the Roman Empire made Irish attacks on Britain possible, while its wealth made it profitable. By the mid-fifth century the Irish seem to have ceased their plundering expeditions and to have become more peaceful. By then the Irish tribes of the east coast, the Laigin, the Déisi and the Uí Liatháin, had set up kingdoms in Wales, while the Dál Riada, who dwelt in the far north-east of Ireland, set up a kingdom in Scotland, which, unlike the Welsh kingdoms, survived. The Isle of Man was named after an Irish deity, Manannan, and remained an Irish dependency for several centuries.

One important result of this extensive contact with Britain was to aid the early introduction of Christianity, which came to Ireland initially from Gaul via the British settlements and through trade.

44   IRISH INFLUENCE ABROAD: 500–800

It is paradoxical that the prime determining factor in encouraging Irish monks to travel abroad was the security, prosperity and veneration the Irish

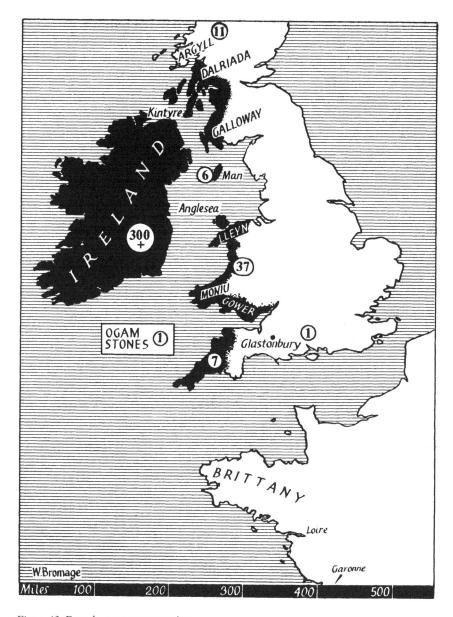

Figure 43 Fourth-century expansion.

church enjoyed at home. Asceticism, not missionary fervour, was the driving force: the impulse was towards what was to an Irishman the ultimate sacrifice – permanent exile. Columcille left Ireland in 563 for Iona in this spirit of mortification. However, once established among the Picts, like so many later travellers from Ireland his missionary zeal led him to spend his life not in solitary prayer but in dedicated evangelism.

Among the most famous of Irish monks abroad were Fursey of East Anglia and north-east Gaul, the patron saint of Péronne, who died in 650; Killian who was martyred at Wurtzburg in 689; Fergal, who had become Bishop of Salzburg by the time of his death in 784; Aidan of Lindisfarne who with Finan and Colman converted Northumbria in the mid- and late seventh century; and Gall of Switzerland, a disciple of Columbanus, who died in 650 and was remembered by an eponymous monastery founded in 720 where he had lived. The greatest name among all of these was Columbanus (540–615). Driven by a combination of political difficulties and unwelcome success in attracting to his monasteries multitudes of disciples and rich endowments, he travelled extensively in Europe founding monasteries, most famously Luxeuil and Bobbio; hundreds of later foundations are said to be descended from his. A distinctive feature of Columbanus's monasteries was his harsh rule, which included penalties of fasting, corporal punishment and exile: he enjoined upon his followers discomfort of body and submission of will.

In his correspondence with political and ecclesiastical leaders, Columbanus showed a magnificence of rhetoric and an intransigence of attitude. He

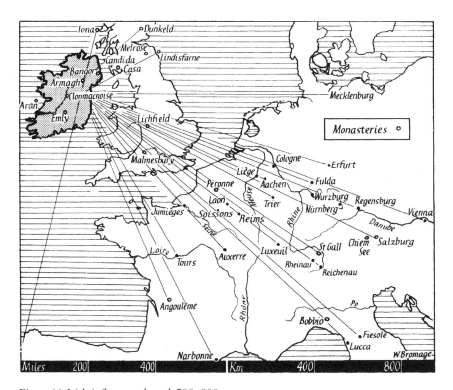

Figure 44 Irish influence abroad: 500–800.

challenged Pope Gregory the Great on the method of calculating the date of Easter – a controversy in which the Irish had been liturgically out of step with the rest of the church for a considerable period. Honorius I in 634 demonstrated papal irritation with Irish obstinacy on this question when, according to the Venerable Bede, he wrote to the Irish 'earnestly exhorting them not to think their small number, placed in the utmost borders of the earth, wiser than all the ancient and modern churches of Christ, throughout the world'.

Although the Irish abroad learned much about Continental art and scholarship from their travels, they maintained much of their institutional individuality, for example their distinctive tonsure and monastic independence of episcopal rule. However, despite their peculiarities, the fervour, dedication and zeal of the Irish monks abroad made them very successful missionaries and great monastic and episcopal leaders. Their reputation as religious pioneers and leaders was secure in Europe by the seventh century, and by the ninth Irish scholars also had a widespread European reputation. Charlemagne had appointed Irish masters to his palace schools, and during the ninth century Irish scholars, many fleeing from the Viking invasions, had an important role in the establishment of France as a centre of learning. Notable among these scholars were the geographer Dicuil and the philosopher and theologian Sedulius Scotus, both of whom taught at Liège, and, most important of all, the greatest scholar and philosopher of the age, John Scotus Eriugena, the author of *De naturae divisione*, who taught at Laon and was described as 'the last representative of the Greek spirit in the West'.

Colonies of Irish scholars existed at Liège, Cologne, Reims, Reichenau, Fulderi and Tours, where they were an interesting contrast to their monastic predecessors. Renowned more for their conviviality than for their asceticism, many ninth-century drinking songs are attributed to them: stories of piety told about the monks are counterbalanced by stories of Irish wit told about the laymen.

45   IRISH COLLEGES IN EUROPE

There was widespread emigration from Ireland by the end of the Tudor period and this continued throughout much of the seventeenth century. There were three main streams of emigrants: soldiers, religious and students. The first were Irishmen going abroad to join foreign armies, the second religious fleeing persecution and the third those who were unable to gain an education at home. These latter included both religious and laymen, and they left – many of them never to return to Ireland – to study at the Irish colleges on the Continent.

Most of the Irish colleges had been established early in the seventeenth century. The lifespan of most of them was between 100 and 150 years; by the end of the eighteenth century most had closed or been closed. Exceptions included the Capuchin college at Charleville, which was abandoned as early as 1684 and the Augustinian Irish College at Rome, which was destroyed during

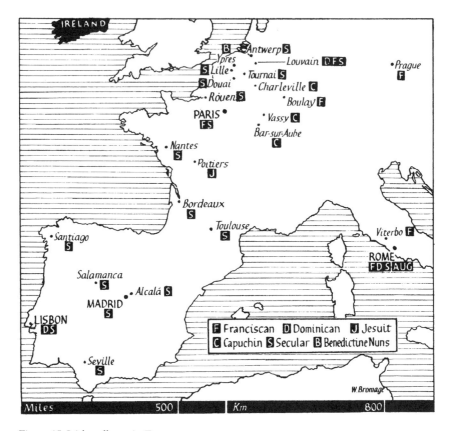

Figure 45 Irish colleges in Europe.

the Napoleonic wars but was later rebuilt and still operates today. Broadly speaking, however, the Irish colleges were at their zenith during the early part of the eighteenth century, when religious persecution in Ireland was at its height, and on the Continent the exiled Stuart monarchy gave an enhanced status to exiled Irishmen whose influence and generosity enormously helped the colleges.

The colleges differed greatly in size. The largest were at Paris and Nantes, where student numbers could exceed 100, and the smallest were Santiago, Seville, Tournai and Toulouse, which always had fewer than a dozen. Finances were precarious and depended largely on Irish patrons, although many Catholics throughout the Continent made generous contributions. Benefactors included Anne of Austria, the kings of France and the Stuarts, particularly Mary of Modena, James II's wife. Students at the colleges were supported either by private money, bursaries or the funds of the individual colleges, while those who were priests could supplement their income by saying Masses or undertaking other religious duties.

One of the most interesting features of the history of these colleges is the spread of Jesuit influence. Although only Poitiers was nominally a Jesuit college, many of the secular (unaffiliated to a religious order) had Jesuit rectors – including, at different times, Rome, Tournai, Lisbon, Salamanca, Santiago and Seville. With the papal suppression of the Jesuits in 1773 the colleges suffered a severe blow to their prestige and this, coupled with economic difficulties and the large-scale confiscations following the French Revolution, brought to an end the career of most of the Irish colleges. By the end of the century only Madrid, Lisbon and Salamanca continued to operate, although some of the others reopened in the nineteenth century.

A significant number of Irish priests settled on the Continent permanently and pursued their pastoral work there. Many lived in extreme poverty, depending on the charity of the Vatican, the Stuarts or other benefactors. A few of them received benefices while abroad, sometimes assisting the local bishops. These should be distinguished from the large body of Irish clerics, particularly bishops, who were exiles on the Continent until the easing of the Penal Laws permitted their return to Ireland; some of them proved very reluctant ever to go home.

Though some girls went abroad to join foreign convents, Ypres was the only wholly Irish convent; other Irishwomen joined convents at Lisbon and elsewhere on the Continent.

46   DESTINATIONS OF THE EMIGRANTS

Emigration became a fact of life for the Irish in the seventeenth century. After the defeat of the Stuarts, thousands of Irish Jacobites and Catholics emigrated to avoid persecution and to find a new way of life on the Continent. This flow began to ease off by the middle of the eighteenth century.

More sporadic emigration had been going on for a long period. Irish vagrants were a familiar phenomenon in Britain in the fifteenth and sixteenth centuries and seasonal migration to help in harvesting was becoming a regular event by the seventeenth century.

Serious permanent emigration really began with the Ulster Scots. Bad harvests, religious discrimination against Presbyterians and high rents set the pattern of a steady exodus. Throughout the eighteenth century an average of about 4,000 a year emigrated, many to Britain, but more to America. Net migration from Ireland to British North America and the West Indies was roughly 165,000 between 1630 and 1775. By 1790 the Irish accounted for 26 per cent of the white population in Georgia, 26 per cent in South Carolina and 24 per cent in Pennsylvania; the majority of these emigrants were Ulster Presbyterians, but the Catholic component was higher than is generally supposed – about 25–30 per cent between 1700 and 1780, most being indentured servants.

Emigration figures increased dramatically at the end of the Napoleonic wars, during which Ireland had enjoyed considerable economic prosperity.

Peace brought an agricultural slump; in 1818 20,000 emigrated. Important factors in encouraging increased emigration were the liberalizing of attitudes to Catholics in America and the rise of the North Atlantic timber trade. The cargo ships carrying timber to Britain returned to North America carrying emigrants at low fares; by 1832 fares to America from Liverpool were only £3 10s. Simultaneously, Canada was opening its doors to emigrants.

Protestant churches generally acted as locations for 'ethnic fusion', interlinking Protestant settlers of Irish, Scots, English and American backgrounds. The Orange Order provided another avenue of social and political association for Irish Protestant emigrants (84a). By 1835 the order had 1,500 lodges around Ireland, 259 in England and 154 in British North America. Lodges were subsequently established in Australia, New Zealand, India and further afield, so by 1877 there were 5,000 across the British Empire. By the end of the First World War (the high watermark of the Canadian Orange Order) there were 2,000 lodges in Canada.

Reliable estimates of emigration cannot be given before the middle of the nineteenth century, but figures for the Irish-born indicate the trend. Donald Akenson estimates the percentage of Irish-born living outside Ireland as: 1841, 6.2 per cent; 1851, 22.3 per cent; 1861, 32.1 per cent; 1871, 35 per cent; 1881, 37.5 per cent; 1891, 38.3 per cent; 1901, 36.3 per cent; and 1911, 27.5 per cent. Of these the vast majority were living in North America. In 1881, for instance, of 3,035,000 Irish-born living abroad, 61.1 per cent were in the USA, 6.1 per cent in Canada, 7 per cent in Australia and, closer to home, 18.5 per cent in England and Wales and 7.2 per cent in Scotland. Almost 9 per cent of the population of New Zealand were Irish in 1886, and there was also a tiny Irish-born presence in South Africa and the West Indies.

Figure 46 shows the numbers and the main destinations of those emigrating between 1841 and 1860: the towns and regions marked bore the brunt. The same pattern of emigration continued as time went on, with the United States being the Mecca for the Irish poor. The years immediately following the famine were appalling for travel, with overcrowding and disease rampant. It took six to eight weeks to reach the United States and months to reach Australia. Not until the introduction of steam ships later in the century did travel become moderately comfortable. Nevertheless, many of the Irish found the hardships of travel to unknown destinations preferable to the grinding poverty that faced them at home.

Nineteenth-century Irish emigrants differed from the European norm. The majority of European emigrants were male, but in Ireland women were equally migratory. Even before the Famine, around two-fifths of Irish emigrants were female and towards the end of the century female emigrants overtook male. These figures are especially marked, given that many women went out unattached. Europeans tended to migrate in family groups, or as unaccompanied men, but from 1820 to 1845 only about half of Irish emigrants to the United States travelled in family groups. This proportion went up during the Famine, but by 1906–14 married couples accounted for only one-tenth of worldwide Irish emigrants.

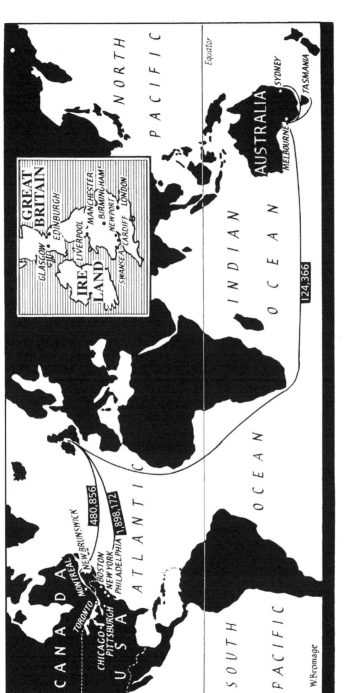

Figure 46 Main destinations of emigrants: 1841–60.

The huge majority of emigrants were unskilled. Even before the Famine, the majority of men classified themselves as labourers, and women as domestic servants, and in later decades four-fifths of all emigrants so described themselves.

47   IRISH CATHOLICISM ABROAD

The mass emigration from Ireland during the nineteenth century posed a serious problem for the Catholic church. Many of these emigrants were Catholics who were settling in countries which had few, if any, Catholic churches or pastors. It was therefore necessary for Irish priests to solve the problem by travelling with their people and founding churches wherever they were required.

Figure 47 shows how far the tentacles of the Irish Catholic church had reached by 1900. Those places named are locations of the earliest recorded activity by Irish clergy, and the date given for each country is that of the first record of an Irish religious arriving either to minister to an immigrant Irish community or to convert the local population. Their early activities are outlined below.

Africa

Irish missionary activity in Africa began in Liberia in 1842 when at the request of Pope Gregory XVI three Irish priests were sent there. In spite of the dangers, comparatively large numbers of Irish priests, brothers and nuns have devoted themselves to missionary work there. The Irish were part of an effort which included French, Belgians, Dutch, Italians and Germans. The major strides were, however, made during the twentieth century when missionary effort in Africa became intensive and widespread; the most effective work of Irish missionaries was in the sphere of education.

Australia

Transportation of Irish convicts to Australia began in 1791. By 1803 there were 2,086 Irish convicts in Australia. Despite the popular belief that these were largely political prisoners, in fact over 60 per cent of them had been sentenced for criminal offences. An Irish priest, James Dixon, transported for political offences, celebrated the first Mass in Australia in 1803. With the increase in transportation and emigration to Australia the need for Catholic priests increased. By 1836 there were 21,898 Catholics in the country – mostly Irish – and almost half of these were convicts. They were severely discriminated against within the colony, the prejudice being anti-Catholic and anti-convict rather than anti-Irish. With the appointment of the first bishop in 1835 began the really serious organization of the Australian Catholic church. There were inner

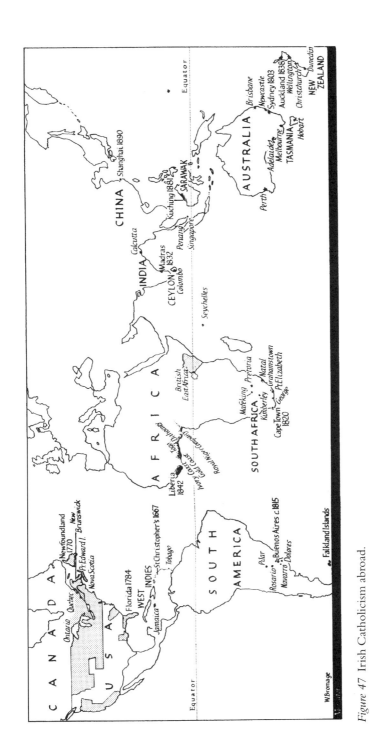

Figure 47 Irish Catholicism abroad.

disputes within the church between those who urged Catholics to be Australians first and those who urged them to identify with their Irish origins. With the appointment of a large number of Irish bishops during the 1860s, to the detriment of successful integration the ultra-Irishness of Australian Catholicism was exaggerated. Cardinal Moran, who arrived in Australia in 1883, moderated this to some extent by refusing to adopt an ultra-Irish position. Nevertheless, the Irishness of his episcopacy and clergy continued to foster the image of the Australian Catholic church as Irish and it is only in recent years that the church has become more Australian than Irish.

The Orient

There is evidence of missionary work in China as far back as the seventeenth century, but the Irish were not involved until much later. Throughout the nineteenth century Irish priests were concentrating their efforts mainly on ministering to their own people in Australia and in North America and there were few available for missionary activity. It is for that reason that most of the work done there was accomplished by nuns and Christian Brothers. By 1900 there were sixteen Irish convents in India. Missionary activity during the twentieth century was much more intensive; there was conspicuous success in the Philippines and steady progress throughout the Orient, although China has proved unconquerable.

Canada

Both Irish and French clergy have borne the responsibility for ministering to the Catholics of Canada. The Irish were dominant throughout the nineteenth century in Newfoundland, Nova Scotia and New Brunswick, and made important contributions in Prince Edward Island, Quebec and Ontario. In west and north Canada, and in Quebec and New Brunswick, the French dominate.

South Africa

Substantial emigration to South Africa began with about 5,000 British settlers in 1820. The Irish among them, and later arrivals, tended to congregate around Grahamstown. As Irish immigration was very limited, Irish priests sent to South Africa were less concerned with ministering to an Irish community than with serving a whole community and undertaking missionary work. Growth was slow; by 1879 there were only 5,500 Catholics throughout South Africa, although there are now around three million. After this period there was a considerable amount of missionary activity, with schools and hospitals also being provided. The Irish contribution was substantial.

South America

By 1832 there were about 2,000 Irish living in Buenos Aires and this had risen to 4,500 by 1848. In the second half of the century immigrants moved to other parts of the country and Irish priests followed. Throughout the country Irish immigration increased until in 1900 it is estimated that there were about 75,000 Irish; since then, however, immigration has been virtually non-existent. On the whole the Irish contribution to South American Catholicism has been marginal.

New Zealand

Irish emigration to New Zealand was quite substantial and in the nineteenth century most priests and nuns throughout the country were Irish. The Catholic population was mainly Irish and the Irish clerical contribution has continued into this century.

United States

The story of the Irish church in America is the story of the Irish people there. Irish priests are strong where Irish settlements are substantial, and during the nineteenth century the priests were mainly ethnic in outlook and much involved in Irish patriotic movements (50, 51). The shading on Figure 47 indicates how widespread was Irish Catholic clerical effort during the century.

48   THE IRISH IN BRITAIN

The history of the Irish in Britain as vagrants, wanderers and seasonal workers dates back to long before the eighteenth century. Many Irish joined the British army and navy during the eighteenth century, including the celebrated Gaelic poet Eoghan Ruadh Ó Súilleabháin (88), who joined both services, travelling with the navy as far as the West Indies. In the Napoleonic wars there were large numbers of Irish on both sides.

Mass emigration to Britain began in the early nineteenth century and Irish immigrants tended to congregate in areas of heavy industry or mining, where their labour was welcome. The great majority of the Irish was in the big towns. In England they were to be found in large numbers in the north-east and the midlands, and also, of course, in London. By 1841 1.9 per cent of the population of England were Irish-born. Only 0.6 per cent of the Welsh population were Irish-born, but over 60 per cent of these were concentrated in Glamorgan, in Swansea and Cardiff. In Scotland they made up 4.8 per cent of the population, a large percentage of these being in Glasgow and Edinburgh.

Politically they were active. Many of them joined the Chartists and became involved in class struggle, while many others supported the Irish movement for repeal of the union (31).

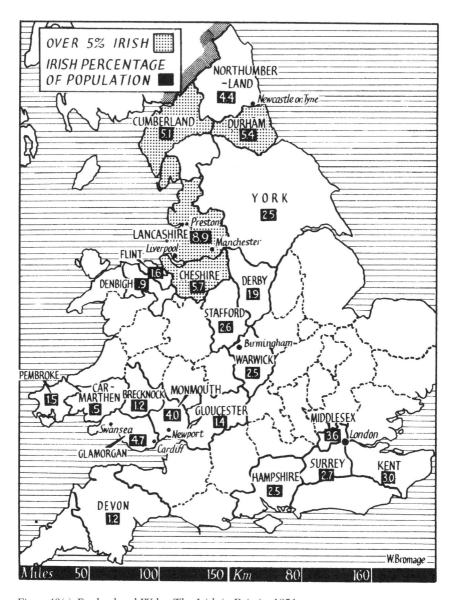

Figure 48(a) England and Wales. The Irish in Britain: 1851.

The 1841 Census showed 419, 256 Irish-born in Great Britain; by 1851 this had risen to 733,866 and was still rising. There was still a strong tendency for Irish immigrants to congregate in the same areas: Figure 48 shows the main areas of concentration. Overall, by 1851 they represented 3 per cent of the population of England and Wales and nearly 7 per cent of Scotland. Like so

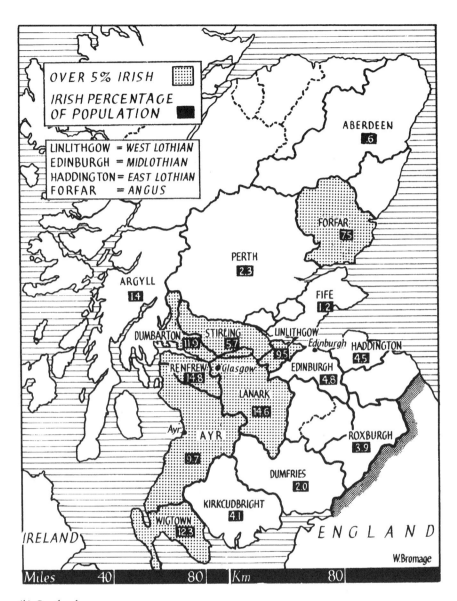

OVER 5% IRISH

IRISH PERCENTAGE OF POPULATION

LINLITHGOW = WEST LOTHIAN
EDINBURGH = MIDLOTHIAN
HADDINGTON = EAST LOTHIAN
FORFAR   = ANGUS

ABERDEEN .6

FORFAR 7.5

PERTH 2.3

ARGYLL 1.1

FIFE 1.2

DUMBARTON 11.9   STIRLING 5.7   LINLITHGOW 9.5   Edinburgh   HADDINGTON 4.5

RENFREW 14.8   Glasgow   EDINBURGH 4.8

LANARK 14.6

Ayr   AYR 9.7

ROXBURGH 3.9

DUMFRIES 2.0

KIRKCUDBRIGHT 4.1

WIGTOWN 12.3

IRELAND   ENGLAND

W.Bromage

Miles 40   80   Km   80

(*b*) Scotland.

many later generations of immigrants they caused resentment and opposition by forming ghettos in large cities: in 1855 Karl Marx wrote: 'Ireland has revenged herself socially upon England by bestowing an Irish quarter on every English industrial, maritime or commercial town of any size.' There were numerous conflicts between Irish and English navvies working on the railways since the Irish also formed a high proportion of mobile workforces. While the

British worker aimed at having a trade, Irish workers were prepared to continue as labourers and unskilled factory workers.

Much of the fear of Irish immigration was justified. Shiploads of diseased and starving Irish landed throughout the second half of the 1840s and the early 1850s. In 1848 more than 60 per cent of the Poor Law funds of Glasgow was spent on Irish immigrants. Since most Irish immigrants were Catholic, they were affected also by anti-Catholic discrimination. Unlike those emigrating to America, the Irish were unwilling to be assimilated in Britain, and their church leaders did not encourage them in that direction. Irish patriotism and religion were intertwined, so consequently they were seen as enemies by many of the British, and there were many popular anti-Catholic demonstrations, culminating in the Stockport riot of 1852 in which an anti-Catholic mob destroyed Catholic property and injured a number of Irish Catholics.

With the ending of discrimination against Catholics and with the abandonment by most Irish-born in Britain of support for revolutionary movements, assimilation has become easier. There are fewer Irish-born in Britain now than there were a century ago; in 1991 they represented only 2 per cent of the whole population.

Although migration to Britain has lessened in absolute terms, Britain is the favourite destination for Irish emigrants. In 1988 there were 40,200 Irish emigrants to the UK, compared to only 7,900 to the USA. Because of the Celtic Tiger (72), ten years later this figure had fallen dramatically – to 13,000 – but Britain remained by far the preferred destination. In 1991 there were 837,000 Irish-born living in Britain compared to an estimated 187,000 in the USA (American visa restrictions obviously account partially for these figures). Despite the activities of the IRA in England, popular prejudice has long since been diverted away from the Irish towards newer immigrants and with the Irish no longer representing an economic threat their integration has become easier and their articulacy and reputation for *joie de vivre* have made them both fashionable and popular. A century ago the Irish were almost exclusively in labouring jobs; they are now to be seen in large numbers in medicine, the civil service, education, business and the media.

Politically the Irish in Britain have tended to identify with the Labour Party, although their loyalty to the Liberal Party, which dated from Gladstone's conversion to Home Rule in the 1880s (32), continued until the 1930s. This political stance conflicted oddly with the comparative lack of success of the Irish Labour Party and – until the advent of New Labour – with the middle-class aspirations of most of the Irish community in Britain, but it is mainly a consequence of a long-standing antipathy to the Conservative Party, which has in part been returned. Also, for class reasons, there has been a disproportionate number of Labour politicians of Irish descent, including around a third of Labour MPs in the late 1960s and, recently, two Labour prime ministers, James Callaghan and Tony Blair.

49   THE IRISH IN THE EMPIRE: SOLDIERS AND ADMINISTRATORS

Apart from ordinary settlers and clergy, there were two major channels for Irish participation in the British Empire: as soldiers and as administrators.

In the early nineteenth century Ireland supplied a disproportionate number of soldiers to the British army (see Figure 49). The Irish share of the UK population was then 32 per cent, but the number of Irish-born in the army was 42 per cent and there were more Irish than English soldiers – overwhelmingly Catholic young men, although Protestants were better represented in the officer classes.

Throughout the century and particularly after the Famine the proportion of Irishmen in the army steadily declined in line with the Irish proportion of the UK population. Yet throughout the nineteenth century Ireland consistently supplied more soldiers than the size of her population warranted and they were significantly overrepresented in officer ranks. Throughout the second half of the nineteenth century about 17.5 per cent of all officers were Irish and were almost entirely drawn from the Protestant Anglo-Irish landowning class.

Figures for Irish troops in the East India Company army are revealing. The East India Company was first allowed to raise troops in Ireland in the 1680s but numbers recruited were very low until the Seven Years War (1756–63) when the ban on Catholic recruits was ignored. During the war almost 17 per cent of recruits to the East India Company army were Irish; by 1778 the proportion had risen to 30 per cent, and between 1816 and 1824, 52.3 per cent of recruits sent to India came from Ireland. By the time of the Indian mutiny (1857) considerably more than half the company's white soldiers were Irish.

Irishmen were also disproportionately represented among officer ranks. While the numbers of Irish among the rank and file declined during the second half of the nineteenth century (25 per cent in the 1870s and 10 per cent in 1900), the numbers of Irish officers remained high (approximately 30 per cent)

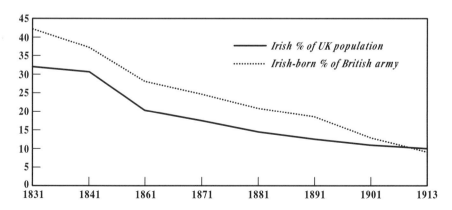

Figure 49 Irish-born percentage in British army compared to Irish percentage of UK population.

until the end of the century. Indeed from 1885 to 1914 the Irish came close to monopolizing the role of commander-in-chief of India. The preponderance of the Irish in the Indian army was immortalized by Kipling, whose character 'Kim' is Kimball O'Hara, son of an Irish soldier.

The Irish generally served with distinction in India: of twenty-two Victoria Crosses awarded in the wake of the Indian mutiny, thirteen went to men with Irish names. Known as 'Rishti' by the native Indian population to distinguish them from the English or 'Angrese', they were capable of brutality and arrogance, with the Connaught Rangers being apparently more respected and feared than any other British unit in India. The Rangers, however, provided the coda to Irish participation in India: in June 1920 they mutinied, unfurled a tricolour, donned Sinn Féin ribbons and demanded the withdrawal of British troops from Ireland.

From the Boer War (1899–1902) onwards, criticism by nationalists of Irish recruitment to the British army grew. Over 28,000 Irishmen served with the British in South Africa, compared to a maximum of 400 who served with the Boers in two Irish brigades, but the symbolic significance of the latter, exploited by nationalists such as Arthur Griffith, was greater. For the first time, from 1910 onwards the proportion of Irish in the army fell below the Irish share of the population. In 1913, 9 per cent of the army were Irish compared to 10 per cent of the UK population.

During the First World War around 140,000 Irishmen enlisted the British army. Approximately 65,000 were Catholics, who until recently were largely ignored by the nationalist version of history and by officialdom. However, they still represent a significant decline in Irish participation in the army compared to the nineteenth century. The percentage of males enlisting in England, Wales and Scotland during the war was 24 per cent, 22 per cent and 24 per cent respectively, but in Ireland was just 6 per cent. Ireland's showing was poor even compared to that of the dominions: 13 per cent in Canada and Australia, 19 per cent in New Zealand and 11 per cent in South Africa.

The extent to which political considerations directly affected the Irish willingness to enlist remains debatable. Ireland's wartime recruitment patterns followed those of Britain – initial enthusiasm, followed by a marked falling off from mid-1916 as the war dragged on. However, unlike in the rest of the United Kingdom, conscription was not applied in Ireland because it was deemed to be politically inflammatory. Of those Irishmen who served in the war, about 30,000 died.

Although, despite Sinn Féin's opposition, a special recruitment campaign in 1918 led to a significant rise in Irishmen enlisting, southern independence three years after the war marked the end of large-scale southern Irish participation in the British army: in 1922 Irish-born accounted for 5.5 per cent of the army. Still, notwithstanding Irish neutrality during the Second World War (23), around 70,000 citizens of the Irish Free State and 50,000 from Northern Ireland served in the British forces: 5,000 died.

Irish colonial administrators were also important to the British Empire. In South Africa, for instance, one-third of the UK-appointed governors, judges and middle-level bureaucrats were Irish. Irishmen were especially numerous in colonial police forces: in New South Wales in 1865 67 per cent of the police force were Irish-born; in Victoria in 1874, the figure was 34 per cent.

India again provides the most revealing case study. About 5 per cent of recruits for the Indian Civil Service (ICS) came from Ireland, until in 1855 open, competitive exams replaced patronage; between 1855 and 1863, when the Irish were 20 per cent of the UK population, 24 per cent of all ICS recruits were Irish-born. Numbers then declined to between 5 and 10 per cent, not least because alarmed English administrators began to rig the entry process. There was less discrimination in the Indian medical service, where Irish recruits never fell below 10 per cent and reached a peak of 38 per cent in the 1870s. Irish administrators in the ICS were in general highly educated – about 80 per cent were Protestant, and 80 per cent came from middle-class backgrounds.

50   THE IRISH IN AMERICA

In the eighteenth century, the demand for labour ensured a welcome for the numerous Irish Presbyterian emigrants to the United States. Massachusetts and Pennsylvania, for example, wanted white labour to help repel the Indians on the frontiers and South Carolina wanted white labour because of a fear of being overwhelmed by black people. 'They were a bold and hardy people who pushed past the settled regions of America and plunged into the wilderness as the leaders of the white advance,' said Theodore Roosevelt. 'The Irish Presbyterians were the first and last set of immigrants to do this.' These natural frontiersmen – passionate about civil and religious liberty, and angry at what they saw as their betrayal by crown and aristocracy – were fertile ground for revolutionary ideas and notoriously ferocious fighters in the War of Independence (1775–83). George Washington, who had twenty generals of Irish descent, is believed to have said: 'If defeated everywhere else, I will make my stand for liberty among the Scots-Irish in my native Virginia.'

Fifteen American presidents have been of Ulster Scots stock: Andrew Jackson (seventh president), James Knox Polk (eleventh), James Buchanan (fifteenth), Andrew Johnson (seventeenth), Ulysses Simpson Grant (eighteenth), Chester Alan Arthur (twenty-first), Grover Cleveland (twenty-second and twenty-fourth), Benjamin Harrison (twenty-third), William McKinley (twenty-fifth), Theodore Roosevelt (twenty-sixth), Woodrow Wilson (twenty-eighth), Richard M. Nixon (thirty-seventh), George Bush (forty-first), Bill Clinton (forty-second) and George W. Bush (forty-third).

But a steady immigration rate of a few thousand Presbyterians was one thing; an influx of poverty-stricken, disease-ridden Catholics was another. There was great ill-feeling between Catholics and Protestants in the period before the American Civil War and anti-Catholic discrimination was common. Not surprisingly the period of main opposition to the Irish within the United States was that of the mid-nineteenth century, when the number of immigrants had grown enormously: from 1847 to 1854 more than 100,000 arrived every year. As the Irish established themselves as the majority group within the Catholic church in America, they went on the offensive rather than the defensive and widespread anti-Irish feeling and discrimination persisted until Irish immigration began to tail off and the influence of Irish churchmen encouraged assimilation. Numbers of Irish-born living in the United States were as follows: 962,000 in 1851; 1,856,000 in 1871; 1,872,000 in 1891; 1,615,000 in 1901; 1,352,000 in 1911.

Useful comparisons can be made between the Irish and some of the other principal ethnic groups in America – the English, Scots and Germans. In 1870 it was estimated that the numbers of foreign-born of these groups in the United States were as follows: Irish 1,855,827; Germans 1,690,410; English 550,688; Scots 140,809.

Their distribution is interesting: the variations between the Irish, English and Scots can be seen in Figure 50.

The German-born congregated mainly in Illinois (12 per cent), Indiana (4.6 per cent), Michigan (3.8 per cent), Minnesota (2.4 per cent), Missouri (6.7 per cent), New Jersey (32 per cent), New York (18.7 per cent), Ohio (10.8 per cent), Pennsylvania (9.5 per cent) and Wisconsin (9.6 per cent).

In their choice of occupations, there is an interesting contrast between Irish immigrants and Germans, one-third of whom were Catholic. The Germans, who came from a more entrepreneurial and industrialized background, were on the whole in better jobs and economically superior to the Irish. Despite Ireland being a predominantly agricultural economy, her emigrants avoided farming, perhaps because of fear of famine, a lack of necessary skills and an innate conservatism that kept them from venturing out of the cities. The percentages of the communities in major occupations are shown in Table 3.

The Catholic Irish progressed quickly economically, politically and socially in America. From the early and mid-nineteenth century, when they competed with African-Americans for the worst jobs, they advanced to better jobs through improved education and greater financial security. They showed an early interest in American politics and quickly gained a reputation for political ruthlessness and corruption; part of the Irish support for the Kennedys was a burning ambition to achieve political respectability, and to get rid of the Tammany Hall image. John F. Kennedy (thirty-fifth president) was famously of Irish Catholic stock, but Ronald Reagan (fortieth) and Bill Clinton (forty-second) also had Irish Catholic ancestors.

Table 3 Occupations of Irish and Germans, 1870 (percentages)

Occupation	Irish	German
Agriculture	7.5	13.3
Personal and professional services	23.0	11.3
Trade and transportation	6.4	6.7
Manufacturing and mining industries	14.3	18.0

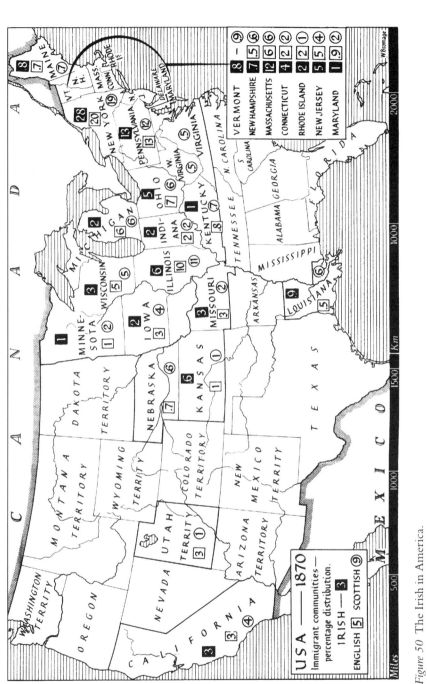

Figure 50 The Irish in America.

51   AMERICA AND IRISH POLITICS

Many of the emigrants who left Ireland for America during and after the Famine brought with them a legacy of bitterness that was soon transformed into political activity and harnessed by John O'Mahony, a Young Irelander, who with James Stephens had fled to Paris after the failure of the 1848 rising. In America he later founded a political group called the Emmet Monument Association, which by 1858 had been renamed the Fenian Brotherhood. Stephens founded a sister movement in Ireland – dedicated to the principle of republicanism – also known as the Irish Republican Brotherhood (IRB) or 'the Organization', and branches of it spread throughout Britain and America. The outbreak of the American Civil War in 1861 destroyed plans for a rising, since American political and financial support was no longer forthcoming. However, it was hoped that following the civil war trained Irish soldiers from both sides would be available to fight for independence, possibly with support from the American government. At the end of the civil war several hundred Irish soldiers arrived in Ireland from America, but the government moved before the Fenians could rise, and crippled the movement to such an extent that its final effort, in March 1867, was a total failure.

Fenianism nevertheless remained a potent force in Britain, Ireland and America. In 1879, under the leadership of the American Fenian, John Devoy, head of the political organization Clan-na-Gael that cloaked Fenianism, elements within the movement joined in a tripartite agreement between Parnell and Michael Davitt in the joint struggle for constitutional and land reform; this alliance, referred to as the New Departure, provided political and financial support (32). During Parnell's American visit in 1880 he collected $200,000.

Although this alliance did not last, Irish-Americans kept a voice in Irish affairs. It was Clan-na-Gael that organized Douglas Hyde's tour of America in 1906 on behalf of the Gaelic League, when he collected £12,500: it was Devoy who was largely responsible for encouraging Thomas Clarke to return to Ireland from America in order to work for revolution. During the time leading up to the 1916 rising, negotiations between the IRB and the German government on arms were conducted through Devoy.

When, therefore, during the Anglo-Irish War of January 1919 to July 1921, Dáil Éireann needed financial and political support, it was natural to turn to Clan-na-Gael and Devoy. De Valera was sent to America with two major objectives: first, to obtain recognition for an Irish Republic from the American government, and consequently a refusal to ratify the part of the Treaty of Versailles recognizing Ireland as an integral part of the United Kingdom; and second, to raise a loan. His mission was complicated by divisions within the Irish-Americans, some of whom preferred propaganda to revolution. De Valera failed to achieve his political objectives; neither the Republican nor the Democratic parties were prepared to offer him any support. However, financially his stay was a great success. Everywhere he went throughout the country he drew enormous crowds. Figure 51 shows the extent of his official tour, from 1 October to 29 November 1919, which took in the main areas of Irish-American strength. Over $5 million were raised for the External Loan.

De Valera had political problems with Irish America. Dissension centred on how to achieve American political support; he rejected the advice of Devoy and Judge Cohalan who, having been snubbed by the Democratic President Wilson, placed their faith in the Republican Party. Cohalan also felt that support from American parties could be won only by stopping short of requesting recognition for the Republic; he recommended that they be asked to recognize only the right of the Irish people to choose their own government. De Valera insisted on taking a hard line, and his resolution was rejected by the conventions of the two parties. Neither Devoy nor Cohalan had given much support to the de Valera campaign, because of both personality differences and their clash of interests; and de Valera claimed that they were Americans first and Irish second. His dispute with the Irish-Americans came into the open in the columns of the *Gaelic American*. By February 1920 there was an open breach.

De Valera left the United States in December 1920. The breach with Devoy and Cohalan had not been healed; indeed, de Valera had founded a rival Irish-American organization called the American Association for the Recognition of the Irish Republic (AARIR). During the Irish Civil War that was to follow, the Republicans received support from the AARIR, while the Free Staters were supported by the older Irish-American movement. The leading spirit of the AARIR was Joseph McGarrity, who later broke with de Valera when he began to act against the IRA (34). His group and their successors continued to give some measure of financial support to the IRA.

When violence erupted in Northern Ireland in 1969, there were many within the Irish-American community who foresaw a civil war and wanted to help the Catholics. Of all the official and unofficial groups collecting American money for Irish republicans during the 1970s and thereafter, the most effective and notorious was the Irish Northern Aid Committee (NORAID), which collected millions of dollars. Ostensibly intended for the families of 'political prisoners', the funds were channelled mainly towards financing the Provisional IRA (87). Until the peace process conferred a new respectability on organizations associated with Sinn Féin, NORAID and other such groups were denounced by leaders of the major Irish political parties and – with possibly more effect – by the then four most influential Irish-American politicians, Senator Edward Kennedy, Senator Patrick Moynihan, Tip O'Neill (Speaker of the House of Representatives) and Governor Hugh Carey of New York. 'The Four Horsemen', as they were known, were close to John Hume, leader of the constitutional nationalist Social and Democratic Labour Party (SDLP), and to the Irish government: they sought to keep Ireland high on the agendas of successive American presidents and helped set up the International Fund for Ireland; latterly, as the Sinn Féin star rose, the only Horseman still in active politics, Ted Kennedy, became close to Gerry Adams, though the relationship came under great strain in 2005 after the Northern Bank robbery and the McCartney murder (24, 87).

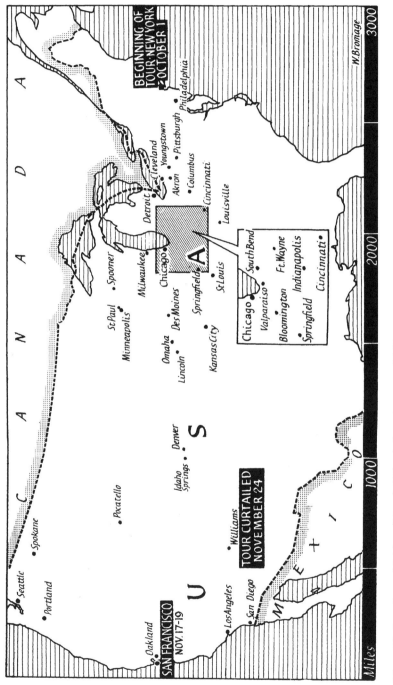

Figure 51 America and Irish politics: de Valera's American tour, 1919.

Although the majority of Irish-Americans had no wish to see their money go to buy bombs or guns, the hard core of IRA supporters provided the Provisional IRA not just with large sums of money but also with shipments of dynamite stolen by construction workers and rifles (particularly the M-1, Enfield and Armalite) purchased easily and legally in the American gun stores. By the late 1970s the Provisional IRA carried weapons more modern than those of the loyalist paramilitary forces or the British army. In 1984, the *Marita Ann* – which had sailed from Boston with 7 tons of arms and ammunition – was seized off the Kerry coast. Sinn Féin has raised millions in the US since the IRA ceasefire, but dissident republicans have been hampered in fund-raising by the designation of both the Real IRA and the Continuity IRA as foreign terrorist organizations.

52 INTERNATIONAL RELATIONS

Under the Cosgrave governments (1922–32) the Irish Free State played an important role in changing the nature of the British Commonwealth. In 1931 the Statute of Westminster formally acknowledged that in future the dominions would have equality with Britain and would not without their consent be bound by Westminster legislation. Although Fianna Fáil had consistently denounced Cumann na nGaedheal as pro-British, it was this change in dominion status which gave the de Valera governments of the next sixteen years the basis on which to build in securing independence from Britain (34).

On 11 December 1936, the day of Edward VIII's abdication, the Dáil passed the External Relations Act which made Ireland a republic in practice, although the British monarch still had a role for the purposes of accreditation of Irish diplomats. In 1937 de Valera introduced a new constitution which affirmed Ireland's independence and made no mention of king or commonwealth: it was approved by the Dáil in June 1937 and by 57 per cent of voters in July; in May 1938 Ireland's first president, Dr Douglas Hyde, was elected. The same year there was an Anglo-Irish agreement that ended the economic war (34) and removed from British control all military and naval facilities in southern Ireland; this latter concession made it possible for Ireland to remain neutral during the Second World War (23).

The 1948 inter-party government decided to clarify Ireland's constitutional position, which was that of a de-jure but not de-facto member of the Commonwealth, and a de-facto but not de-jure republic. In December 1938 the External Relations Act was repealed by the Republic of Ireland Act. This final step marked the end of Ireland's almost total preoccupation in foreign affairs with Anglo-Irish relations.

Although Ireland had joined the League of Nations in 1923 and had been elected to its council in 1930, and although de Valera was a respected president of the council in 1932 as well as president of the assembly in 1938, Ireland showed little interest or faith in the league. Not until 1955, when it was elected

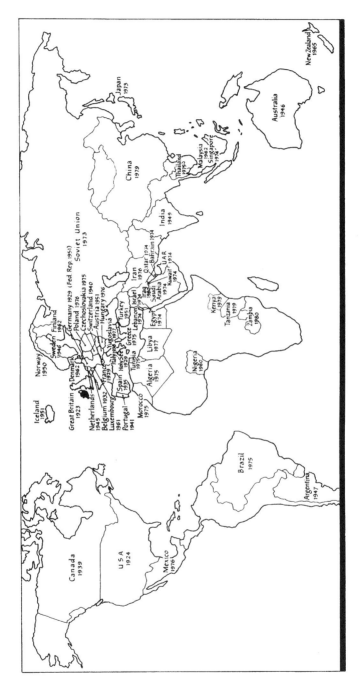

Figure 52 International relations: dates of diplomatic recognition to 1980.

to the United Nations, did Ireland begin seriously to consider itself to have a worthwhile international role. Since 1958, Irish defence forces have had a continuous presence on peacekeeping missions, including the Congo (1960–64, 6,191 personnel) and Lebanon (1978 to date, almost 10,000). Since the end of the Cold War, members of the defence forces have served as observers and peacekeepers in Central America, Europe, Russia, former Yugoslavia, Cambodia, Iran, Iraq, Afghanistan, Kuwait, Zaire, Namibia, Western Sahara, Somalia, South Africa, Cyprus and East Timor. By 2004 eighty-two personnel in total had died on duty, around 900 – about 10 per cent of army strength – were currently serving overseas and Ireland was ranked sixth in the world as contributors to UN peacekeeping. Ireland is also committed to participation in an EU rapid-reaction force and although up to now it has been protected by NATO – which it refuses to join – its jealously-guarded neutrality has little basis in logic and may not survive the next stages of European integration.

From modest beginnings in 1974, Ireland's overseas aid rose twelvefold in five years and in 2003 reached around €440 million. The priority of what is now called Development Cooperation Ireland (DCI) is 'the reduction of poverty, inequality and exclusion in developing countries'. Financial and other assistance is provided through the UN, the EU and other international organizations including non-government organizations (NGOs). In 2003 partnership agreements promised the following over three years: €39 million to Concern, €34.3 million to Trocaire, €32.1 million to Goal, €6.9 million to Christian Aid and €4.5 million to Self Help Development.

It was Ireland's joining of the European Economic Community that required it to establish new priorities in foreign policy and move beyond the isolationism of its early days as a state. As Figure 52 shows, within seven years of joining the EEC Ireland had established diplomatic relations with twenty-eight more countries, including communist China. In 2004 Ireland had diplomatic relations with 107 countries and forty-seven embassies abroad.

53   IRELAND AND THE EUROPEAN UNION

Ireland's most important foreign-policy action decision since the Second World War was taken in 1961 when it applied to join the European Economic Community (EEC). Ireland's reasons for joining were a natural consequence of Seán Lemass's 1958 programme of economic growth and internationalization that challenged de Valera's traditional vision of a culturally and economically protectionist Ireland (71).

Initially membership was blocked because of French president de Gaulle's veto of UK entry, but along with Denmark, Ireland and the UK finally joined on 1 January 1973.

Membership of the EEC, subsequently the European Community (EC) and now the European Union (EU), has had a profound effect on Ireland in all spheres – financial, economic, social, political and diplomatic – and these are touched on in other chapters. For instance, since 1973 Irish agricultural policy has essentially been dictated by the EU (60).

The EU is a unique organization – less than the full federation some of its founders envisaged but far more than either the simple free market envisaged by others or even than a traditional system of interstate cooperation. It has a 'quasi-constitution' in the form of a set of treaties, on which the Irish people vote in referenda, and a body of law, with which all member states must comply. Once passed, these laws or directives become part of (and if necessary override) national law. Irish gender-equality legislation, for instance, owes much to EU law in this field; between 1975 and 1986 five anti-discrimination directives were adopted. Similarly, in the mid-1980s, the EU began regulating health and safety requirements for its members, and most environmental protection measures have come through EU enforcement.

The EU institutions similarly include both traditional intergovernmental forums of cooperation and 'supranational' authorities largely independent of member states. Intergovernmental relations between sovereign states are regulated by the European Council, where the heads of government meet: supranational authority is represented by the Court of Justice, the Court of Auditors, the Commission (the EU bureaucracy or civil service) and the European Parliament. Rulings from the European Court of Justice have meant, for instance, that the Irish state has had to pay compensation to women for discrimination in social-security legislation. The EU representative institution is the 732-strong European Parliament, to which the Irish Republic sent thirteen and Northern Ireland three members (MEPs) in 2004; it has some budgetary, but mostly only consultative, powers.

The Irish Republic's membership of the EU has brought huge benefits, especially for infrastructure, trade and industry (VIII, IX) and it is no surprise that most Irish are enthusiastic Europeans. From the outset of Ireland's membership, successive governments have been committed to further integration and strengthening of the European project, in terms of support for further liberalization of the single market, the enlargement of the European Union and the creation of a single currency (the euro) which became legal tender on 1 January 2002. This is in marked contrast to 'Eurosceptical' nations, especially the UK, which has been a counterbalance to the Franco-German dreams of integration and, like Denmark and Sweden, has refused to join the single currency. In Northern Ireland, unionists and republicans tend towards Euro-scepticism, while constitutionalist nationalists are generally Euro-enthusiasts. The Republic, however, has a deserved reputation for slowness in implementing directives about which it is unenthusiastic, most strikingly in matters environmental (Figure 72a).

Support for the EU has generally been higher in Ireland than elsewhere; the 83 per cent in favour of joining in 1973 was the highest majority of any member state. Four subsequent referenda for ratifying treaties to increase or clarify the EU's functions also had strong, if decreasing, majorities in favour (see Figure 53). Then in 2001 the unthinkable happened: in a derisively small

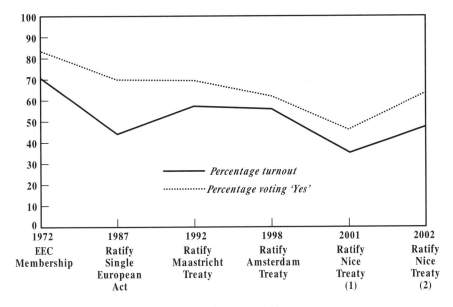

Figure 53 Irish voting on Europe: referenda, 1973–2002.

turnout of 34.8 per cent of the electorate, 46.1 per cent voted in favour of ratifying the Treaty of Nice, and 53.6 per cent against; 14,800 votes were spoiled.

The Nice Treaty was a coda to the Treaty of Amsterdam, ratified two years earlier, and dealt with the institutional reform necessary to further enlargement by taking in ten East European countries. The Irish people's No vote was seen not as a rejection of the countries of the former Soviet bloc, nor as fear that Ireland would lose out on structural funds as poorer nations joined. Fears of an increased military role may have played a part, as 'No' parties such as Sinn Féin and the Greens claimed that Ireland's neutrality would be affected. However, the main reason seemed to be that the people had no idea what they were being asked to vote about; taking Irish Europhilia for granted, the government had run a lazy campaign. Since the adoption of the treaty required unanimity, the vote was regarded in Brussels as catastrophic; using the low turnout as an excuse, the government controversially put the question to the electorate again, one year later, in October 2002 and this time gained the usual solid majority of 62 per cent in favour. But the message was clear: the love-in was over. Ireland, like its fellow EU-members, was wary of a project which seemed over-extended, confused, remote, and dogged by corruption scandals. In an extremely successful Irish presidency in the first half of 2004, Bertie Ahern and his colleagues succeeded in persuading twenty-five governments to agree on a formal constitution for the EU. However, ratification by the Irish electorate is not a foregone conclusion.

In Ireland, the EU elections of June 2004 had little to do with European issues. In the Republic, they were dominated by general dissatisfaction with Fianna Fáil (34) (see Table 4).

In Northern Ireland, the vote essentially reflected fights for supremacy within nationalism and unionism; the centre parties were the losers (86) (see Table 5).

Fine Gael and Ulster Unionist Party (UUP) MEPs are members of the largest party in the European Parliament, the conservative Christian Democrat, EPP-ED (European People's Party and European Democrats); Labour's MEP is a member of the PES or PSE (Party of European Socialists); Sinn Féin's MEPs of the small, largely communist GUE-NGL (European United Left/Nordic Green Group); and Fianna Fáil MEPs of the even smaller nationalist UEN (Union for a Europe of Nations). The Democratic Unionist Party (DUP) is non-aligned.

Whatever the future of the EU, there is no doubt that membership has transformed the Republic and has meant that over the past thirty years, Europe has joined the UK and the USA as a major destination for Irish emigrants and as a strong cultural influence on Irish life. However, as the figures for growth show, hungry little Ireland, which has flourished compared to complacent and less flexible fellow members in the EU, is now looking at real competition from the east (Figure 72b).

Table 4 Republic of Ireland EU elections, 1999 and 2004, in percentages

	Seats/First preference votes (1999)	*Seats/First preference votes (2004)*
Fianna Fáil	6/38.6	4/29.5
Fine Gael	4/24.6	5/27.8
Labour	1/8.7	1/10.6
Green Party	2/6.7	0/4.3
Sinn Féin	0/6.3	1/11.1
Others (not including the PDs, who ran no candidates)	2/15.0	2/16.8

Table 5 Northern Ireland EU elections, 1999 and 2004, in percentages

	Seats/First preference votes (1999)	*Seats/First preference votes (2004)*
DUP	1/28.40	1/32.00
SDLP	1/28.10	0/15.94
UUP	1/17.61	1/16.60
Sinn Féin	0/17.33	1/26.31
Others	0/8.57	0/8.27

VII   Land

The land question dominated Irish politics for four centuries from the period when the first plantations were attempted under the Tudors. Previously, although the Viking and Norman invasions resulted in the dispossession of many native Irish from their lands, there were too few settlers to expel the Irish from occupying at least a part of their old territory. The main pre-Tudor victims were the Gaelic leaders, who lost their power to the invaders, rather than the mass of the population, whose way of life did not alter radically.

Mary Tudor – who recognized it was necessary to import settlers in substantial numbers in order to change the composition of the population – was the first monarch to pursue actively the possibilities of plantation. She failed because she offered insufficient incentives for prospective settlers, and because although she made a number of grants of estates, the newcomers could not expel the native Irish. Elizabeth Tudor similarly made a large number of grants, and although in the case of the Desmond lands the grantees met little opposition, this was a direct result of the catastrophic effects of the Desmond rebellion on the lives of the natives rather than an indication of any acceptance of the newcomers. In fact, the result was similar to that obtained by Mary in Laois and Offaly: the grantees obtained nominal control, but eventually the natives resumed their old lands and their old way of life.

James I was the first ruler to consider the problem of plantation systematically. He saw that no plantation could succeed without the importation of enough settlers to re-people the land in large numbers. He was fortunate in that the long-standing associations of the Scots and Northern Irish (XI) had given the Scots a familiarity with Ireland that encouraged them to accept the challenge of emigrating there. Poverty at home was another powerful incentive, as was later the persecution which the Scots Presbyterians were to experience at the hands of James I in his capacity as James VI, King of Scots.

The plantation of Ulster therefore succeeded in bringing about radical change; the native Irish who remained in planted areas were forced either to accept vastly inferior land or work as labourers for an alien people. The confiscations that followed the Cromwellian invasion and the defeat of the Stuarts had a similar effect. Both the middle and lower classes, as well as the aristocrats, suffered directly from the confiscations and were forced to move away from their traditional homes or to work as labourers.

The Penal Laws of the eighteenth century continued the movement in the ownership of land from Catholics to Protestants and intensified the trend towards absentee landlords who – via middlemen – let land to a multitude of tenants. Even resident landlords encouraged the development of the small farm, since from 1793 – with the enfranchisement of the 40-shilling freeholder (31) – political power could be extended by increasing the number of smallholders. Realizing that unchecked subletting would eventually lead to economic disaster, more farsighted landlords resisted the proliferation of holdings, but to do so involved evictions and the imposition of great misery in the short term. Indeed since there was virtually no way of making a living except through occupation of a piece of land, any landlord expelling tenants was probably condemning them to death.

The greatest hardship was experienced in Connacht, western Munster and western Ulster, since those were the areas with the poorest land and the highest populations. The introduction of the potato – a subsistence food which could grow in the poorest land – enabled whole families to survive on a few acres, and after the Napoleonic wars the practice developed, in the poorest areas, of subletting already small plots. In Leinster and the midlands, there were some industries, land was better, farmers were richer, there was more diverse farming, subletting was not allowed and the population was lower.

Ulster was more prosperous both because of its widespread domestic industries, which were usually combined with farming, and because its tenants had better conditions. Not until the Land Acts of the late nineteenth century was any serious attempt made to give by law to all Irish tenants those protections that were available in Ulster by custom: tenant right, or the Ulster Custom, gave tenants security of tenure and some compensation for improvements made to their land. Still, although they alleviated the situation in the short term, even the granting of these concessions failed to attack the root of the problem, which was that the country was farmed by tenants rather than owners. Once this was recognized by the government the land question was on its way to being answered, and the transference of the land to those who worked it was accomplished with speed (59).

54   TUDOR PLANTATIONS

After Henry VIII had broken the power of the house of Kildare (27) in 1534, he set out to become king of Ireland *de facto* as well as *de jure*. He accomplished the latter in 1541, when his title was changed by an Irish parliament from Lord of Ireland to King of Ireland, and he planned to achieve the former by a steady process of establishing his claim to the whole of Ireland.

Henry already commanded the Pale and he had confiscated the Kildare lands, although he had permitted the Irish occupiers to remain. He believed that it would be possible to persuade the semi-independent Gaelic and Anglo-Irish lords outside the Pale to accept his authority, if in exchange he offered them greater security in their territories by giving them legal title to their lands. The principle by which rulers of various territories surrendered their lands to the crown and received them back *in capite* by re-grant under certain conditions is usually known as 'Surrender and Re-grant'. Forty of the most important lords accepted this principle, some of them receiving English titles: O'Neill, for example, became Earl of Tyrone, O'Brien Earl of Thomond, MacWilliam Burke of Galway became Earl of Clanrickard, and MacGillapatrick Baron of Upper Ossory.

The apparent success of his policy caused Henry to leave these grantees undisturbed. He was prepared to rule indirectly through them, although he managed during the course of his reign to extend his immediate rule throughout Leinster and into Munster. With the succession of Edward VI, a more aggressive policy was pursued by the English government. In reprisal for insurrection, O'Connor of Offaly and O'More of Laois were imprisoned and their lands declared forfeit. In 1556, under Mary, a plantation scheme for most of Laois and Offaly was declared, the counties being renamed Queen's County and King's County: 160 families, mostly from England and the Pale, were granted estates. The natives resisted, and there were many risings of varying degrees of seriousness during the rest of the century.

Under Elizabeth, determined encroachments upon independent territories caused so much mistrust as to lead to insurrection. The Fitzgeralds of Desmond, for both religious and territorial reasons, rebelled twice, between 1569 and 1573, and 1579 and 1583. In 1583 the Earl of Desmond was killed. In 1586, with a view to a plantation, his whole territory – 374,628 acres in counties Cork, Limerick, Kerry and Waterford – was formally confiscated. Ultimately, however, only 210,000 acres were actually settled; they were divided mainly into estates of 12,000, 8,000, 6,000 and 4,000 acres, although Sir Walter Ralegh received about 40,000. While there was little resistance from the native population, many of them having died during the Desmond wars and many more having fled to safer parts of the country, the plantation did not prove sufficiently rewarding financially to Elizabeth to encourage its repetition. When MacMahon of Monaghan was attainted in 1591 and his land confiscated, rather than attempt another plantation she divided the territory between the MacMahons and MacKennas. This was typical of Elizabeth's pragmatism. In 1567, after the death of the rebellious Shane O'Neill, she had confiscated his land, but although over the next decade she made a number of abortive grants to Englishmen (including the Earl of Essex and Sir Thomas Smith) she ultimately permitted Turloch Luineach O'Neill to rule the whole territory formerly held by Shane.

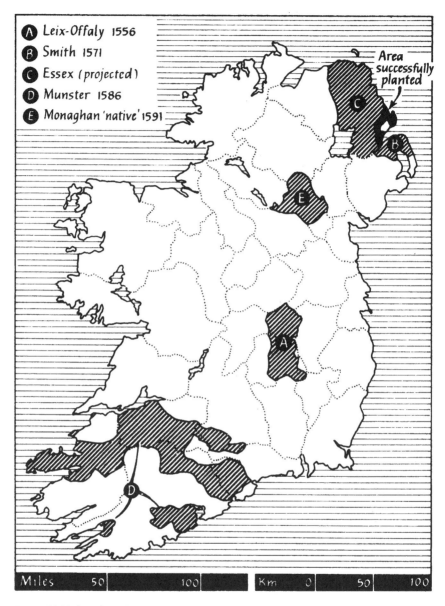

Figure 54 Tudor plantations.

55 PLANTATIONS OF JAMES I

After the submission of O'Neill and O'Donnell in 1603 (15), James restored them to their lands. However, his imposition of English law and government upon Ulster proved unacceptable to the proud northern chiefs; they left for exile in Italy in September 1607, accompanied by more than ninety other Irish leaders. This exodus afforded an opportunity for confiscation of their lands, and the six counties of Armagh, Coleraine (later Londonderry), Donegal, Tyrone, Fermanagh and Cavan were duly escheated to the crown. Monaghan, which had been subject to surrender and re-grant in 1591, was exempt from this confiscation.

This land comprised about 3.8 million acres, of which 1.5 million acres were either partly or wholly infertile – this portion being restored to the native Irish. Of the remaining land, substantial grants were made to the established church, royal schools, military forts and towns. An agreement was made between James and the city of London, according to the terms of which the county of Coleraine – renamed Londonderry and slightly extended in size – was to be granted to the city in exchange for financial backing for the plantation: one consequence was that a number of English planters settled in the county. The city's failure to observe regulations concerning Irish tenants was to result in the confiscation of the county by Wentworth (16). The Articles of Plantation of Ulster, issued in May 1609, scheduled the remaining 500,000 acres of fertile land for colonization.

There were three divisions of settlers:

Undertakers:	Scots and English of high rank who were to receive estates of 2,000, 1,500 or 1,000 acres at a rent of £5 6s. 8d., per acre and who could have English or Scots tenants only.
Servitors:	Mainly administrators or military men who were granted estates of similar size at a rent of £8 per 1,000 acres; Irish tenants were permitted in certain cases.
Native Irish:	These paid £10 13s. 4d. per acre and were allowed Irish tenants; their estates were usually between 100 and 300 acres.

The undertakers and servitors receiving 2,000 acres were required to bring in a minimum of forty-eight Scots or English tenants to settle on their estates.

This plantation was successful. Although the planned number of English and Scots did not materialize, a substantial number did arrive. By 1618 it is estimated that there were about 40,000 Scots in Ulster who had emigrated to obtain land and escape religious persecution.

A simultaneous plantation was taking place in Antrim and Down. In 1605 the north-east of Down was granted to Hugh Montgomery, and the north-west to James Hamilton; Sir Arthur Chichester was granted a large stretch of land in Antrim. Hamilton and Montgomery brought in Scottish immigrants; about 10,000 were settled in Down by 1614. Although Chichester established an English colony, many Scots also settled in the south of Antrim. These private plantations proved very successful, but, nevertheless, throughout Ulster, the natives usually managed to remain, often surreptitiously and frequently as virtual serfs to the new owners.

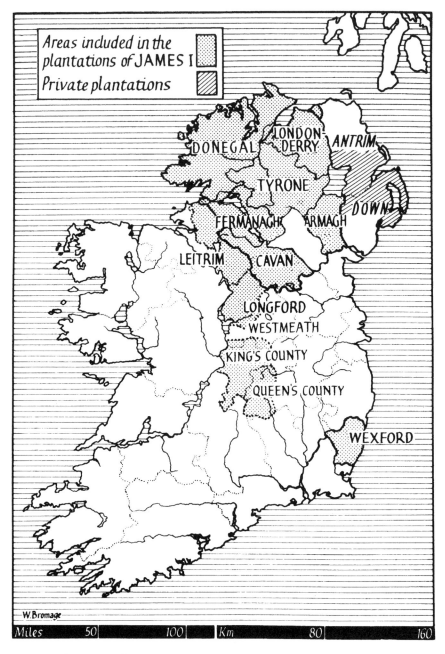

Areas included in the plantations of JAMES I

Private plantations

DONEGAL
LONDON-DERRY
ANTRIM
TYRONE
DOWN
FERMANAGH
ARMAGH
LEITRIM
CAVAN
LONGFORD
WESTMEATH
KING'S COUNTY
QUEEN'S COUNTY
WEXFORD

W.Bromage

| Miles | 50 | 100 | Km | 80 | 160 |

Figure 55 Plantations of James I.

Emboldened by the success of the Ulster plantation, the government followed it up by a series of minor plantations in distinctively Irish areas where a legal quibble could prove the crown's title to the land. During the remainder of James's reign, plantations were carried out in Irish-held territories in Leitrim, Westmeath, King's County, Queen's County and Longford. Although there was some success in establishing a strong Protestant element in Wexford and Ely O'Carroll (the baronies of Clonlisk and Ballybrit (3) in King's County), these plantations achieved only a very limited success.

56   CROMWELLIAN LAND CONFISCATIONS

After 1650 the Cromwellian parliament saw Ireland mainly as a vehicle for paying debts which were primarily to soldiers and adventurers who had subscribed money between 1642 and 1646 for the conduct of the war. Twenty-two counties were surveyed under the supervision of Petty (7), enabling the government to dispose of land with some degree of accuracy.

The Irish population were dealt with decisively. Many soldiers went to serve in European armies; beggars were sent to the West Indies. A series of acts of 1653 decreed that Irish landowners were to be transplanted to Connacht and Clare and their lands in the rest of the country confiscated for the creditors of parliament. This of course involved massive confiscations throughout Connacht and Clare also, in order to cater for the transplantees. Figure 56 shows the percentage of land confiscated in each county and also shows the class of assignee to whom the land was given.

Of the 11 million acres confiscated in Leinster, Munster and Ulster, nearly 8 million were considered profitable land. Additionally, north-east Mayo and all of county Sligo were taken later. Precise figures of the number of planters are not available. There were over 1,000 adventurers and it was originally intended that 35,000 soldiers should be granted land in Ireland. The vast majority of these, however, sold their entitlements and it is thought that fewer than a quarter of them actually settled in Ireland.

There was a logical plan for the dispersal of planters, with soldiers being concentrated in areas where military security was important, for example in the land surrounding Connacht. The plan did not, however, work as well as had been expected. The numbers of planters were much fewer than had been planned for, and they showed an early tendency to intermarriage with the Irish. Nevertheless, it was overall a remarkable operation. By the Restoration the whole character of the ownership of land throughout Ireland had changed and Charles II did little to alter the position. Ownership was now largely in Protestant hands. The ensuing problems posed by a country owned by an ever-decreasing number of Protestant owners with an ever-increasing number of Catholic tenants would dominate the later history of Ireland.

Another important development came from the confiscation of property in all the cities and towns that had been held by the Confederate forces (16). City

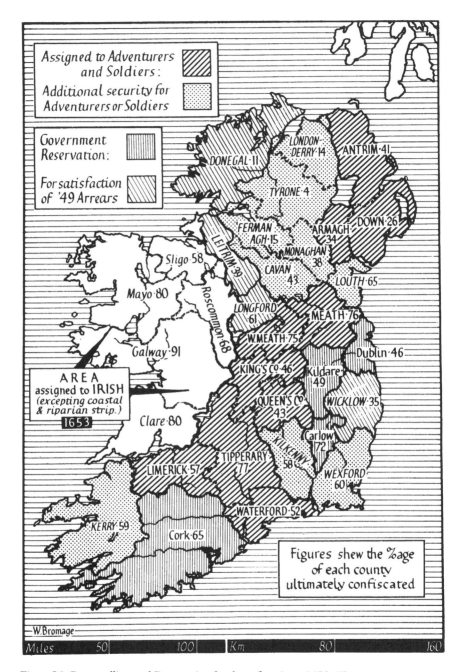

Figure 56 Cromwellian and Restoration land confiscations: 1653–65.

government was henceforth to be a Protestant monopoly, except during a brief period under James II. This also set a pattern that would store up problems for the future.

57   THE TRANSFER OF LAND OWNERSHIP: 1603–1778

At the end of the Tudor monarchy, in 1603, despite the Tudor confiscations and plantations, 90 per cent of Irish land was still in Catholic hands. By 1641, mainly due to the success of the Ulster plantations, this proportion had been reduced to 59 per cent, a figure that was further reduced by the Cromwellian plantation. By the accession of James II in 1685, only 22 per cent of land was left in Catholic hands. After the implementation of the Treaty of Limerick, with yet more changes in land ownership, Catholics held only 14 per cent. By a series of restrictive acts, the Penal Laws reduced this proportion even more.

An act of 1704 dictated that no Catholic could purchase any interest in land other than a lease of thirty-one years or under, nor could he acquire land from a Protestant by marriage or inheritance. A Catholic could not dispose of his estate by will; it was automatically divisible on his death among all his sons. However, if the eldest son became a member of the established church he would receive the whole estate and if he conformed during his father's lifetime, his father became a life tenant only and could not dispose of the property.

This act was vigorously enforced and had a profound effect on the disposition of land. Failure to conform to the Church of Ireland brought economic ruin to Catholic families. By the 1770s, when the relaxation of the Penal Laws began, only 5 per cent of land was left to the Catholics.

In addition to losing their land, economic recessions forced the majority of the Irish people to make their living from agriculture. Absentee landlords became more common and their estates were let to one or several middlemen who usually divided and let the land, which was often then sublet again. Proportionately, the highest rent was paid by the farmer at the bottom of the pyramid. The pattern of too many tenants paying inflated rents for inadequate land was to have disastrous consequences in the nineteenth century.

Concessions to Catholics on landownership began in 1772, when the Bogland Act was passed, allowing Catholics to acquire leases of up to sixty-one years on 50 acres or under of unprofitable land. Gardiner's Relief Act of 1778 permitted Catholics to acquire leases of land for indefinite tenure if they took an oath of allegiance and they could also inherit land in the normal way. In 1782 Catholics were finally allowed to buy, hold or inherit freehold land and leases on almost the same terms as Protestants. As a safeguard against Catholics now asking for the re-examination of earlier claims to land, Yelverton's Act confirmed earlier land settlements.

The graph in Figure 57 shows the stages of change in landownership over 175 years between the Stuart accession and the Relief Act of 1778.

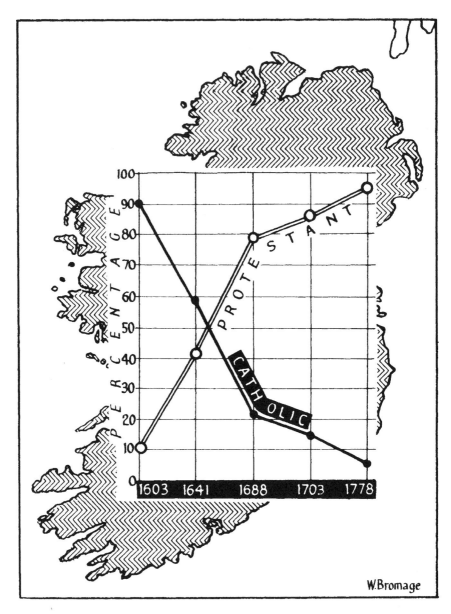

Figure 57 The transfer of land ownership: 1603–1778.

58   PRE-FAMINE AGRICULTURE

Famines were not uncommon in Ireland in the nineteenth century: potato famines occurred in 1800, 1816, 1817, 1822 and 1836. Usually, failure of the potato crop was partial and was for one season only. In the Great Famine of

1845–8, however, the blight, which was selective in 1845, was general in 1846. There was an unblighted though small crop in 1847 and a partial failure again in 1848.

Agricultural and economic conditions throughout most of the country were such that a crop failure of this magnitude was bound to end in disaster. Because of untrammelled subletting, combined with a massive growth in population, more and more people came to depend on less and less land for the means of survival. As Figure 58a demonstrates, in 1841 the areas with the worst over-crowding also had the poorest land. The proportions of arable land in each county are illustrated – that is, the amount of land suitable for the growth of crops and the pasturing of cattle. Throughout the country there was a very uneven distribution of such land; most of the east and south-east had rich land and a manageable population, while in the west there was appalling over-crowding and poor soil. In Kildare for example, over 85 per cent of the land was arable, supporting 187 people per square mile, while Mayo, with 36 per cent arable land, was supporting 475 people per square mile.

In the north-east of Ireland, though agricultural conditions were poor, the textile industry continued to give employment to a large proportion of the population. The textile industry which had existed in other parts of Ireland had declined during the early nineteenth century, so that while Ulster peasants had an extra source of income, for most peasants in the rest of Ireland agriculture was the only means of survival.

When the full extent of the famine was realized, the British government attempted to deal with it by means of relief works and also by public food distribution centres. Although government reports and studies by independent observers had for years been prophesying an agricultural and social catastrophe, contemporary attitudes to state intervention made it impossible to avert or significantly ameliorate the disaster.

A consequence of the practice of subletting was a continual trend in the years before the famine towards uneconomic farm sizes. Early nineteenth-century observers believed that it was possible to support a family on as little as 7 acres of reasonably good land. In Ireland, in 1841, the majority of families were living on farms of under 7 acres.

The famine, by reducing the population, brought a rapid change in farm sizes in Ireland, and during the rest of the century the trend towards larger farms continued. The figures in Table 6 indicate the radical nature of the change.

Table 6 Farm sizes, 1851–1901, percentages

Farm size	1841	1851	1871	1901
1–5 acres	44.9	15.5	13.7	12.2
5–15 acres	36.6	33.6	31.5	29.9
15–30 acres	11.5	24.8	25.5	26.0
30 plus acres	7.0	26.1	29.3	31.9

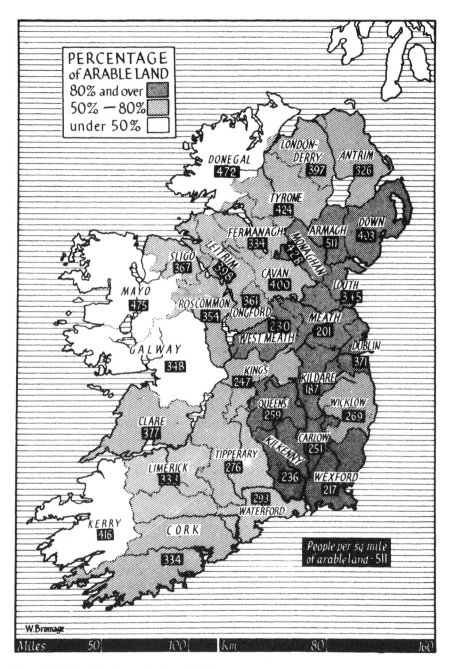

Figure 58(a) Pre-Famine agriculture, 1841.

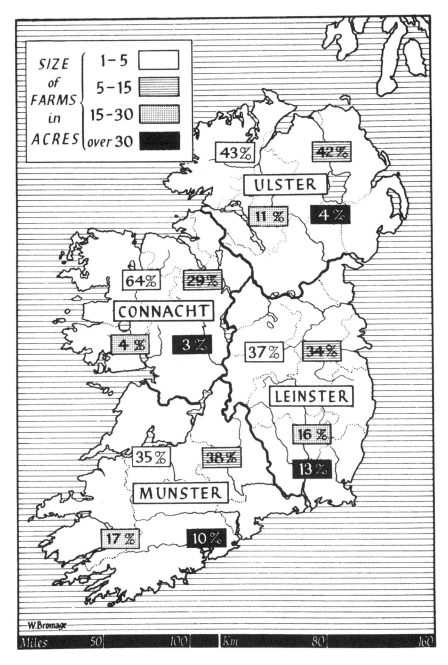

SIZE of FARMS in ACRES
- 1–5
- 5–15
- 15–30
- over 30

ULSTER
43% 42%
11% 4%

CONNACHT
64% 29%
4% 3%

LEINSTER
37% 34%
16% 13%

MUNSTER
35% 38%
17% 10%

W.Bromage

Miles 50 100
Km 80 160

(b) Farm sizes, 1841.

With this increasing concentration on larger farms and a more professional approach to agriculture came a drop in the proportion of the population depending on farming for a way of life.

59   THE TRANSFER OF LANDOWNERSHIP: 1870–1916

In 1870, after the passing of the first Land Act, only 3 per cent of Irish householders owned any land. By the time of the 1916 rebellion that figure had grown to 63.9 per cent and the battle for landownership was won. That this happened in so short a time was a tribute to radical and far-seeing measures passed by successive British governments. It was also due to a change in government economic thinking.

Seventeen years after the union, in 1817, the Irish and British exchequers were amalgamated and the Irish contribution was set at a ratio of 2:15. For decades a rigid view prevailed which dictated that all Ireland's economic needs should be met from its own contributions. This – as interpreted by the doctrinaire Whig governments – was to frustrate attempts to introduce adequate relief measures to cope with the famine. In the 1890s there was a radical policy change that facilitated the transfer of landownership by making adequate funds available for land purchase. Without this development, the Land Acts would have been ineffective.

Deasy's Act of 1860 converted feudal relations into a contractual agreement and was intended as a protection for tenants. Gladstone's Landlord and Tenant (Ireland) Act (1870) attempted to implement this in a practical way by requiring landlords to pay some compensation for improvements and giving tenants theoretical security of tenure if they paid their rents. The Act, however, did not have the teeth to bring this about in practice and so had little effect. At this period, about 80 per cent of profitable land in Ireland was owned by fewer than 4,000 people; nearly 10 per cent of the whole country was owned by twenty people. To deal effectively with landowners of such power, more sweeping laws were required.

The Irish Land Act (1881) was far more effective. It extended the Ulster Custom to the whole country and gave the 'Three Fs' – fair rent, fixity of tenure and free sale, as well as setting up a Land Court and a Land Commission, among whose responsibilities were the establishment of fair rents and the provision of money to tenants to buy land.

Although these measures helped, they did not solve the problem of the tenants who had no capital whatsoever and could not avail themselves of the offer of two-thirds of the money under the 1870 act or three-quarters under the 1881 act. Not until the Land Acts of 1885 and 1891 made all the purchase money available to tenants did the transfer of land on a large scale become a reality. Under the 1885 Ashbourne Act £5 million were made available for loans from the Land Commission and, as an incentive, annuity payments were set lower than rents. The Conservative governments of Salisbury and Balfour

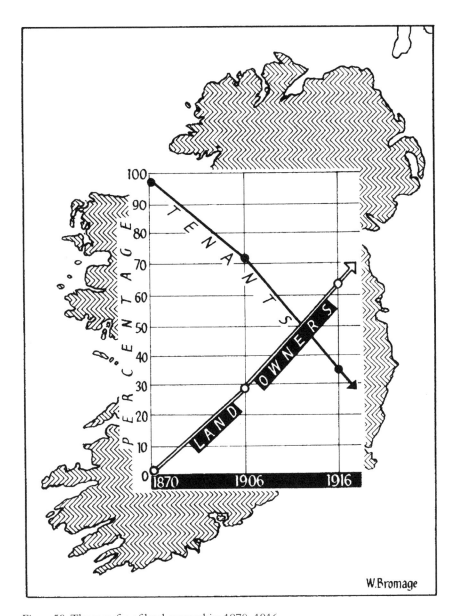

Figure 59 The transfer of land ownership: 1870–1916.

became committed to the idea of land purchase, made substantial sums of money available and encouraged landlords to sell their lands by offering them good prices and using active moral persuasion. In 1891 £30 million was made available for land purchase and in 1903 the Wyndham Act allocated £100 million for the same purpose. These acts brought about a major breakthrough.

As a consequence of the Wyndham Act, 252,400 tenants purchased their holdings and after the Birrell Act of 1909, which provided for powers of compulsory purchase, a further 66,500 followed suit.

In 1891 the Congested Districts Boards were set up to deal with the poorest parts of rural Ireland: their initial terms of reference confined them to areas in Donegal, Leitrim, Sligo, Roscommon, Mayo, Galway, Kerry and West Cork, but they were later permitted to extend their sphere of influence. Although many of their experiments with new industries were not particularly successful, they improved economic conditions considerably in many parts of the country, helped 59,510 tenants to buy their land, and gave assistance with improving land and setting up fishing centres and light industries.

Although land transfer created a social and economic revolution, it was essentially a conservative revolution that created a dominant class of peasant proprietors who would long constitute an obstacle to any kind of liberalization or social progress.

60   AGRICULTURE IN THE TWENTIETH CENTURY

In 1923 the Land Commission was reactivated by the Free State government and given responsibility for the functions of the Congested Districts Board and the difficult task of redistributing large subdivided properties to labourers and smallholders, without interfering with property rights. Though untenanted land could be compulsorily acquired, the scope for such redistribution was limited, but in the following decade the commission reallocated 450,000 acres. It was also responsible for moving, in the 1930s, some hundreds of smallholders from non-viable holdings in the west to vacant land in Leinster.

Agriculture was the most important sector of the newly independent country's economy, employing over half the workforce and prioritized by the government. In the 1930s the sector as a whole suffered through a combination of factors: the worldwide depression, protectionism, the Anglo-Irish economic war of 1932–8 and Fianna Fáil's pro-tillage policy. De Valera believed that tillage encouraged self-reliance, would bind farmers to the soil, would create more employment and would shift the balance away from the big farmer and livestock towards the more labour-intensive smallholder; accordingly, he subsidized wheat and sugar beet. The area dedicated to wheat acreage grew from 24,000 acres in 1932 to 254,000 acres in 1936, of which 147,000 acres were in Leinster and only 14,000 in Connacht, thereby belying de Valera's attempt to improve the lot of the small farmer on the south-western seaboard. Compulsory tillage also meant soil exhaustion and declining milk yields.

Ireland failed to capitalize on the opportunities offered by the Second World War. In the late 1940s tillage was abandoned in favour of livestock cultivation, and Irish farming remains today predominantly grass farming with cattle and dairy products being pre-eminent. However, during the 1950s sluggish British demand and competition from other exports meant livestock production did less well than projected. Irish agriculture remained backward by British and north European standards: in 1963 holdings of fewer than 30 acres still accounted for half the total holdings, and there was little investment in new equipment or in modernizing techniques.

In the late 1960s, as other industries and exports took off, agriculture finally stopped being regarded as the primary economic sector. In 1971, at the eve of Ireland's entry to the EEC, agriculture employed 26 per cent of the population, half the figure of fifty years previously.

Then came the Common Agricultural Policy. Since the country joined the EEC in 1973 Irish agricultural policy has been EU agricultural policy. This is because the CAP is the most integrated of the EU's sectoral policies and also the largest – in 2004 it still accounted for over half of total annual expenditure. It is the one area of EU policy where Brussels has completely dominated national policy-making.

The CAP, enshrined in the Treaty of Rome, aspires to ensure certainty of supply, stable prices and the opportunity for farmers to stay on the land. Since the thinking behind the CAP was (and is) that it is undesirable to allow farmers' incomes to deteriorate to the point where they are forced off their land into cities in search of employment that may not exist, they are therefore subsidized. Agricultural prices are subject to considerable fluctuation because weather affects production: price fluctuation, as well as creating insecurity for farmers, fuels inflation, so prices are guaranteed at a level that does not necessarily reflect products' market value. In agriculture, therefore, the single market is thus a free-trade system, run on anti-market principles. Guaranteed prices for a wide range of foodstuffs have meant EU prices have been consistently above world prices and EU consumers have subsidized their farmers.

Irish farmers have done extremely well out of the CAP, much better, for instance, than Mediterranean farmers, since dairy, cereals and beef have been the main products subsidized. Between 1970 and 1978 real incomes per capita in agriculture in the Republic more than doubled, the price of farmland more than quadrupled and the price of agricultural produce trebled. Between 1979 and 1986 real incomes and land prices fell rather dramatically but then picked up again. During the late 1990s, the Celtic Tiger (72) helped drive up the price of land: between 1997 and 2001, it doubled in value to €5,626 per acre.

The CAP had, of course, a discernible effect on exports. In 1972, 74 per cent of agricultural exports still went to the UK (including Northern Ireland) and 15.6 per cent to other European countries: twenty years later 38 per cent went to the UK and 43 per cent to the rest of the EU. The sector that saw the biggest increase was dairy, which accounted for 16 per cent of exports in 1972 and 38 per cent in 1992. Sheep farming also rose from the 1980s onwards. During this period Irish farms expanded: in 1972 two-fifths of Irish farms were 50 acres or more; in 1991 almost 50 per cent.

In Northern Ireland, the trend was similar. During the 1990s, the number of full-time farms (that is, those generating at least the average income of a male manual worker) fell from 6,800 to 3,000.

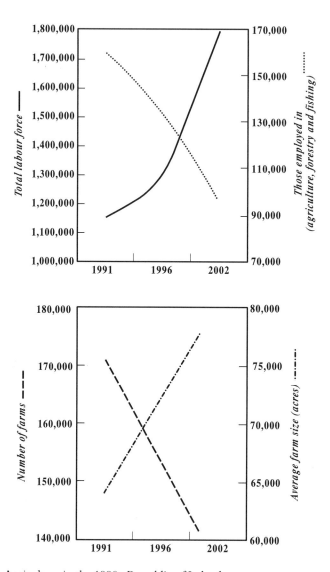

Figure 60 Agriculture in the 1990s: Republic of Ireland.

Still, although it raised rural living standards, the CAP created huge problems which made it a vulnerable target for Eurosceptics. Obsession with 'certainty of supply' meant that intensive farming, which was bad for the environment, was encouraged and very quickly there were huge surpluses – the milk lakes and beef and butter mountains which were a source of embarrassment to Brussels. Eventually quotas had to be imposed.

Despite the surpluses, there was little regeneration of economic activity. In

Ireland employment in agriculture declined by 42 per cent between 1973 and 1986 and by 1998 was down to only 8 per cent. Growth was poor: gross agricultural product (GAP) fell from 18 per cent of GDP in 1973 to 8.2 per cent in 1993. Additionally, benefits were not equitably spread across the sector, and bigger farmers were favoured: in 1988–93 the top quartile of Irish farmers ended up with more than half the available aid. According to the then Irish EU Commissioner, Ray MacSharry, 20 per cent of Europe's farmers received 80 per cent of CAP payments.

The government had no strategy for agriculture beyond making big short-term killings from Brussels. There were no long-term national policies concerning the role of agriculture in the overall development of the economy. Outside the EU umbrella, Irish agriculture might have been forced to become more efficient.

Serious reform of the CAP has been in progress since 1992. Supply and demand are being brought more closely into balance and agriculture's share of the EU budget fell from 60 per cent in 1989 to 50 per cent in 1994. The accession of the East European countries in 2004, including some such as Poland with strong agricultural bases, will bring renewed problems.

VIII   Infrastructure

Until comparatively recently, the physical difficulties of travel in Ireland were daunting. The combination of mountains, drumlins, rivers, lakes, bogs and extensive woods (8) made progress difficult, and roads were insufficient in number and badly maintained. The roadways constructed in early Ireland were not improved upon substantially until the Norman invasion, and even then the woods continued to bar effective progress until their virtual eradication during the seventeenth century.

The most common method of travel throughout the early and medieval period was by water, especially for purposes of trade. Treacherous though the coasts undoubtedly were in many parts of the country, on the south and east they were easier for the transportation of goods than were the inadequate roads. Inland waterways were often used also (66a). During this period the Irish were fine sailors.

During the medieval period improvements in roads were marginal: the Pale usually kept in touch with Waterford, Cork, Limerick and Galway by sea. During the Tudor period a good deal of attention was paid to improving communications. Efforts were made to free main rivers of weirs that blocked transport, and military considerations accelerated road- and bridge-building, yet methods were somewhat unscientific and planning was haphazard. In 1614, however, a Highways Act initiated a more systematic approach by outlining schemes for linking the principal towns of the plantations which were taken up enthusiastically in some parts of the country, especially by the hardworking planters of Ulster who were very conscious of the need for a decent infrastructure. Still, standards throughout the country were very variable and however good the roads might be, normal transport was limited to horseback and was therefore slow, and for long journeys very uncomfortable.

The eighteenth and nineteenth centuries saw a series of transformations in transport, first with a new road network and the introduction of jaunting-cars (small horse carts) for passenger transport, then with the construction of canals and, after that, the railways. With the twentieth century came the upheavals in the transport system caused by the introduction of the motor car and the aeroplane and a revolution in communications in general through the development of radio, television, telephone, fax, e-mail and the Internet.

61 EARLY INFRASTRUCTURE

The exact routes followed by roads in early Ireland cannot be delineated with certainty but, drawing on contemporary evidence, Figure 61 reflects the most likely routes of the major roads. Certainly there can be no doubt of the existence of wide, soundly constructed roads (*slighe* in Irish). Where the Irish learned their expertise in road construction is unclear, but the Celts used wheeled vehicles which would have required paved roads and it is also likely that contact with Roman Britain taught the Irish to appreciate the strategic importance of roads and the skills required to build them.

That early Irish roads were of military importance is unquestionable. They were good enough to make possible the movement of soldiers about the country, and the comparative speed of progress of the Norman invaders was to a considerable extent the result of the road system.

The locations of roads obviously depended to a considerable extent on the location of places of importance, for example royal seats such as Rathcroghan, Ailech, Tara and Cashel, and monasteries hospitable to visitors, such as Derry, Clogher, Fore, Durrow and Roscrea. In addition to the roads shown in Figure 61 there were of course many lesser roads – like that from Limerick to Cork – which were of great importance.

The early roads appear to have been paved with stone, wooden causeways being constructed over bogland. The routes are as follows.

An tSlighe Mhór

The Great Road. A low ridge of eskar (post-glacial gravel) known as Eiscir Riada marked a dividing line between north and south and enabled journeys to be made across the bogland of the centre of Ireland. This route seems to have formed a basis for the construction of An tSlighe Mhór, stretching from Dublin to the west coast.

Slighe Dhála Meic Umhóir

The Road of Dála, son of Umhóir, was designed mainly to link Tara with the south-west coast: it followed a route to the south of the Kildare boglands, through the Curragh, across the Barrow and by Slieve Bloom.

Slighe Assail

The Road of Assal was considered to be the route connecting Tara with Rathcroghan, the capital of Connacht, at a very early period, and dividing Meath into north and south. It diverged from the Slighe Mhidhluachra north of Drogheda, travelled through the gap of Mullingar, between Loughs Owel and Ennell, and across marshy land to Rathcroghan.

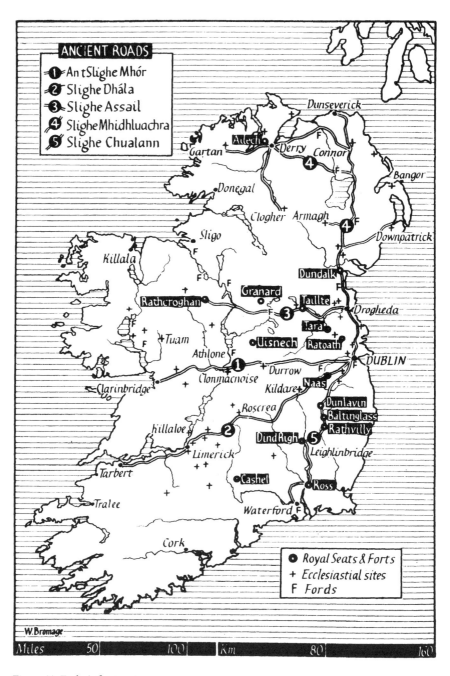

Figure 61 Early infrastructure.

Slighe Mhidhluachra

The Road of Mid-Luachair was the main northern road, from Tara across the plain of Louth to Dundalk and then via the Moyry Pass up to Gartan in Donegal, with branches to Armagh, Downpatrick, Dunserverick and Derry.

Slighe Chualann

The Road of Cuala was the great road linking Dublin with Waterford, passing by the foot of the Wicklow Mountains across the Liffey to the Barrow, crossing it at Dind Righ and thence to Waterford.

62   INFRASTRUCTURE IN THE EIGHTEENTH AND NINETEENTH CENTURIES

In the eighteenth century there was a significant improvement in communications with the introduction of turnpike roads, which were built as commercial ventures. During the 1730s and 1740s there was an intensive period of road-building throughout most of the country, but it did not prove sufficiently profitable for the Grand Jury of each county to plan roads and finance them from the rates. Still, by 1800 it was considered that Irish roads were comparable with those of Britain.

The eighteenth century had also seen the beginning of canal-building. The Newry Canal, the Lagan Navigation (Belfast to Lough Neagh), the Tyrone Navigation and the Strabane Canal were all completed by 1796. The first half of the nineteenth century saw the completion among others of the Grand Canal, the Royal Canal, the Ulster Canal and navigation works on the Boyne, Barrow, Nore, Suir, Slaney and Shannon rivers, but with the advent of the railway enthusiasm for canal-building waned rapidly.

At this period methods of passenger transport were still slow and expensive: few could afford the mail coach. Although canals initially conveyed a significant number of passengers (in 1837 the Royal Canal Company carried 46,450), they became more and more restricted to freight (the Royal Canal's tonnage peaked at 112,181 tons in 1847) and 1849 saw the end of the last passenger service. (Towards the end of the twentieth century canals were systematically restored for recreational purposes.) A dramatic improvement in transport was made in 1815 when Charles Bianconi introduced to Clonmel jaunting-cars for public transport; by 1845 his cars were operating over 3,000 miles of road, covering Munster, Connacht and much of Leinster. With the arrival of the railways Bianconi was astute enough to adapt his road services to complement rather than to compete.

Railways operated in Ireland from 1834, when the Dublin–Kingstown route was opened, but their development was comparatively slow: in 1839 the Ulster Railway Company opened the Belfast–Lisburn line; in 1842 it was extended to

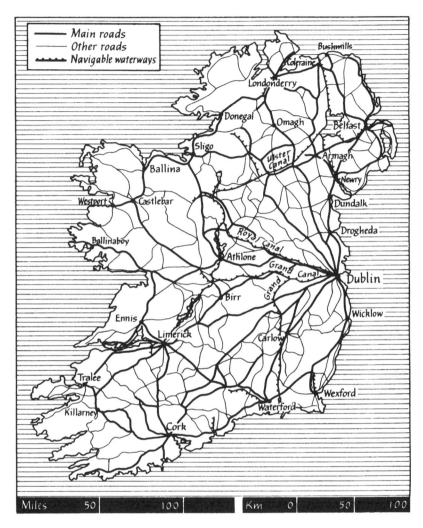

Figure 62 Infrastructure: early nineteenth century.

Portadown; and by 1844 the Dublin–Drogheda line was in operation. During the 1840s and 1850s there was a boom in railway construction and by the early 1850s lines were open from Dublin to Belfast, Galway, Limerick, Cork and Waterford. Although there was little railway construction in the poorer areas, by 1866 there were 1,909 miles of railway, a figure which by 1978 had been reduced to 1,250. In the late nineteenth century light railways were set up to more remote rural districts, but these did not have a very long life. By the 1920s competition from the motor car began the decline of railway services.

63 MODERN TRANSPORT

Rail

In 1924 the government amalgamated all the railway companies operating in the Irish Free State into one company, the Great Southern Railway (GSR). In 1926 the GSR carried 15.5 million passengers; five years later this had declined to 11.9 million. In response to complaints that railways suffered unfair competition from road competitors, the 1932 Road Transport Act prohibited the operation of scheduled passenger transport services except under licences issued by the state; in 1933 railways were permitted to acquire road-transport companies. This legislation was intended to create monopolies and prevent the under-utilization of the railways, which the government regarded as an important national asset; by 1938 the railways had eliminated 1,098 independent bus services. However, losses continued to mount during the 1930s and 1940s despite the closure of branch lines and reduction in services. Under the 1944 Transport Act, a new company, Córas Iompair Éireann (CIE) – a merger of the GSR and the Dublin United Transport (formerly Tramways) Company – was established to run the rail system, city buses and provincial coaches: it was brought into the state sector in 1950.

The Transport Act of 1958 enabled CIE to terminate uneconomic rail services; by 1968 the rail network had been reduced to 1,910 miles, from 2,697 miles ten years earlier. By the 1980s CIE operated three loss-making companies: Iarnród Éireann, Bus Éireann and Dublin Bus. Iarnród Éireann operates the national rail services, the Dublin–Belfast Enterprise service (with Northern Ireland Railways) and the Dublin Area Rapid Transport (DART), an electrified above-ground suburban rail system, running along the coastline from Howth to Greystones. In 1989 CIE had a deficit of £100.3 million and was financed by a state subvention of £109.8 million. Over the next decade it recorded passenger increases in all its services – mainline railway numbers increased by 34 per cent, DART by 23 per cent and Bus Éireann's inter-urban routes by 166 per cent. However, CIE continued to operate at a loss: in 2002 Iarnród Éireann's deficit was €22.5 million.

Northern Ireland Railways was founded in 1968 to operate the railway services of the former Ulster Transport Authority, which in turn had taken over the three private railways (Great Northern Railway, Northern Counties Railway and Co. Down Railway) in Northern Ireland between 1948 and 1957: its rail network extends to 342 kilometres and in 2002–3 it received a £17.7 million subsidy. With Citybus and Ulsterbus, it is now part of Translink.

Air

Aer Lingus (an anglicization of 'aer loingeas' – airfleet) was registered as a private airline company by the Irish government; its first transatlantic service was 1958. The Republic has three state-owned airports, operated by Aer Rianta (Dublin, Cork and Shannon). Since deregulation in 1986, regional, privately owned airports with international services have opened at Knock, Galway, Waterford, Kerry, Sligo and Donegal. Between 1978 and 1985 air-passenger traffic between Ireland and Britain declined by 6 per cent, but after the 1986 liberalization, reduced fares led to an immediate increase: in 1989 the number of passengers between Dublin and London was more than double that of 1985.

Irish air-passenger traffic grew at an average annual rate of 13.9 per cent from 1993 to 1998, largely because of Ryanair's aggressive fare-cutting. In 1992 Ryanair operated six routes; in 1997 fifteen routes; and by 2003 it operated 133 routes to over eighty-five destinations in sixteen countries and was the fastest-growing airline in Europe; it is currently the largest airline in Europe. Ryanair profits for 2002–3 were €239.4 million, up 53 per cent from the previous year. After years of loss-making in the 1990s, Aer Lingus has been successfully repositioned as a low-fare, profitable airline to rival Ryanair.

Airfreight traffic also grew in the 1990s in response to the Celtic Tiger: from 1990 to 1998 the total volume increased by 144 per cent.

Belfast International Airport, which is the most technically advanced airport in Ireland, services over 3.7 million passengers a year and is the fifth largest regional air cargo centre in the UK. Belfast City Airport, with a new £21 million terminal, serves more than 1.3 million passengers.

Sea

The B & I Line (originally the British & Irish Steam Packet Company), which transported many generations of Irish emigrants, was acquired by the Irish government in 1965, privatized in 1991 and is now part of Irish Ferries. With the growth in cheap airlines, sea travel has declined in popularity, but it remains a key means of transporting freight. The Celtic Tiger was responsible for large-scale growth in port traffic: between 1988 and 1997 the overall volume of goods handled by ports grew by 51 per cent. The island of Ireland has thirty ports, but sea trade is dominated by ports on the east and south coasts and by Shannon. Between them, Dublin, Cork, Rosslare and Shannon handle 80 per cent of trade: Shannon handles bulk traffic, servicing the needs of industry in its hinterland. The ports are generally under direct state ownership, except for Greenore (privately owned) and Rosslare, which is owned by CIE.

Northern Ireland has five commercial ports – used by more than eighty international shipping lines – out of which leave 90 per cent of its total freight traffic and almost 50 per cent of that of the Republic. Belfast is the busiest port in Ireland: almost 9,000 ships, carrying 17 million tonnes of cargo, leave it each year.

Road

In Ireland, as in all developed countries, the fastest-growing transport sector of the twentieth century was road. In 1911 there were only 9,169 registered motor

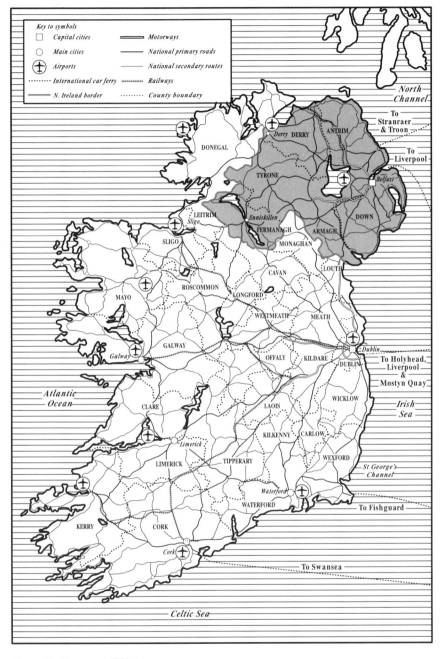

Figure 63 Transport: 2004.

Source Bartholomew Ltd, 2003.

vehicles in the country; by 1935, in the Republic, there were 46,751; in 1965, 447,129 and in 2002, as a result of the Celtic Tiger, 1,447,908. Dealing with this steadily rising number of vehicles required strong investment in roads. In 1975, just after joining the EU (then EEC), the Republic spent the lowest GDP share on transport (0.6 per cent, compared to the average 1.5 per cent) and had among the worst roads in Europe, but by the 1990s the situation was much improved: EU funds had financed improvements and extensions of national primary roads and national secondary roads. However, bad planning, inadequate public transport and increasing numbers of cars have given rise to serious problems of traffic congestion, air pollution and accidents.

The greatest challenge facing the Republic's transport sector is how to reduce traffic in Dublin as its population continues to expand. The lack of an underground metro system means the city has some of the worst traffic problems in Europe. Solutions such as bus corridors and a new – but long-delayed – tram system (the LUAS) are only stopgaps in dealing with the traffic problems of a geographically small city with over a million inhabitants apparently tied umbilically to their cars.

Northern Ireland has a well-developed road infrastructure and little traffic congestion, though its pattern of transport use was distorted after 1969 by the damage caused to tourism and the prevalence of military traffic.

64   TELECOMMUNICATIONS

Northern Ireland's broadcasting services, being integrated with those in the rest of the United Kingdom, have been run by the British Broadcasting Corporation (BBC) since 1926; commercial television and radio are now under Ofcom. For economic and social reasons, the Republic lagged far behind in offering a choice of stations. Regular radio broadcasting began in Dublin on New Year's Day 1926; broadcasting from Cork began the following year and reception became widespread when the Athlone transmitter came into service in 1933. Originally referred to by its call-sign of 2RN, in 1937 the service became known as Radio Éireann. Ireland came late to television and was unable to receive a clear transmission until 1955, when the BBC increased the power of its transmitter in Belfast, so enabling it to be picked up in Dublin; there was no national channel until 1961 when Telefís Éireann began broadcasting. In 1966, the joint broadcasting service became Radio Telefís Éireann (RTE). Gay Byrne launched what would be the hugely influential *Late Late Show*; more than forty years later this national institution is still going strong – now under Pat Kenny. In 1962 only 3.3 per cent of the population had TV licences; this had risen to 24.5 per cent by 1996 (about one per household). RTE 2 began broadcasting in 1978; ten years later it changed its name to Network 2, ten years later again, to N2 and in 2003 back to RTE 2. The 1988 Broadcasting Act established legal commercial radio and television, thus opening the way to TV3 (which took eight years to get up and running). An Irish-language channel, Telefís na

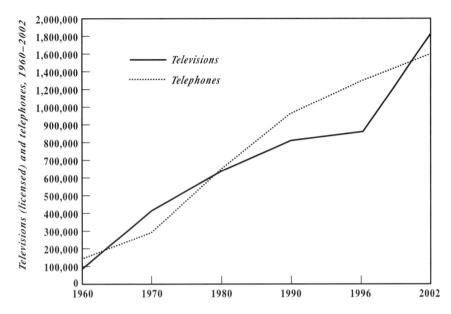

Figure 64 Telecommunications in the Republic: 1960–2002.

Gaelige (now TG4), was started in 1996 and has proved successful. Cable and satellite penetration is growing fast and, as in Northern Ireland, the government is keenly encouraging the trend from an analogue to a digital service.

Telephones were also slow to penetrate in the Republic, largely because of supply problems: in 1960 there were 5.3 telephones per 100 people; by 1976 the penetration was only fourteen per 100 compared to thirty-eight in the UK. Mainly due to under-capitalization, the system was backward and inefficient. In the succeeding decades, helped by EU funds, Ireland became a leader in the telecommunications sector, though penetration remained comparatively low, largely because prices were so high. More competitive pricing from Telecom Éireann – privatized as Eircom in 1999 – in all areas of telecommunications is closing the competitive gap with the rest of the EU; mobile-phone usage is high and computer use and Internet access are increasing sharply. In 1998 18.6 per cent of households had home computers; this rose to 33 per cent in 2000 and 43.5 per cent in 2002. Households with Internet access went from a fifth in 2000 to a third in 2002. However, there is a startling difference between levels of broadband penetration north and south. The Republic has one of the lowest broadband penetrations in Europe, while, partly because of competition, Northern Ireland is expected to have 100 per cent coverage in 2005.

IX The economy

Like most island people, the Irish were for many centuries a maritime race; their warriors (43) and merchants had close contacts with Britain and Europe, and their fishermen fished not only for the domestic market but also for export. As far back as the first century AD there are references in history and legend to foreign merchants attending great fairs to exchange their wines and spices for hides and cloth. With the coming of Christianity military expeditions abroad ceased, but commercial intercourse continued.

While initially the Vikings (11) disrupted Irish life, their contribution to the growth of organized trade was to be crucial: they introduced Irish goods to Viking settlements in Britain and on the Continent. Trading was a way of life for the Vikings, for their familiarity with the seas and their scattered settlements, extending as far as Russia, gave them security from which to operate. For their commerce, the east coast of Ireland was ideally placed geographically, since Dublin had easy access to their settlements in Scandinavia, Britain and the Continent.

Although the Viking settlers initially resisted the Norman invaders (12) they soon made peace with them and took advantage of the founding of new towns and the new opportunities for more widespread trade with Britain. Despite the many disruptions that occurred during the medieval period, the coastal towns suffered less than many other parts of the country, and Dublin in particular was a haven of commercial peace. Even though domestic markets were severely limited by poor communications and political and military upheavals, the Viking and Norman inhabitants of the coastal towns – reinforced by merchants from the Continent (66) – continued to trade profitably.

By the seventeenth century, items to be traded included the produce of cottage industry; weaving and spinning provided a supplementary income in many parts of the country. The influence of the Huguenots and the Quakers (40) on the development of textile industries was significant, especially in the north-east where they settled in comparatively large numbers and concentrated on linen manufacture.

Throughout the eighteenth century brewing and glass industries grew steadily and despite British protectionism the domestic market was large enough to encourage the growth of the woollen industry.

The development of the linen industry was encouraged by the government to meet the demands of the English market: money was invested and a Linen Board set up in 1711 to assist its growth. Dublin merchants, however, provided most of the capital for the industry during the eighteenth century, despite its increasing concentration in the north-east. Initially the industry was mainly in north-east Ulster, in Antrim, Armagh, Down and Londonderry, but it spread south gradually, first into Tyrone, Monaghan and Cavan and later, in Leinster, to Louth, Meath, Westmeath and Longford. Auxiliary industries, such as the spinning of the yarn, were more widespread, extending as far as Roscommon, Mayo, Sligo, Galway, Kerry and King's and Queen's counties.

Unlike the linen industry, the woollen industry was more urban in emphasis, although for a period there was some domestic weaving rurally, especially in the midlands and the south-west.

Other industries were operating with some success by the beginning of the eighteenth century, catering mainly for the domestic market. Many of these had of necessity to be concentrated in the ports or nearby towns, because of their dependence on imported coal. Distilling, brewing, sugar-refining, glass-making and ironworking were particularly dependent on coal, while milling of grain, paper, wool and flour tended to be concentrated along rivers. There was, however, increasingly a tendency towards the centralization of industry to take advantage of technological innovations and economies of scale.

There was ample capital available in Ireland to finance industrial expansion. Banking increased in extent greatly during the first half of the eighteenth century, and although later economic crises brought about a number of bankruptcies, nevertheless by the early nineteenth century banks were widespread throughout the country. Apart from banking investments, financial backing was available from landowners, merchants and the government, the latter making substantial grants for industrial development.

Irish trade, and hence industry, was hampered from the mid-sixteenth century by the English government's acquisitiveness. Until then trading had been extremely lucrative, both for the merchants and for the towns in which they operated. Even widespread piracy could not greatly affect the prosperity of their enterprises. But by the early seventeenth century Irish trade was suffering from government intervention, which had imposed heavy customs duties, as well as from the effects of the political and military instability which had affected many towns during the Nine Years War. However, northern ports began to achieve a new significance through the work of the Ulster Scots in improving them and increasing exports. A period of stability before the middle of the seventeenth century, combined with Wentworth's encouragement of certain industries and his success in ridding the seas of piracy, helped to stage a recovery, which was, however, frustrated by the political upheavals of the rest of the century. The late seventeenth and early eighteenth centuries were to see British protectionism at its height succeed in limiting the nature and extent of Irish trade.

The introduction of power-spinning to the Irish linen industry in the 1820s spelled the end of domestic spinning, and concentrated the industry more narrowly in the north-east. By this time the woollen industry was dying; the superiority of cheaper English wool had finally had its effect. This was to impoverish the west of Ireland further, as milling and weaving ceased: in 1838 Ireland had to import 86 per cent of its woollen cloth. Cotton, which had also begun as a domestic industry, had been industrialized in the 1770s when machines for spinning were introduced, mainly in Belfast, Dublin and Cork. The industry did not have a long period of success, however. By the 1820s the Lancashire cotton industry, like the Yorkshire woollen industry, was gradually strangling all opposition in the British Isles.

The concentration around Belfast of the linen industry, which resulted from the investment in power-spinning, was in Ireland the most dramatic result of the Industrial Revolution, for mechanization changed the whole industry from a widespread domestic activity to a purely urban industry. The same kind of concentration was to be seen in brewing and distilling. Within fifty years of 1785, malt houses in Ireland dropped in number by 83 per cent while increasing productivity by 100 per cent. Milling was expanding also, and agricultural industries, like bacon production, maintained their importance up to the Famine.

Although free trade was a reality by the end of the eighteenth century, Irish trade had already become so restricted in its scope that its prosperity was short-lived. By the early nineteenth century Irish exports were very narrowly based. The only really significant manufactured export was linen, and as a result of the Industrial Revolution it was now being produced only in one small part of the country, where the transformation of industry from domestic to factory-based production was in progress. Banking had developed more extensively in Ulster than elsewhere and thus capital was more readily available. By this period Belfast, which had been in existence for only two centuries, was the second most important city in Ireland and had extensive trading contacts: it centralized the trade in agricultural produce, the only other main export and the only important product of Connacht, Munster and much of Leinster.

The effects of the famine were to prove the need for diversity in industry and trade: it was necessary to learn the lesson that disproportionate dependence on any one product could mean disproportionate hardship should markets change rapidly.

By the middle of the nineteenth century, after the Famine, a number of smaller industries like paper, glassworks, ironworks, tanning and shipbuilding were expanding steadily. Improvements in communications resulting from the advent of the railways were to be another force for centralization, since local industry was faced with stiffer competition, though there were compensatory local benefits in the extension of the range and variety of retail and wholesale trades.

During the second half of the century this centralization adversely affected such industries as glass-making, tanning, sugar-refining, paper-making and milling and by 1885 parliament found it necessary to appoint a committee to inquire into Irish industry. The work of organizations like the Congested Districts Board (59) helped to some extent, but industrial recovery was a result more of improvement on the agricultural side – particularly in the dairy industry – than of any overall recovery. There was, however, a gradual improvement in industry: with even more centralization in industries like milling, baking, wool and clothing, there was greater efficiency of production, and distilling and brewing prospered. In the north-east, while linen kept its pre-eminence, ship-building and engineering prospered.

By the time of partition, however, the industrial landscape still resembled that of the seventeenth century, with the north-east the only significantly industrialized part of the country.

When Arthur Griffith died in August 1922, his economic policy of promoting rapid industrialization with the help of protective tariffs virtually died with him, though the policy was revived in the 1930s by de Valera's government (34). Greater industrialization followed, as did the creation of semi-state services like Aer Lingus, the Electricity Supply Board (ESB) and Bord na Móna (the Peat Board). In the 1950s state intervention was stepped up as part of an effort to expand the economy by encouraging exports, and there was a marked improvement in the range and quality of economic planning. During this period began the highly successful policy of attracting investment by means of incentives (71). Despite inevitable problems with, for instance, balance of payments deficits, inflation and unemployment, most years in the 1960s and 1970s saw a growth in output in the Republic that exceeded that of most European nations. During the 1980s, membership of the EU and Ireland's consequent desirability as a manufacturing and trading base for global enterprises created the conditions for the 1990s phenomenon of the Celtic Tiger, with its startling implications for halting emigration and encouraging immigration.

65   MEDIEVAL TRADE

The lack of adequate documentary evidence makes any account of medieval Irish trade somewhat conjectural, but there is ample proof of significant trading contacts with Britain and the Continent; the most important of the known contacts are shown in Figure 65. We know the main goods that were exchanged, although we cannot gauge the extent or profitability of the trade.

Although there was some sporadic foreign trade before the Vikings established coastal towns, it was they who introduced an organized trade to Ireland. The development of their towns, and later the widespread Norman foundations, helped this trade and encouraged contacts with Britain and France: Gerald of Wales testifies to the flourishing nature of Irish trade with France at the time of the Norman invasion. Apart from the conjectural sea routes indicated on the map, Irish goods travelled throughout the Continent by means of well-established inland trading routes, although there were direct links between Ireland and a number of major trading towns.

Broadly speaking, the Irish exported necessities and imported luxuries. Their staple exports were hides, wool and grain, although salmon, hake, herring, linen

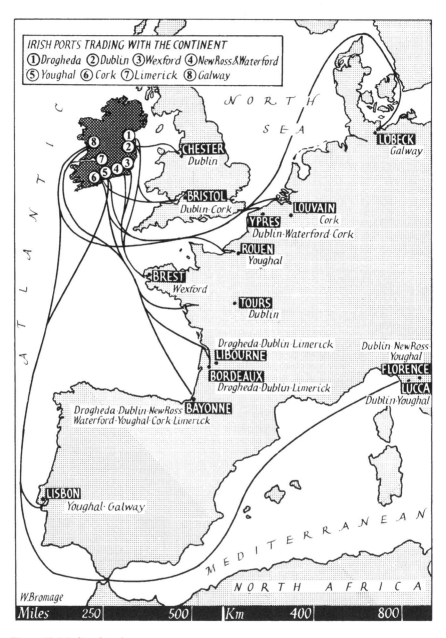

IRISH PORTS TRADING WITH THE CONTINENT
① Drogheda ② Dublin ③ Wexford ④ NewRoss&Waterford
⑤ Youghal ⑥ Cork ⑦ Limerick ⑧ Galway

NORTH SEA

LÜBECK
Galway

CHESTER
Dublin

BRISTOL
Dublin·Cork

LOUVAIN
Cork

YPRES
Dublin·Waterford·Cork

ROUEN
Youghal

BREST
Wexford

TOURS
Dublin

Drogheda·Dublin·Limerick   Dublin·NewRoss
                                   Youghal
LIBOURNE   FLORENCE

BORDEAUX   LUCCA
Drogheda·Dublin·Limerick   Dublin·Youghal

Drogheda·Dublin·NewRoss
Waterford·Youghal·Cork·Limerick BAYONNE

LISBON
Youghal·Galway

MEDITERRANEAN

NORTH AFRICA

W.Bromage

Miles 250   500   Km 400   800

Figure 65 Medieval trade.

cloth, timber, butter, gold, gold vessels and ornaments are frequently mentioned as subsidiary exports. By the thirteenth century Irish linen and serge were popular abroad. Important imports were spices from Lisbon, Florence and Lucca, corn and English cloth, and salt, coal, silks and metals, but the major import was wine, which came mainly from France. Brian Ború is alleged to have exacted as a tribute from the Vikings of Dublin 150 vats of wine and from the Limerick Vikings a daily barrel. Dublin's main trade was with Bristol and Chester, and it had a highly profitable slave trade during the twelfth century. Bristol was given Dublin by Henry II in the twelfth century, so even when Dublin secured its independence there were very close ties between the two ports.

Economic considerations made the towns bastions of conservatism and loyalty to the established order. The citizens were of many races: Irish, Vikings and Normans formed the majority, with a substantial minority of Welsh, and some Flemish and French merchants and Italian bankers and financiers. The Florentine banking family of Frescobaldi stationed members of the family in Dublin, Waterford, Youghal and Cork in the thirteenth century, and during the same period the Ricardi, a family of money-lenders, were active in both eastern and western coastal towns.

66   TUDOR TRADE

In 1436, the anonymous author of the polemic called the *Libelle of English Polycye* urged upon the English government the patriotic necessity of maintaining a strong navy in order to protect and expand English trade. In the course of his tract the author drew attention to the economic possibilities of Ireland and urged that England take an active interest in the trade of a land 'so large, so gode, so plenteouse, so riche'. That the English government was successively too weak and too preoccupied with other concerns to interest itself effectively in Ireland's trade until the middle of the sixteenth century was a matter of good fortune for Ireland, which had continued its Continental trade undisturbed.

The eastern ports, particularly Dublin and Wexford, traded mainly with Britain, although Dublin maintained trading contact with the French wine-growing areas. The eastern ports also had a widespread internal trade. Despite having a bad harbour, because of its political importance Dublin was an important port. Yet its traffic – which was mainly imports of luxury goods from England – was not especially profitable. The southern and western ports traded far more widely. Galway had an extensive foreign trade, mainly with Spain and Flanders, and supplied most of Ireland with wine. The city benefited from a considerable degree of fiscal autonomy, being free for much of this period from the necessity of paying any customs duties to the King. (The removal of this privilege in 1584, in addition to increasing political instability, was to herald the steady decline of Galway from the mid-sixteenth century onwards.) Galway's main commercial contacts were with Castile, Andalusia, Gascony and Iceland. A

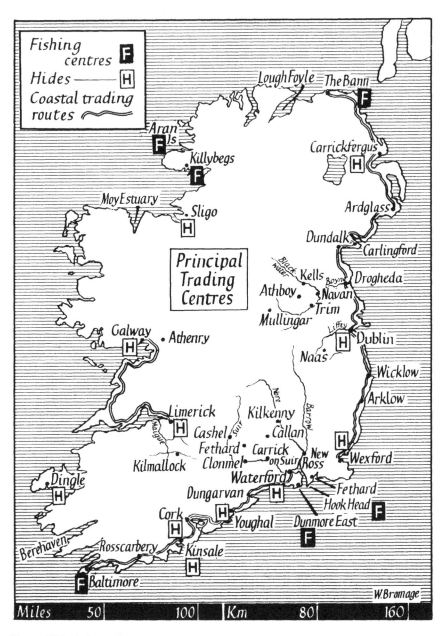

Figure 66(a) Tudor trade.

(b)

port of call for Bristol ships sailing to Iceland, she also controlled coastal commerce between the Shannon and Donegal. Galway's great commercial rival in the wine trade was Limerick, whose main contacts were with the Iberian peninsula and which also began to decline towards the end of the sixteenth century.

Cork also depended largely on its foreign trade, which began to suffer after the Desmond rebellions. Its main contacts were with Flanders, western France and the Iberian peninsula, but its privileges were fewer than those of Waterford.

Waterford had an extensive interior trade, especially along the Barrow, Nore and Suir and an excellent harbour, and although it never had quite the independence of Galway, it was the pre-eminent Irish port, having connections with France, Portugal, Spain and the fishing lands of Newfoundland. Wexford had a rivalry with Waterford akin to that of Limerick with Galway and from a similar position of inferiority: its harbour was so poor that few foreign ships could enter it, and it was obliged to build its own ships for foreign trade, which was mainly with Bristol.

Of the smaller ports, New Ross, Dungarvan, Youghal, Kinsale and Dingle were important until the mid-sixteenth century. All of them traded with England and the Continent, mainly with France. Other small ports, such as Carrickfergus and Ardglass, and the more important Drogheda, traded mainly with Scotland, although they had some contacts with Brittany. Carrickfergus was the main centre of northern trade.

Internal trade was mainly conducted around the coast or by means of inland waterways. Figure 66a shows the main internal trading contacts, though it should be noted that the trade between ports was usually by sea and not by land.

The main exports were the traditional hides, cloth, fish and timber, with wine, oil, spices, salt and iron being the main imports. In other words, exports were still basic necessities and raw materials, while imports were mainly manufactured goods and luxuries.

With the political disturbances of the Elizabethan period, the Munster rebellions, the Nine Years War and the restrictions placed by the government on foreign trade came great changes. The western, southern and south-eastern ports – which relied mainly on trade with the Continent – went into decline, and the northern ports – notably Drogheda, Dundalk, Carlingford and Carrickfergus – went into the ascendant. Yet their main trading contacts were with Chester and Liverpool, to which they became subordinate, and their exports were mainly yarn and tallow and lacked the variety of the past.

67   SEVENTEENTH-CENTURY TRADE

Despite the late-sixteenth-century decline in Irish trade with the Continent, a study of the main import, wine, has shown that links with the Continent were still very strong. Although Anglo-Irish trade was increasingly dominant in Irish commerce, wine, salt, hops and iron were still imported from further afield, while Ireland continued to export fish, hides, wool, linen and provisions.

Figure 67 shows the wine trade in 1614–15, and demonstrates the increasing trading contacts with Britain and the new importance of the northern ports. The strong links between the south-western ports and Spain and France still persisted, although a sizeable proportion of the imported wine was carried in English ships. This indirect dependence on England is shown in the contemporary shipping figures: of a total of 143 ships engaged in importing

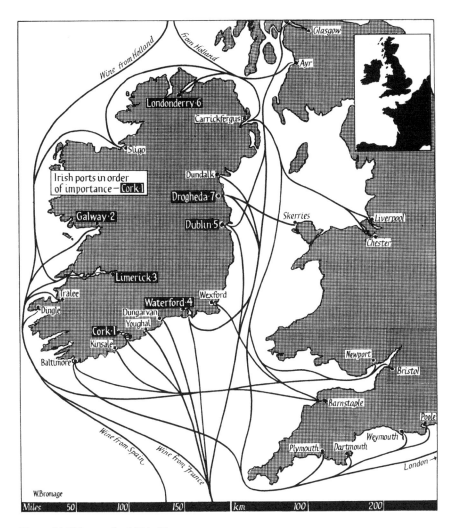

Figure 67 Wine trade: 1614–15.

wine into Ireland, only thirty-one were Irish; of the remainder, fifty-one were English and thirty-one Scottish.

As the century progressed, Ireland became increasingly dependent on trade with Britain. Irish cattle became so important and successful an export that from about 1621 there was economic pressure on the English parliament to control imports of Irish cattle because of the threat posed to the English farmer. Protectionism did not succeed initially, and until the 1640s Irish trade was reasonably successful; wool and butter also became important exports. During this period the agricultural potential of the country was just beginning to be exploited. For the first time there was a sustained period of peace in the country, and woodlands were being cleared on a large scale. However, the increasing concentration of Irish exporters on agricultural products restricted trade, since Europe had little need of agricultural products, and European outlets became fewer in number.

The wars between 1641 and 1652, the plague of 1650 and the famine of 1652 all contributed to the disruption of Irish economic life, while the Cromwellian land confiscations inhibited agricultural and commercial stability. Customs revenue, which had reached £60,000 in the 1630s, slumped to £12,000 in 1656.

A fundamental recovery was, however, in evidence by the end of the decade, and exports rose steadily, though dependence on the English market was increasing. The demand for cattle and wool continued and Irish beef was shipped to the British colonies in the West Indies.

In 1663, the poor state of the market for cattle in England led to the passing of a bill imposing heavy duties on Irish cattle or sheep imported from July to December each year. Then in 1667 a bill was passed which forbade the importing of any Irish cattle, sheep, pork or beef. Heavy as was this blow to Irish trade, there were compensations in the increased demand for Irish wool. Nevertheless, Irish trade was in an unhealthy state at this time; there was little demand anywhere for agricultural produce.

The economic prosperity of many of the Irish ports was affected by these and other measures, including the Navigation Acts of 1671–85, which forbade the importing of many products, including sugar and tobacco, except indirectly from England. Many ports began to sacrifice their earlier importance to increased centralization. Dublin, Cork and Belfast grew enormously in size and importance, while there was a marked decline in the importance of Carrickfergus, Youghal, Kinsale and many other similar smaller and less well-placed ports.

Despite the measures discriminating against Irish trade, until the mid-1680s exports continued to rise: Ulster was developing a prosperous linen industry. However, yet again, peace proved transitory, and with the outbreak of war in 1689 Irish trade once again suffered. The steady recovery of the mid-1690s was largely a consequence of famines in France and Scotland that produced an artificial demand for agricultural produce. Nor was the recovery unimpeded. Mainly because of the alarm shown by English merchants at the competitiveness of Irish wool, a bill passed in 1699 outlawed the export of woollen cloth from Ireland overseas, even though prohibitive duties already made it uneconomic to export Irish woollen goods to England. Direct interference by the English government with Irish trade was to continue during the eighteenth century (68).

68   EIGHTEENTH-CENTURY TRADE

Although the laws discriminating against Irish trade were serious in their effect on Irish prosperity, they were only a part of a general economic decline. A revaluation of the Irish currency brought about a fall in prices at home which – coupled with a slump in European markets occasioned by war – had a serious effect on the Irish export trade. Occasional years of recovery during the next few decades were accompanied by harvest failures and a gradual fall in the value of foreign trade. Only the linen trade was really prosperous; by 1730 it made up over a quarter of all Irish exports. Recovery during the 1730s depended largely on the linen trade and on a high demand in the colonies for Irish products, particularly beef and butter. This provision trade was hindered by a series of embargoes on trade with countries hostile to England, which affected Irish trade with France though not with French colonies. In 1776 a general embargo was placed on the provision trade except to Britain and her colonies. From this came the Irish provisions trade's ultimate dependence on Britain.

The linen trade was largely dependent on England from 1696 when duties were abolished on Irish linen entering England. During the eighteenth century Irish linen became supreme in English markets: from making up about 23 per cent of exports to Great Britain in 1698, linen reached 80 per cent sixty years later. The woollen industry improved also with the abolition in 1739 of all duties on its entry into England and the repeal in 1779 of the 1699 act. Another important factor in improving Irish trade was the demand for cattle, beef and butter in England in the 1750s which led to the suspension in 1758 and 1759 and the repeal in 1776 of the Cattle Acts and those acts prohibiting the export of beef and butter.

The centralization of the ports, which had been occurring during the seventeenth century, was virtually complete by the mid-eighteenth century. A comparison between the ports' relative importance in the early seventeenth-century wine trade and in the 1750s illustrates the position. Of the ships employed in Irish trade during 1753, Dublin – with 2,360 – dominated, Cork was second with 732, Belfast third with 468, Waterford fourth with 208, Drogheda fifth with 200 and Dundalk sixth with 179; no other port had more than 100 ships. The eastern and northern ports concentrated on the export of linen and Cork and Waterford on the provisions trade. Irish shipping was classed as British and could trade with Britain and the colonies directly, so while the story of Irish trade during the late seventeenth and eighteenth centuries is of the contraction of foreign trade, mainly due to British protectionism, British support for the linen trade and Ireland's special position in the British market were a considerable compensation.

By 1779, under pressure from the Volunteers, England had no option but to concede 'free trade', which meant the opening of the colonial trade to Ireland. By the end of the eighteenth century, therefore, although the scope of Irish trade had become restricted, it was otherwise in a flourishing state.

Between 1700 and 1800 Irish exports went up in value from £1.2 million to £7.6 million, while imports rose even more from £1.2 million to £11 million. The increasing dependence on Great Britain for both imports and exports is illustrated in Figure 68.

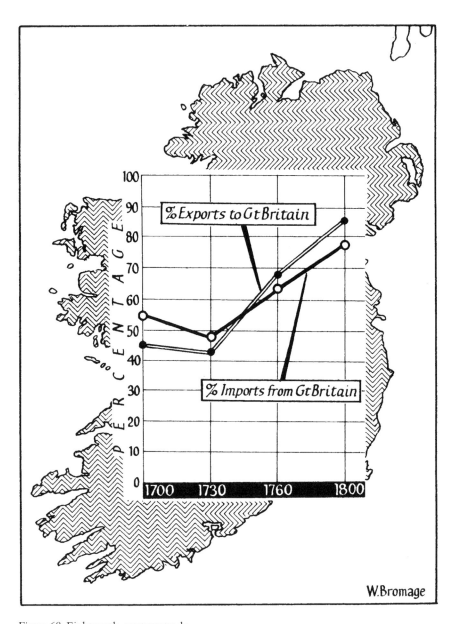

Figure 68 Eighteenth-century trade.

69   PRE-FAMINE TRADE

The main Irish exports of the eighteenth century were linen, woollen goods and provisions. By the end of the century woollen goods were no longer competitive with their English counterparts. The concentration of the industry in urban areas and its inferior craftsmanship meant that ultimately it was producing a product higher in price and lower in quality than the English alternative, although it continued largely to satisfy the home market.

One feature of Irish trade before the famine is the enormous expansion in the provisions trade, an anomaly in a period when there was so much starvation throughout the country. The linen industry continued its steady expansion; while foreign trade continued to contract, the heavy demand of the British market for linen continued, and overall, between 1810 and 1825, linen exports increased by over 100 per cent.

While the best period for the provisions trade was during the Napoleonic wars, its growth continued. By the 1830s, 700,000 tons of agricultural produce were being exported annually. Although Dublin was still the premier port, handling 28 per cent of all exports and imports, with Belfast having 15 per cent, Cork 13 per cent and Waterford 12 per cent, the strength of the first two was in linen, while the latter two specialized in provisions. Estimates of the value of the exports and imports handled by the major ports during the 1830s indicate their specializations.

The message of these figures is clear. The south-eastern, southern and western ports were heavily dependent on a single export – either provisions or cereals. With the disruption caused by the famine of the 1840s this trade was to collapse catastrophically. The north-eastern and northern ports were healthier, since the three main ports had linen as their main export, and of the three smaller ports, only Dundalk had a very heavy dependence on food exports (see Table 7).

Table 7 Trade in the 1830s

Port	Main export	% of total	Main import	% of total
Londonderry	Linen	30	Sugar	6
Belfast	Linen	62	Linen yarn	26
Newry	Corn, meal, flour	33	Woollen manufactures	10
Dundalk	Corn, meal, flour	62	Coal	18
Drogheda	Corn, meal, flour	34	Tobacco	31
Dublin	Linen	29	Tea	12
Wexford	Corn, meal, flour	56	Woollen manufactures	19
Waterford	Corn, meal, flour	43	Cotton manufactures	30
Cork	Provisions	69	Cotton and woollen manufactures	32
Limerick	Corn, meal, flour	52	Tobacco	22
Galway	Corn, meal, flour	86	Tobacco	21
Sligo	Corn, meal, flour	50	Sugar	15

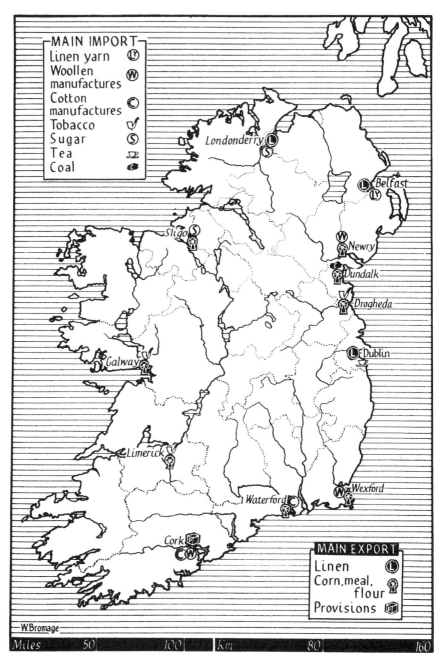

Figure 69 Pre-Famine trade.

Until the famine, however, the provisions trade continued to flourish, although it lost most of its colonial markets at the beginning of the century when the Americans captured the Newfoundland and West Indies markets. Its main elements were bacon, beef and butter, which in the 1830s made up 45 per cent of the trade, with corn, meal and flour providing 37 per cent and livestock 18 per cent.

The importance of the inland waterways in making the provisions trade possible must not be forgotten. Since the sources of agricultural produce were widespread, and the ports dealing with it were few in number, good communications were vital; the canals and navigable rivers were of great importance. During the 1830s, about 700,000 tons of agricultural produce were exported annually; total tonnage carried by all waterways was about 600,000, of which the vast majority must have been provisions.

After the Famine the emphasis of the provisions trade changed. Bacon, beef and butter declined in importance as exports, while the livestock and corn trade increased.

70 PRE-FAMINE INDUSTRY

The 1841 Census calculated the whole population of Ireland as being over eight million, of whom about 40 per cent were classified as having an occupation. Of these just over one million were classified as working in industry, fishing or transport and over half of these were in Ulster. The greatest industry by far was textiles. There were more textile workers in Ulster than in the rest of Ireland put together and more people worked in the clothing industry in Ulster than in any other province.

The figures show that about 80 per cent of the population relied on agriculture or textiles for employment; many of those depending on textiles were experiencing economic disaster as a result of the mechanizing of the industry.

Agricultural industries were based mainly in the south, where indeed, as in the west, there was very little else in the way of industry. Milling continued to grow, both in the eastern and western coastal towns, with small mills being scattered throughout the country; during the 1830s there were almost 2,000 mills in Ireland. It is possible that with more enterprise from local landlords enough small industries could have been initiated or kept going to mitigate the universal poverty. The hitherto widespread textile industry had contracted; cotton, wool, muslin and silk, which in earlier times had brought prosperity, were now in decline, and linen was concentrated in the north-east of the country.

Although brewing and distilling had prospered before the 1840s and were to do so again, they suffered a serious setback with the campaign in Ireland in the 1830s of Father Theobald Mathew, a Tipperary-born Capuchin friar who led a remarkably successful temperance campaign. Drunkenness was (and is) certainly a problem in Ireland and was greatly reduced by his Total Abstinence Societies,

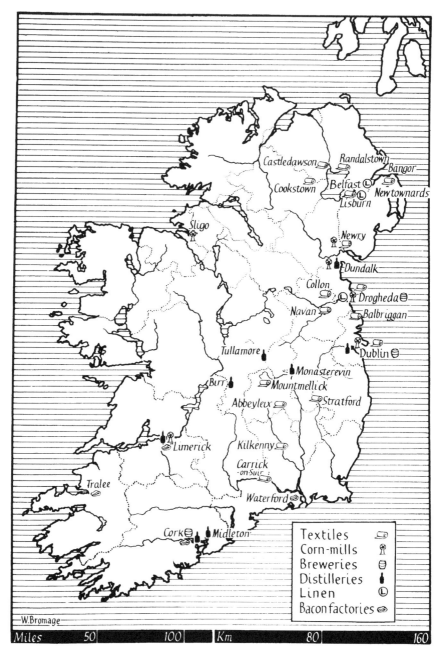

Figure 70 Pre-Famine industry.

but the slump in the home market was a serious blow to the industry, although it had partially recovered by the mid-1850s. Concentration in these industries led to increasing prosperity for a few big firms like Guinness, Beamish and Crawford.

One of the remarkable lacunae in Irish industrial development was fishing. Fish in earlier centuries had been an important export, but by the nineteenth century the industry was barely in existence. Although fish were plentiful – whether cheap fish like herrings or the more exotic salmon, oysters and lobster – the lack of a proper industry seems to have been due to a simple reluctance on the part of an erstwhile maritime people to venture onto their dangerous coastal waters.

Sir Robert Kane, in 1844, published *Industrial Resources of Ireland* in which he surveyed, among other aspects of industry, the country's mineral potential and charted its mineral wealth – which is widespread though very limited in quality. Although extensive coalfields could be found in the south and south-west, they were made up of poor-quality seams too narrow to be economically mined. Iron mines existed mainly in the east, lead in the east and west and copper in the south and east. Unfortunately, minerals mined in Ireland proved uncompetitive by foreign standards because of expense of production and lack of quality.

Overall therefore, pre-Famine Ireland was seriously under-industrialized outside the north-east. The most prosperous industry in the south was the agricultural industry, which was to suffer seriously with the cataclysmic upheaval of the Famine.

71 TRADE AND INDUSTRY IN INDEPENDENT IRELAND: 1920–90

The first ten years of the Irish Free State were characterized by extreme fiscal rectitude as the new government sought to impress Britain with its discipline and caution, and tried to repair the physical devastation caused by the Civil War without excess borrowing. Government expenditure was reduced from £42 million in 1923–4 to £32 million the following year and £24 million in 1926–7; income tax fell from 5 shillings (25 new pence) in the £1 in 1924 to 3 shillings (15 pence) in 1926 – 6d (2½ pence) less than in England – with increases in indirect taxation and reductions in social-security payments.

Partition cut the Free State off from the most industrialized part of the island, but this did not overly worry Cumann na nGaedheal, which did not prioritize industry. According to Patrick Hogan, Minister for Agriculture: 'National development in Ireland is practically synonymous with agricultural development.' Agriculture in the 1920s employed half the workforce and most of the exports were food and drink products. Private industrial entrepreneurship was given little incentive, but government-sponsored initiatives included the

Shannon hydro-electricity scheme (1925–9) and the establishment of a sugar-beet factory in Carlow.

When Fianna Fáil came to power in 1932, de Valera embarked on a radical policy of national self-sufficiency: he sought to create an indigenous protected manufacturing sector and to shift from livestock to tillage in agriculture, on the dubious basis that more tillage meant more employment and was in the interests of the small farmer. Trade disruption caused by tariffs was exacerbated by a 1932–8 economic war with Britain, which started when Westminster imposed revenue duties in response to de Valera's refusal to pay land annuities. This hurt Ireland far more than Britain. However, the young, energetic and talented Seán Lemass, as Minister for Industry and Commerce, presided over an industrialization drive that saw gross industrial output rise from £55 million in 1931 to £90 million in 1938. This industrial base was uncompetitive and not strong enough to meet the challenges of the Second World War. Post-war, America's Marshall Aid to Europe helped keep the economy buoyant. Although Ireland's wartime neutrality meant it was not in the front line of aid recipients, the £40 million provided financed nearly half of state investment from 1949 to 1952 and was used for afforestation, land reclamation and construction programmes and for the Electricity Supply Board.

Protectionism was not an unusual response to the drastic slump in international trade in the 1930s, but Ireland continued this policy for another two decades and suffered severe economic stagnation in the 1950s while the rest of Europe boomed. Finally in 1959 Lemass took over as Taoiseach and laid the foundations of a period of sustained economic growth by implementing the recommendations of T. K. Whitaker, secretary to the Department of Finance, in a Programme for Economic Expansion which made a shift from protectionism to free trade and encouraged foreign direct investment: the Anglo-Irish free trade agreement was signed in 1965.

The transition to free trade was difficult: Irish firms could not compete and all sectors were affected by the sudden flood of cheaper, better imports; clothing, textiles, footwear and chemicals suffered particularly and car assembly was wiped out. However, firms soon adapted and the rapid growth in exports saw GDP reach unprecedented levels – averaging 4.4 per cent a year growth between 1960 and 1973 (figures surpassed only in the 1990s), during which period living standards rose by 50 per cent. Foreign firms began to invest in Ireland – between 1960 and 1978 the Industrial Development Authority (IDA) attracted 656 companies to Ireland – and the first ever growth in population since the famine was recorded in 1966. In 1958 manufactured exports had made up only a quarter of exports: in 1972 they were level with agriculture. However, Irish firms still lacked self-confidence and self-reliance and there was still little indigenous industry; over half of all investment was financed by the state, either directly or in aid to the private sector. In 1974 60 per cent of manufacturing output was generated by foreign firms attracted to Ireland by tax breaks.

Ireland's reliance on British markets steadily lessened. In 1924 84 per cent of Irish exports went to Great Britain; the 1979 figure was 39 per cent. Exports to

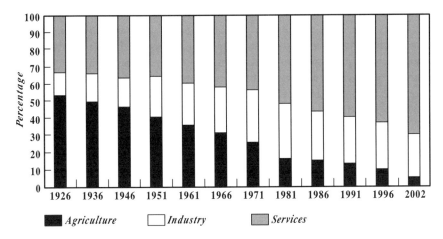

Figure 71 Republic of Ireland: employment trends: 1926–2002.

the US moved from 0.5 per cent in 1938 to 5 per cent in 1979, while exports to the EEC countries went from 4.6 per cent in 1958 when Britain was not a member, to 77 per cent in 1979. Imports from the EEC rose from 11.1 per cent in 1958 to 72 per cent in 1979, while Britain, which had supplied 69 per cent of imports in 1924, supplied only 46 per cent in 1979.

The economy and employment continued to grow until the late 1970s, but if Ireland's GDP appeared high, it was because rates everywhere else slowed in response to the oil crises, to which Ireland responded by embarking on a ruinous policy of massive public spending financed by borrowing. Although 'balancing the books' had been economic orthodoxy since the foundation of the state, the coalition government in 1973–4 projected a budget deficit of 1.5 per cent of GNP; foreign debt under the coalition rose from £126 million in 1973 to £1,040 million at the end of 1976. Towards the end of their term the coalition began to make cutbacks, but when Fianna Fáil came to power in 1977 it kept its election promises of increased public spending with disastrous consequences. Their projected 1978 budget deficit was raised from 3.8 per cent of GNP to 6.2 per cent, borrowing reached an extraordinary 13 per cent of GNP and the consumer boom did little for inefficient Irish businesses but pushed up imports. Within two years the economy showed signs of trouble and during the 1980s growth stagnated, emigration went up and in 1987 unemployment reached 18 per cent.

At the outset of its existence, Northern Ireland was largely dependent on agriculture, linen and shipbuilding, all of which were damaged in the 1920s by the end of the post-war boom and in all of which wages were depressed. Agriculture, which employed 26 per cent of the workforce in the early 1920s, suffered from competition with more intensive farming in the rest of the UK:

4.4 per cent of Northern Irish farms were 100 acres, compared with 8.8 per cent in the Irish Free State and 20.9 per cent in England and Wales. In 1924, 51.77 per cent of the workforce was making linen, for which the market was going into a worldwide decline. Shipbuilding was hit by a fall in demand coupled with protectionism abroad, but nonetheless, the high reputation of Harland and Wolff enabled it to launch both the biggest ship and largest tonnage in the world in 1929, just before the Wall Street crash plunged it into crisis and Northern Ireland into poverty: 27 per cent of the insured workforce was unemployed between 1931 and 1939.

The war greatly boosted employment, and a post-war policy of encouraging inward investment brought about a high growth rate and almost 30,000 new jobs, many in engineering and textiles in the 1960s. Northern Ireland was still poorer than the rest of the United Kingdom, but significantly richer than the south until the Lemass reforms began to take effect. However the international oil crisis of 1973–4, which particularly hit Northern Ireland's synthetic fibre industry, coupled with the violence and devastation that repelled investors (in the late 1970s the IRA began specifically targeting businessmen (87)) began a long economic decline despite immense efforts by the Westminster government to entice foreign investment.

72   THE CELTIC TIGER

The phrase 'Celtic Tiger' was coined by an American investment bank, Morgan Stanley, in a report on the Irish economy, published on 31 August 1994. The IRA announced a 'cessation' of military activity that day, grabbing all headlines, but within three years the term 'Celtic Tiger' was commonly used to describe Ireland's phenomenal growth rate, which at times surpassed that of such East Asian 'tiger' economies as South Korea and Taiwan.

The Celtic Tiger phenomenon took by surprise most commentators, grown accustomed to Ireland's gloomy prospects, but by 1998 a combination of indicators led even the most cautious economists to hail Ireland as the EU success story of the decade. Foremost was the growth rate: GDP was a remarkable 9.1 per cent in 1998, compared to 2.7 per cent in the UK and 3.5 per cent in the US. Job creation was also spectacular, with 513,000 extra jobs being created between 1986 and 2000 – an increase of 47 per cent – the bulk of them after 1994. Unemployment fell to 6.4 per cent in November 1998, well below the EU average, and the decades-old problem of emigration was reversed. In 1996 Ireland had the highest immigration rate in the EU (1.6 per cent) relative to its population, of which 69 per cent were returning nationals, most of whom were bringing skills to the economy. Other positive indicators included a budget surplus, slowly rising workers' incomes, low inflation and interest rates, and a dramatic reduction in the national debt from 125 per cent of GNP in 1987 to 54 per cent; in 1999. Although Ireland had enjoyed good growth in the 1960s, the Celtic Tiger marked the longest period of economic success ever sustained in the independent state, and in terms of comparison with other countries, certainly the most spectacular.

Economists explain the Celtic Tiger by pointing to a combination of favourable conditions: the government, chastened by the 1973–85 experience, helped by creating a stable economic environment and returning to the old orthodoxy of fiscal reform and rigour; 1987 saw the largest cut in public spending ever made and this was followed up by reductions in the rate of borrowing (borrowing was 9.4 per cent of GNP in 1987 and just 3.1 per cent the following year); membership of the EU gave access to the single market; and Ireland put substantial EU structural and cohesion funds to far better use than did Greece or Portugal – the other major recipients. Structural funds amounted to a mini-Marshall Plan to help Ireland out of its recession. Invested in infrastructure such as ports, roads, airports and telecommunications, and in human capital (largely in training) the structural funds produced a multiplier effect on the economy which is estimated to have raised Ireland's GNP by 2–3 per cent in the 1990s.

Ireland's traditional success in attracting Foreign Direct Investment (FDI) was another key factor. Between 1992 and 1996 Ireland attracted 37 per cent of all US investment in the EU (just behind the UK) and also attracted 31 per cent of UK investment in the EU. In 1998, according to the IDA, there were 1,137 foreign firms in Ireland, making up 47 per cent of all manufacturing jobs and 71 per cent of exports, and paying corporation tax of over £700 million. The reasons for foreign companies choosing Ireland included exceptionally low corporation tax and the presence of a young, well-educated, English-speaking

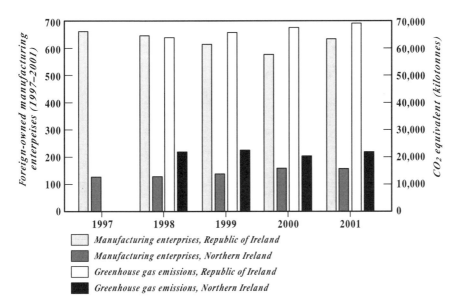

Figure 72(a) Foreign investment and domestic pollution: 1997–2001.

workforce. Despite relative peace in Northern Ireland, compared to the south it is an 'also-ran' in the quest for inward investment. However, as Figure 72a shows, there are disadvantages to rampant growth.

Ireland's traditionally high birth rate and high emigration of working adults had meant that for years it had an exceptionally high dependency ratio (170 dependants for every 100 workers in 1960; by 1985 the ratio had risen to 230:100). In the 1990s, for the first time in thirty years, the dependency ratio fell owing to the declining birth rate and reversal of emigration: the forecast for 2010 is 125:100.

The years of phenomenal growth were 1994–2000; thereafter growth began to tail off. GDP in 2002 was still a healthy 7 per cent but in 2003 it fell to below 2 per cent (though this was still above the EU average). The fall was a result of

Figure 72(b) EU members 2004: GDP per capita in million $ and world ranking; real growth rate and world ranking 2003.

the general global economic downturn, the appreciation of the euro (of which Ireland became a member in 1999) and the rise in inflation and in wages and the inherent problems of the Celtic Tiger – principally over-reliance on multi-nationals. As in the 1960s, there had been a reliance on foreign companies to generate growth along with a neglect of indigenous industry. Even during the boom years this posed a problem, since multinationals made vast amounts of money in Ireland which they then sent home; furthermore, the low rate of company tax induced them to declare all their profits in Ireland – transfer price fixing – thus inflating and distorting Ireland's GDP figures. Furthermore, after 2000 many multinationals began to move out of Ireland, attracted by the lower wages and the well-educated workforces of eastern europe.

Ireland still has a strong position in high-technology industries and has flexible working practices; however, the economy is extremely export-based and dependent on FDI, and is therefore vulnerable to the patterns of world trade.

The Tiger has thrown up other problems: it has had a disappointing trickle-down effect, with money being concentrated in the hands of the few. In 1997 – in the middle of the boom – one-third of the population were living on 60 per cent of the average income, and though unemployment in general fell, the problem of the long-term unemployed was not tackled – 52,000 people were still categorized as long-term unemployed at the end of 1998. Health care and social welfare did not benefit from the boom. Most alarming of all were house prices, which climbed steadily and inexorably, from £60,000 for an average Dublin house in 1990 to £144,000 in 1999, to £250,000 (€300,000) in 2003; by 1998 Dublin houses were 8.2 times the average income. Inept government intervention helped to open the door to property speculators and put buying a house beyond the reach of ordinary people.

By the beginning of the twenty-first century Ireland's per capita income was well above the EU average but the infrastructure (e.g. housing, public transport) and social provision (e.g. health care, social welfare) were well below. Irish tax revenue in 2002 was at least 7.5 per cent below the EU average (measured in terms of GNP). This was not as a result of insufficient income tax – which was close to the EU average – but of inadequate taxes paid by those moneyed people, among whom enthusiastic tax avoidance (legal) is the norm and tax evasion (illegal) all too frequent.

However those doomsayers who predicted the Tiger bubble would burst and plunge Ireland into recession have to date (2005) been proved wrong. The boom years have evened off to stable growth and Ireland remains one of the most confident, competitive and optimistic countries in the EU.

X Social change

For most people, life in Ireland before the eighth century was more pleasant than it would be for more than a millennium. After the Celtic invasion had given way to a permanent settlement (IV), the life of the people was stable, the population was small and food was ample and varied: the staple diet was meat, fish and corn, with milk and ale in large quantities. Complex laws determined a man's position in society and dictated the work he did, the clothes he wore and the food he ate: although restrictive, these laws served to protect those it bound and defend them where necessary. While there were no towns and the inhabitants lived in small communities, they were not isolated. They had a strong cultural tradition, the druids – as well as the poets and the lawyers – being inheritors of an oral tradition. Feasts were quite common and musicians and poets provided entertainment.

By the eighth century, just before the Norse invasions were to disrupt the life of the community, Christianity had introduced certain changes into Irish life. Christians had brought a written culture which was cultivated in the monasteries with dedication and artistry; small groups of people lived around monastic settlements. The country was almost totally agricultural, and the diet was enhanced by the cultivation of crops. Houses, though primitive, were probably overall somewhat superior to those inhabited by many peasants during the nineteenth century. And there continued to be a widespread popular culture; entertainments were provided at feasts and fairs, and storytelling was a pastime of many.

It would be misleading to give the impression that the Ireland of this period was a land overflowing with milk and honey and peopled with merry and cultured farmers. Life was certainly difficult; work was hard for those who were required to perform it and there were serious agricultural recessions during the eighth century. Neither was the country wholly peaceful. Cattle raids, warfare between *tuatha* and personal violence were not infrequent. Nevertheless, for the majority of the people, it was a life of stability which in normal circumstances yielded adequate food, comfort and cultural stimulation.

This life was to be considerably disturbed by the Norse raids, although many would be completely unaffected by two centuries of intermittent warfare. The greatest social changes were brought about by the establishment of Norse and

Norman towns; hitherto only scattered proto-urban settlements had existed. In the rural community conditions did not change so much. Though the Normans introduced feudalism, it was not radically different from the social system that had pertained in earlier centuries and although its law was different from Brehon law and the introduction of primogeniture was an alien concept, the serfs of the feudal system were similar to the slaves of the *tuatha* (IV). In the Gaelic areas the cultural traditions continued and the way of life changed little, although there was more disruptive military activity than in earlier centuries. In the Norman areas a new culture had been introduced which was primarily French in origin and was to have an influence on the later literature of Ireland. Norman architecture was radically different from Irish architecture; stone churches, monasteries and castles were constructed throughout the country within a short time after the invasion.

The greatest social upheavals occurred during the fourteenth century with the bubonic plague, which in 1348 alone killed about 14,000. Outbreaks of the plague or Black Death also occurred in 1361, 1370, 1384 and 1398. Earlier in the century there had been epidemics of other diseases, a number of famines and the ruinous and destructive Bruce invasion (14). Of those who died from the plague, the Normans were the worst affected, since urban communities were the most vulnerable. It is estimated that almost half the colonists and their tenants were eliminated along with huge numbers in the towns, but while the plague brought some deaths to Gaelic Ireland the toll was not large enough to affect the fabric of society.

During the later Middle Ages there was a strong Gaelic cultural revival in which many of the Norman colonists took a close interest; the itinerant poets were popular and revered members of the community who received patronage from both Gaelic and Norman lords. Yet as far as most people were concerned, the cultural revival was of little relevance. Their lives were still virtually unchanged: their houses were still primitive, their work hard agricultural labour, their food meat, corn and dairy products, their main drink ale (with wine for the middle and upper classes, and whiskey becoming popular), their entertainments were dancing and storytelling and occasional festivals.

The wars of the sixteenth and seventeenth centuries affected the lives of the common people, since they were so widespread, but a more significant social development was the rapid rise in the population which began at the end of the seventeenth century. By the end of the eighteenth century the country was suffering from overcrowding, and the mass of the population were living in inferior conditions to those of their ancestors, and on a restricted diet. By the early nineteenth century meat and fish were rare items in their diet, and more and more families were beginning to rely on the potato for food, with milk as the only drink.

The social disasters of the nineteenth century are described in detail in this section and in section VII; it took massive depopulation as a consequence of famine and emigration to restore the living conditions of the majority of the Irish people to a sustainable level. In the territory that became the Republic of

Ireland, the destruction of families and communities, intense urban poverty and destructive internecine warfare would leave a legacy of bitterness and inertia which – combined with state subservience to a conservative church – led to social paralysis; most cultural dissidents emigrated. In the more prosperous region that became Northern Ireland, the tribal stand-off would similarly encourage inflexibility and cultural stagnation. It would take the EU to broaden the cultural horizons of the south and a bitter war to jolt the north out of its insularity.

73   URBANIZATION

Before the Vikings, around major monastic centres like Armagh, Clonmacnois and Clonfert there were semi-urbanized communities probably composed mainly of craftsmen and labourers working at the monastery. The Vikings set up some coastal towns as strongholds and later as commercial centres. Of these foundations, Dublin, which was set up in the ninth century, became within a century extremely powerful and had dependencies as far north as Strangford Lough and as far south as Waterford. Limerick was occupied by the Vikings in the ninth century but did not become a proper town until the tenth century, when for many years its inhabitants waged sporadic warfare with Dublin. From being a dependency of Dublin, Waterford became an important town in its own right in the tenth century, as did Cork.

By the time of the Norman invasion therefore, Ireland had a small number of powerful towns on the coast, but none inland. The Normans set up towns around their major castles to which either the King or the lords of a liberty would grant charters permitting the setting up of a community court, the election of a mayor and certain kinds of trading. The proliferation of towns in Leinster and Munster was a consequence of these provinces being the Normans' area of influence while Connacht and Ulster were mainly held by the Irish. Exceptions are Galway and Athenry in Connacht, founded respectively by the de Burgos and the de Berminghams, and Carrickfergus in Ulster, which was founded by John de Courcy.

The prosperity of most of the towns kept them loyal to the Dublin administration. Although they contained large numbers of native Irish, these attracted considerable hostility from the rest of the urban population and during the fourteenth century many attempts were made to limit the numbers of Irish in towns and to control their behaviour. Simultaneously, Irish communities were springing up outside the walls of the towns.

Towns outside the Pale were almost completely independent, many of them in practice controlled by a small number of powerful families who went to great lengths to keep control in their own hands: with the Tudor conquest this independence was gradually eroded. There were some Tudor foundations as a result of the plantations, but the main wave of new foundations came with the Stuarts, particularly in Ulster. Since that period foundations have been very

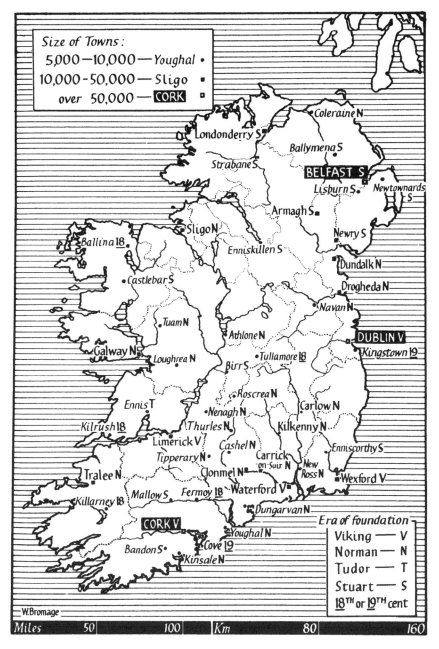

Figure 73 Irish towns, 1841.

Vikings in good inland ports
Stuart – Northern Ireland

limited. Before the Famine Ireland was primarily a rural community and only 20 per cent of the population lived in towns or villages compared with 50 per cent in England and Wales. It took the disaster of the Famine to bring the Irish people to accept and even welcome urban living.

74 TOWNS: 1841–2002

In 1841 only 20 per cent of the population of Ireland lived in towns: in the Republic in 2002 the figure had risen to 60 per cent (still well under the EU average of 75 per cent). However, as a result of the massive depopulation of the country, this shift from a rural to an urban society was accomplished without – until recently – greatly increasing the actual town populations. In 1841, 1,475,106 people lived in towns of over 500; in 1971, for the Republic, the equivalent figure was 1,648,962; and in 2002, 2,334,300 lived in towns of over 1,500. The main change has been therefore less in the size of town populations than in the concentration of the population in bigger towns. Figure 74 shows how variable the history of Irish towns has been during this period; many of the less important towns have lost many of their inhabitants to larger towns.

In 1841 there were only three towns with more than 50,000 inhabitants: Dublin (232,726), Belfast (75,308) and Cork (80,720). In 1971 there were three more within that category: Dún Laoghaire (52,990), Limerick (57,137) and Londonderry (51,617), while Dublin had grown to 566,034, Belfast to 358,991 and Cork to 128,235. The big development of the end of the twentieth century was the expansion of Dublin. Greater Dublin with just over one million, accounted for 25.6 per cent of the population, while Galway was added to the towns of more than 50,000 inhabitants. The biggest change in the past thirty years has been in the growth of medium-sized towns: in 2002 in the Republic, the number of towns of 10,000–50,000 was up to twenty-five from only thirteen in 1971.

The extent to which Ireland has moved from a rural to an urban society is somewhat deceptive. Irish society is in fact less urban in character than the rest of the British Isles, but the speed with which the rural population declined exaggerated the social consequences of the change. In 1841 5 per cent of the population of Ireland lived in cities of more than 50,000 while the equivalent figure for England was 30 per cent. By 1911 the percentage had risen to 15 per cent for the future twenty-six-county-area and 31 per cent for the six-county-area, while Wales was 27 per cent, Scotland 40 per cent and England 51 per cent. Since that date the rate of urbanization in most of the British Isles has slowed down considerably but Ireland is still catching up.

The most striking trend since the early 1990s has been the growth of the Dublin commuter belt. Among the areas showing huge population increases between 1996 and 2002 were Navan (54 per cent), Mullingar (48 per cent) and Naas (30 per cent). The populations of Kildare and Meath increased by over a fifth in the same period and increases in the populations of Westmeath, Laois,

Towns 1926

Towns with population
5,000–10,000:

Carlow, Athlone, Enniscorthy,
New Ross, Bray, Ennis, Youghal,
Killarney, Dungarvan, Ballinasloe,
Clonmel, Mullingar, Limavady,
Strabane, Downpatrick, Cookstown,
Enniskillen

Towns with population
10,000–50,000:

Kilkenny, Drogheda, Dundalk,
Wexford, Tralee, Galway, Sligo,
Limerick, Waterford, Derry,
Ballymena, Newtownards,
Carrickfergus, Coleraine, Lurgan,
Bangor, Lisburn, Newry

Towns with population
50,000–100,000:

Cork

Towns with population 100,000+:
Dublin, Belfast

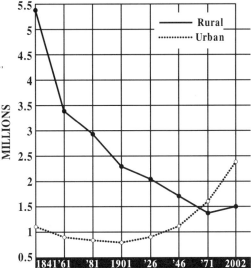

Towns 2002

Towns with population 5,000–10,000:

Arklow, Cobh, Ballina, Wicklow, Enniscorthy, Mallow, Shannon, Portmarnock,
Tramore, Midleton, Longford, Dungarvan, Thurles, Rush, Youghal, New Ross, Nenagh
Ashbourne, Cavan, Athy, Tuam, Monaghan, Trim, Kildare, Westport, Carrick-on-Suir,
Dunboyne, Gorey, Buncrana, Bandon, Ballymoney, Portrush, Portstewart, Cookstown,
Craigavon, Newcastle, Dungannon, Magherafelt, Kilkeel, Ballyclare, Holywood, Omagh

Towns with population 10,000–50,000:

Waterford, Tralee, Ennis, Clonmel, Kilkenny, Carlow, Athlone, Drogheda, Dundalk,
Bray, Letterkenny, Sligo, Navan, Naas, Wexford, Droichead Nua, Celbridge, Athlone,
Mullingar, Leixlip, Malahide, Killarney, Portlaoise, Greystones, Castlebar, Carrigaline,
Tullamore, Maynooth, Antrim, Newtownards, Newry, Armagh, Portadown, Larne,
Ballymena, Banbridge, Carrickfergus, Dundonald, Lurgan, Downpatrick, Strabane,
Enniskillen, Limavady, Dunmurry, Lisburn, Coleraine

Towns with population 50,000–100,000:
Limerick, Galway, Derry, Newtownabbey, Bangor

Towns with population 100,000+:
Dublin, Dun Laoghaire-Rathdown, Cork, Belfast

Figure 74 From a rural to an urban society: the Republic.

Louth and Carlow reflect a widening of the commuter belt. Many of these areas
are neither rural nor urban but suburban, and the housing sprawl has done little
to enhance the countryside. This has come about as a result of bad planning and
the preference of Irish people for living in detached (44 per cent) and semi-
detached (27 per cent) houses rather than in apartments (8 per cent) or terraces

(18.5 per cent). The tendency for rural houses to be bungalows is so marked that this has been termed the 'bungalization' of the Irish countryside. Between 1985 and 1996 about 30 per cent of all new houses were bungalows. Many of these bungalows in the most remote and picturesque areas do not even serve a demographic need but are holiday houses, used principally for the summer season.

The big problem facing Irish people at the beginning of the twenty-first century as a result of the overheating of the economy (72) is how to buy their houses – detached, terraced or otherwise. In the ten years between 1990 and 1999, house prices more than doubled, and then almost doubled again between 1999 and 2004 (72). In Northern Ireland, prices have gone up much less – 45 per cent between 1997 and 2002 – which is one reason why average household sizes there are small (2.58 to the Republic's 2.94).

Although Ireland will probably continue its remorseless urbanizing trend, the social problems have been severe. In other parts of the British Isles including Northern Ireland, where urbanization has been gradual and the overall population has risen steadily, urbanization has not meant rapid depopulation of the rural areas, whereas in southern Ireland the population of the towns in 130 years has risen only slightly while there has been a massive rural depopulation, with demoralizing social consequences.

75   POPULATION CHANGES: 1841–51

From 1841 to 1851 the population of Ireland dropped from 8,175,124 to 6,552,386, a fall of 20 per cent; and since by 1845 the figure was probably closer to 8,500,000, the fall was actually more than 23 per cent. This enormous reduction in population was due to death and emigration, mainly as a result of the Great Famine of 1845–8. Estimates can be made of the number of deaths, but all figures must be viewed with caution. In many areas of the country death was so common that bodies were thrown into communal graves without any records being kept.

Figure 75 shows the changes in population in all the Irish counties and shows how variable these changes were. The figures can give a misleading idea of the severity of the famine in certain areas. Although the west of Ireland was unquestionably the worst affected, there are even more severe falls in the population of some of the midlands counties. One reason for this is that the slightly better-off tended to emigrate first. Unless public assistance was forthcoming, the completely penniless could not emigrate until a relative or friend gave them the money, so the drop in population in the poorer counties generally relates to a disproportionately heavy death rate.

The censuses of 1841 and 1851 give a number of useful figures on the changes in population from province to province (see Table 8).

In the decade 1851–61, when the mass deaths had ceased, and emigration was the main reason for population decrease, the population fell by 5 per cent in Ulster; 13 per cent in Leinster; 19 per cent in Munster; and 10 per cent in Connacht.

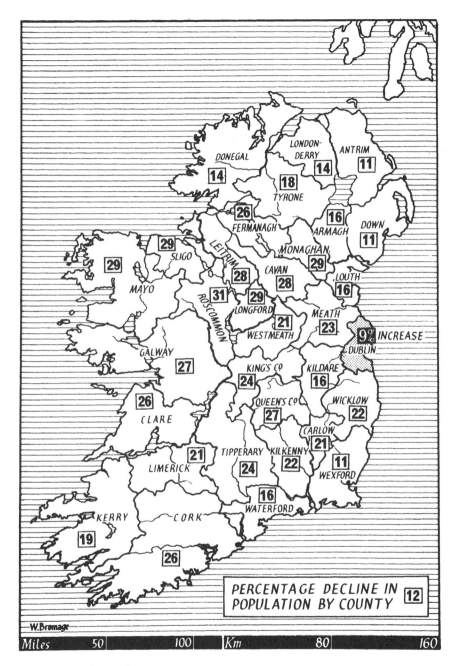

Figure 75 Population changes: 1841–51.

Table 8 Provincial population change, 1841–51

Province	1841	1851	Fall
Ulster	2,389,263	2,013,879	16%
Leinster	1,982,169	1,682,320	15%
Munster	2,404,460	1,865,600	22%
Connacht	1,420,705	1,012,479	29%

Another valuable statistic relates to deaths during this period. Recorded deaths between 1841 and 1851 totalled 1,622,738, with men making up 56 per cent of the total.

The 1851 Census provided a painstaking analysis of the death statistics while admitting that many must have gone unrecorded. Changes in the age groups between 1841 and 1851 are also significant. Children under ten were the group affected most; there were 34 per cent fewer one-year-olds in 1851 than in 1841, 38 per cent fewer one- to five-year-olds and 25 per cent fewer five- to ten-year-olds. For ten- to twenty-year-olds the decrease is only 10 per cent.

76   POPULATION CHANGES: 1841–2002

No accurate estimates can be made of the Irish population before the nineteenth century. It seems likely that by the eighth century there were about half a million inhabitants – giving a population density of about sixteen per square mile. In 1659 a helpful if rather inaccurate estimate of the population calculated that it was over half a million. Although later evidence suggests that this is an underestimate (Sir William Petty in 1672 estimated 1.1 million), it nevertheless indicates how static the Irish population had remained for almost 1,000 years due mainly to continuous wars, famines and plagues. By the end of the century after a period of comparative peace this figure seems to have shot up to nearer two million. The estimates from sources of varying reliability, such as the Hearth Money Collectors, suggest that during the first half of the eighteenth century the population grew comparatively slowly, not achieving three million until the 1770s. A second and greater population explosion began in the late eighteenth and early nineteenth centuries, when a long period of almost unbroken domestic peace (excluding the casualties of 1798), combined with what has been described as 'a gap in the famines' and a very high birth rate, brought about a massive increase in population. The population virtually doubled in the fifty years between 1791 and 1841. When it reached its highest recorded level of 8,175,124 in 1841, the population density was 254 people per square mile.

The population figures since 1841 for the areas of the present Republic and Northern Ireland are given in Table 9.

Ireland is the only country known to have had a declining population during the century from 1850. The area of the country which became Northern

Table 9 Population changes, 1841–2001/2★

Date	Republic	% increase or decrease	Northern Ireland	% increase or decrease	Ireland	% increase or decrease
1841	6,528,799		1,646,325		8,175,124	
1851	5,111,589	−22	1,440,797	−12	6,552,386	−20
1881	3,870,020	−24	1,304,816	−9	5,174,836	−21
1901	3,221,823	−17	1,236,952	−5	4,458,775	−14
1946	2,955,107	−8	1,334,168	+8	4,289,275	−4
1961	2,818,341	−5	1,427,000	+7	4,245,341	−1
1971	2,978,248	+6	1,527,593	+7	4,505,841	+6
★2001/2	3,917,203	+32	1,685,267	+10	5,602,470	+24

★ Census 2002 in the Republic: 2001 in Northern Ireland.

Ireland, being much more industrialized than the south, suffered less during and after the Famine, and its population remained relatively stable. While in 1971 the population of the Republic was only 46 per cent of that of 1841, the Northern Irish population had dropped by only 7 per cent, and in 2002 Northern Ireland's population was very close to that of 1841. In the Republic, from the 1960s onwards, the depopulating trend began to reverse.

During the twentieth century a major social problem was the depopulation of the west of Ireland. The effects of the famine varied considerably in different provinces, but the west of Ireland, and Connacht in particular, suffered more than any other part of the country. By 1926 the population of Leinster had dropped to 58 per cent of the 1841 figure; by 1979 it had risen to 88 per cent; by 2002 it had actually exceeded the 1841 population (by 100,000 people) and was the only province to do this. The 1926 population of the whole of Ulster was 65 per cent of that of 1841; the 1971 figure was up to 73 per cent; the 2002 figure was 80.9 per cent. The 1926 population of Munster was 40 per cent that of 1841; the 1979 population was still only 41 per cent and the 2002 population 46 per cent. The 1926 population of Connacht was 39 per cent of that of 1841; the 1979 figure was still lower at 29 per cent. In the last decade of the twentieth century Connacht experienced a small population growth but it is too soon to tell if this has reversed the trend. Its 2002 figure was 33 per cent that of its 1841 figure, but most of the increase from 1979 was in Galway; other counties remain sparsely populated (see Figure 76b).

The population increase of the late twentieth century therefore affected Leinster disproportionately. The tourist boom has of course brought increased prosperity to the west, but a feature of picturesque counties such as Kerry and Clare is holiday homes which are only occupied several weeks of the year. However, one success story in the west is Galway, where the population continues to grow – between 1996 and 2002 it increased by a massive 10 per cent. This is because Galway city has been successful in establishing itself as the third major city in the Republic of Ireland, after Cork and Dublin. It has a large

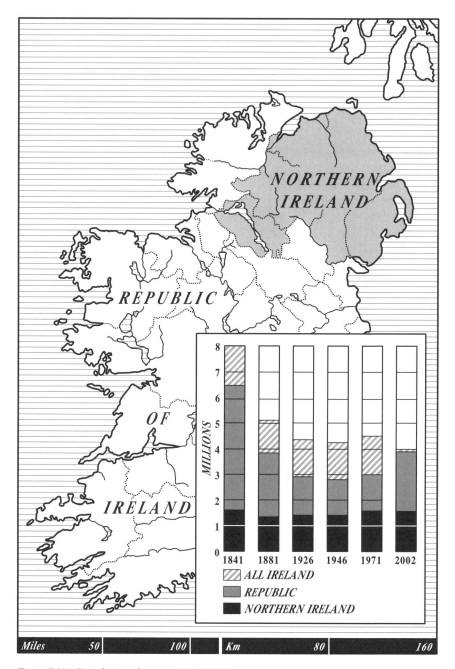

Figure 76(a) Population changes: 1841–2002.

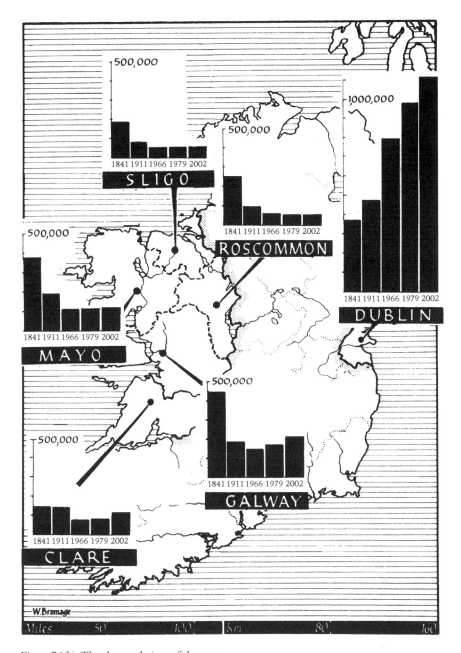

Figure 76(b) The depopulation of the west.

university, a thriving arts scene, and during the Celtic Tiger years, was able to attract its share of foreign direct investment.

77   EMIGRATION: 1881–2002

Migration statistics are notoriously unreliable for Ireland before 1871, although some estimates can be made of the numbers of those who left the country before this time. In the main post-Famine emigration period, 1845–55, almost two million left the country for North America and Australia and probably about 750,000 left for Britain. After 1855 the flood of emigrants began to wane somewhat, but it has nevertheless remained a way of life until the present day.

Throughout the second half of the nineteenth century the annual rate of emigration remained very high. Between 1871 and 1891 about 1.4 million emigrated – an annual rate of about 70,000, of whom about 20 per cent were from the territory that became Northern Ireland. To the shame of the new state, independence did nothing to change emigration patterns; indeed, despite pious protestations, it was a relief that unemployment levels were thus kept within reasonable bounds. Only the high birth rate kept the population stable between 1926 and 1951. The high emigration during the 1950s (when 14 per cent of the population left) was responsible for the historically low population level of 2.8 million recorded in 1961. The population began to rise again during the economic boom of the 1960s, and this continued into the 1970s; between 1971 and 1979, immigration exceeded emigration (by 14,000) for the first time since 1841. However, emigration resumed in the 1980s, only to drop in the 'Celtic Tiger' years, when many 1980s emigrants returned. In 1997, there were 29,000 emigrants as against 44,000 immigrants.

Irish emigration goes in peaks and troughs. Despite the recent levelling off, the Irish remain more mobile than most other Europeans, with strong communities worldwide (there are few cities without Irish pubs) and a tradition of emigrating during recessions.

Northern Irish emigration has been steadier than the Republic's, as is evident from the stability of its population, but has also been subject to fluctuation. In the 1950s, it lost over 90,000 people, about 6 per cent of its population, and during the 1970s the figure rose to 111,000, undoubtedly as a result of the Troubles. A worrying trend for the majority population has been the increasing tendency of young Protestants to go to university in Britain and stay there subsequently.

78   EDUCATION: 1800–2004

The appalling illiteracy figures of the pre-Famine period can be somewhat misleading, for it must be remembered that many of those who could not read or write retained some of the oral culture of previous generations. Nevertheless

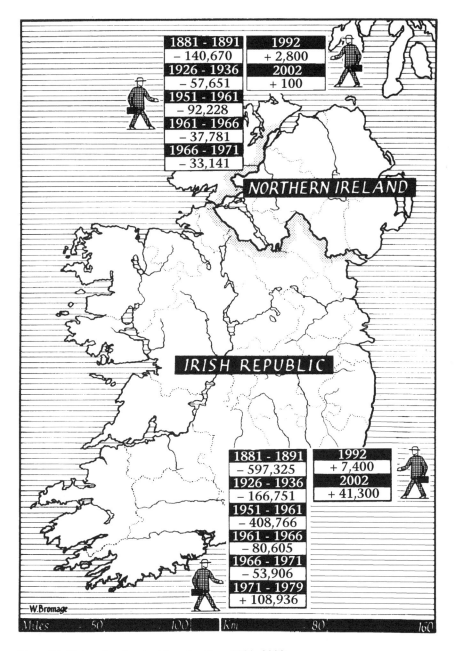

Figure 77 Net emigration/net immigration: 1881–2002.

Highest literacy in N. Ireland tied to religious orientation

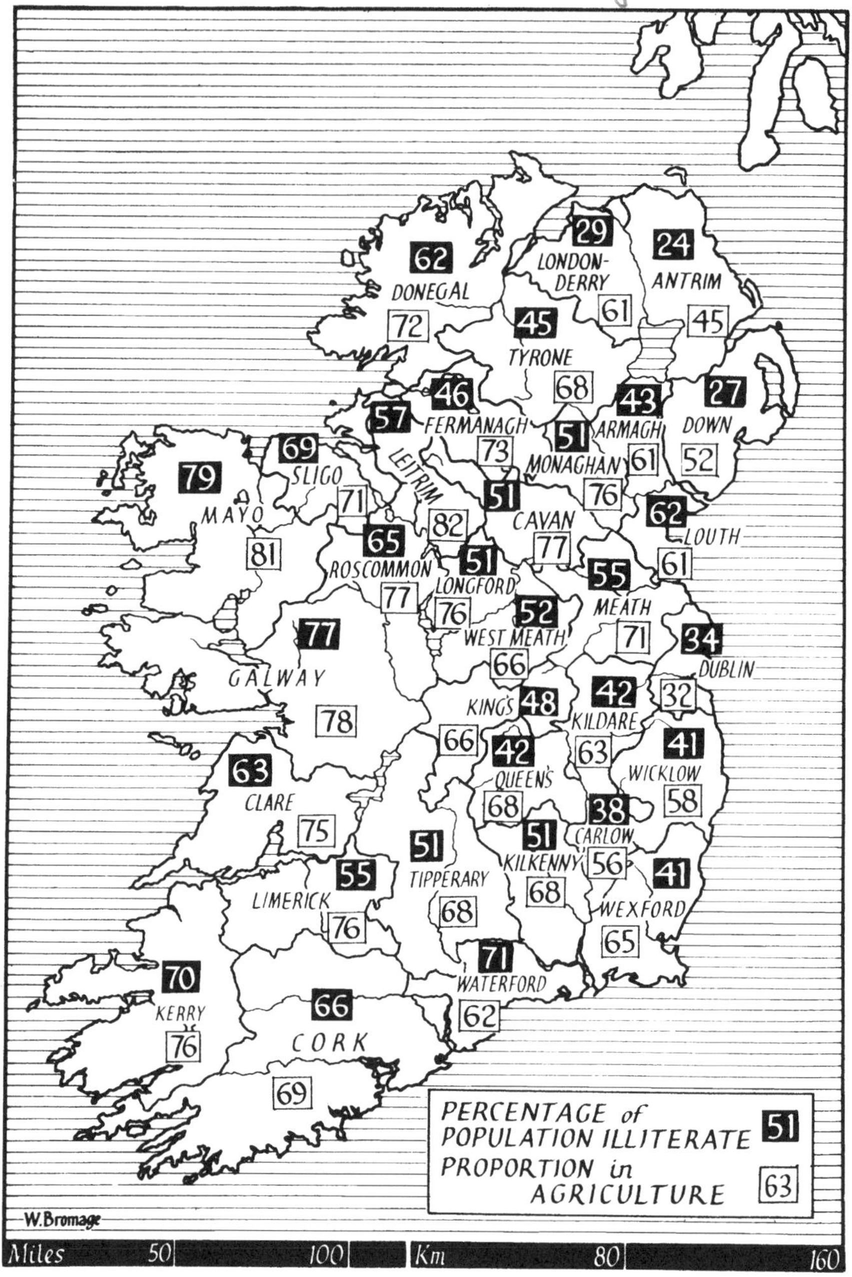

Figure 78 Illiteracy, 1841.

the relevant statistics for 1841, as shown in Figure 78, indicate how backward was Irish education at this point.

At the beginning of the nineteenth century, for the mass of the population the only schooling available was obtained from 'hedge' schools – literally schools held in the open. With the founding of the Irish Christian Brothers, schools for boys were introduced to the main towns. The Presentation Sisters and Ursuline Sisters opened girls' schools, also in urban areas and also catering exclusively for the Catholic population. There were a number of endowed schools for the Church of Ireland, and an educational body called the Kildare Place Society which offered non-sectarian education but was unacceptable to the Catholic church. This was typical of the kind of problem that arose in an era when education was the preserve of the churches. In Ireland – as in England and Scotland – there were inter-denominational jealousies and deep mutual suspicions that militated against any kind of constructive cooperation; opposition to government attempts to introduce non-denominational and coordinated education was more intense and long-lasting in Ireland than elsewhere: the Catholic clergy considered an illiterate flock preferable to one subjected to the dangers of non-Catholic education. This conflict was to continue throughout the nineteenth and twentieth centuries in inter-denominational squabbles about education and was to frustrate the British government in many of their attempts to provide an education for the mass of the population. (At the beginning of the twenty-first century, Protestants and Catholics are rarely educated together in either part of the island.)

In 1831 the Whig government set up a national primary education system which vastly increased the scope of education throughout the country. From only 789 schools in 1831, there were 3,501 national schools twenty years later, and during that period pupils increased by about 400,000 to over half a million. At the time of the Famine, however, the disparity of educational opportunities between different provinces was very marked, with Ulster having about 40 per cent of the schools and Connacht only 10 per cent. The initial concentration of schools in urban areas meant that illiteracy was particularly high in rural areas and tended to be closely related to occupation; Figure 78 shows the close correlation between illiteracy and the dependence on agriculture.

There was also a close correlation between illiteracy and religion, as might be expected since the mass of the population were Catholics. The relevant proportions of illiterates according to religion in 1861 are shown in Table 10.

Table 10 Illiteracy by province, 1861

Province	Roman Catholic	Protestant
Ulster	44.4%	15.2%
Leinster	39.9%	8.2%
Munster	48.4%	9.9%
Connacht	59.4%	13.9%
Total	45.8%	13.7%

The problem of illiteracy had been virtually beaten in Ireland by the end of the nineteenth century. The illiteracy figures for the whole country are as follows: 53 per cent in 1841; 47 per cent in 1851; 39 per cent in 1861; 33 per cent in 1871; 25 per cent in 1881; 18 per cent in 1891; 14 per cent in 1901; 12 per cent in 1911.

In 1878 with the introduction of the Intermediate Education Act the problem of secondary education was tackled, since grants were made available both for private and state schools. In 1923 the Intermediate Board virtually went out of existence.

University education had been very limited, since the only university in Ireland was Trinity College Dublin, established in 1592. Its initial welcome to Catholics evaporated after the 1641 rebellion and in the eighteenth century religious tests precluded Catholics and Dissenters from taking college positions or degrees, although some took undergraduate courses. After these tests were abolished in 1794, many Catholics were educated at Trinity until in the mid-nineteenth century, on sectarian grounds, their own bishops banned them from attending; restrictions were not fully lifted until 1970.

In 1793, a Catholic seminary, St Patrick's, was established in Carlow, and another St Patrick's in 1795 in Maynooth. In 1845 the Queen's Colleges (Ireland) Act controversially provided non-denominational colleges at Belfast, Cork and Galway and in 1854 the Catholic University was founded in Dublin with the future Cardinal Newman as rector. Reorganized in 1882 as University College, it was controlled by the Jesuits from 1883. An examining body, the Royal University, set up in 1879, was empowered to confer degrees. In 1908 it was replaced by the National University of Ireland (NUI), comprising the three constituent university colleges of Dublin, Cork and Galway; and Queen's College, Belfast, was made an independent university. From 1910 Maynooth became a 'recognized college', in 1966 it opened its courses to the laity and in 1997 it became a fourth constituent college of the NUI. All negotiations on university education were marred by long-drawn-out disagreements, mainly involving the clergy of the Catholic church.

In Northern Ireland, the plans of the first Minister for Education to provide all children with non-denominational education were demolished by Catholic and Protestant clergy alike and the government ended up financing state schools with a Protestant/unionist ethos and Catholic-managed schools with a nationalist outlook. (Although there are now some integrated schools, the vast majority of children are still religiously segregated at school.) Still, the province benefited from Westminster reforms which brought free secondary education, and increased funding for universities and mandatory grants. In 1968 the New University of Ulster was established in Coleraine; in 1984 it merged with the Ulster Polytechnic and the Ulster College of Art to form the multi-campus University of Ulster. The number of full-time undergraduates rose between 1996 and 2001 from 35,000 to 40,000.

In the south there were few post-independence educational changes until, during the 1960s, the government accepted that education was its responsibility rather than that of the church, and in 1967 it abolished fees in most secondary schools. Participation in third-level education increased hugely (in 1948–9 there were 6,796 full-time students; in 1990–91 38,336). National Institutes of Higher Education were created in Limerick in 1970 and Dublin in 1976; both became universities in 1989. As a result of a combination of university grants (third-level undergraduate education was actually free from the mid-1990s but fees were introduced again later) and the creation of more university places the take-up accelerated. The number of full-time undergraduates rose between 1997 and 2002 from 90,000 to 112,000.

79 IRISH-SPEAKERS: 1851–2004

The Irish literary tradition was almost exclusively oral in character, although important elements were written down in the Irish language during the period when Latin dominated as the medium of education and culture. Latin was the normal language of the Irish church for centuries, Norman French was spoken for a time, especially among the administrators, but English was the language of the professional classes by the late sixteenth century. A medieval Irish literary tradition existed alongside all of them. The displacement of Latin by English was accelerated by the Reformation. Anyone with any educational, professional or commercial aspirations was required to learn English, with the result that at the time of the union English was spoken by the middle and upper classes while Irish was spoken by the mass of the rural population outside Ulster. Therefore, with the collapse of the traditional Gaelic culture and the disappearance of the Gaelic professional learned class, Irish ceased to be a language of culture and gradually became the language of the poor and the uneducated.

The decline of Irish continued throughout the nineteenth century. In 1851 25 per cent of the population could speak Irish; by 1911 only 12 per cent. Inspired by the work of German and French scholars of the Gaelic language, the Gaelic League, founded in 1893, made valiant attempts to revive the language and the culture. Its success was mainly academic and political.

In 1925 the Gaeltacht Commission was set up to consider those areas – the poorest in the country – where Irish was still the main language. The Commission distinguished between two types of Gaeltacht: in the Fíor-Ghaeltacht, at least 80 per cent of the population spoke Irish; in the Breac-Ghaeltacht, between 25 per cent and 80 per cent. Of those areas designated as Gaeltacht areas, despite government aid, the numbers of Irish speakers continued to decline (see Table 11).

Table 11 Irish-speakers, 1936–61

	1936	1946	1961
Fíor-Ghaeltacht	83.1%	76.3%	71.9%
Breac-Ghaeltacht	41.5%	33.8%	35.3%

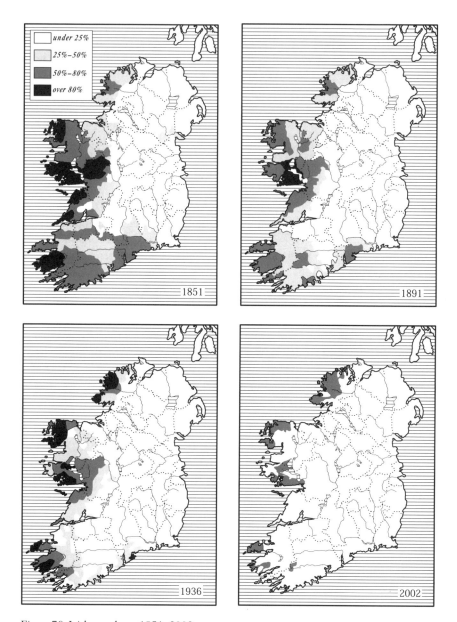

Figure 79 Irish-speakers: 1851–2002.

In 1956 the Gaeltacht Areas Order redefined the Gaeltacht to cover areas in which most of the population spoke Irish; these areas were roughly equivalent in area to the Fíor-Ghaeltacht. The population of this new Gaeltacht in 1956 was 85,700, in 1961 79,323, and in 1971 70,568. In recent years numbers in the

Gaeltacht have held steady as a proportion of the population (now around 86,000), but there is serious doubt over the veracity of many of those claiming grants as Irish speakers. The Gaeltacht is facing inevitable decline: the young do not wish to be restricted by their language to an extremely limited range of jobs or locations.

The Irish constitution specified that Irish was the first official language, with English also an official language, but in practice although obeisance is paid to Irish – the sentence or two in Irish at the beginning of politicians' speeches are recognized as sanctimonious hypocrisy and known as the *cúpla focal* ('couple of words') – English is the working language of the state; for that reason, the Irish government did not until recently request that the EU incur the expense of making Irish an official working language. However, in 2003, the Official Languages Act was introduced which provided an extensive and expensive statutory framework for the delivery of services through Irish.

Knowledge and use of Irish in the population as a whole is difficult to quantify. It is a compulsory subject at school and for entrance to university, so most (41 per cent in 1996 claimed to be able to speak it) have a passing knowledge of it, but may never use it. Since 1973 a knowledge of Irish is no longer required for entry into the public service, although there is considerable resentment that it remains a necessary qualification for teaching.

There has, however, recently been something of a mini-renaissance in the image of Irish. The imaginatively run TV channel, TG4, brought in young audiences, and also created jobs, finally giving Irish an economic *raison d'être*; more Irish-language schools opened; and the general self-confidence of the Tiger years helped make the language seem vibrant rather than a dull school-room necessity. In Northern Ireland, where once Irish was of interest mainly to antiquarians from both communities, Sinn Féin put it high on the political agenda – thus making it popular in some republican circles and gaining it large state subsidies, while alienating Protestants, who now see it as the exclusive property of Catholic nationalists, and lovers of the language, who feel it has been hijacked.

80   THE STATUS OF WOMEN: 1841–2004

Before the Great Famine in the 1840s, more than half the non-agricultural labour force was female; women were also valued workers on farms. The collapse in domestic industry that followed the Famine, coupled with the shift from tillage to livestock that reduced the need for farm labour, produced a disastrous reduction in job opportunities for women. Except in Ulster, where factory work was available, most women were left with the options of domestic service, marriage, the convent, emigration or dependence on relatives.

The agricultural bias of the economy kept an enormous number of young men on farms awaiting their inheritance and deferring marriage; poor youths would usually marry only a woman with a dowry; and an authoritarian church

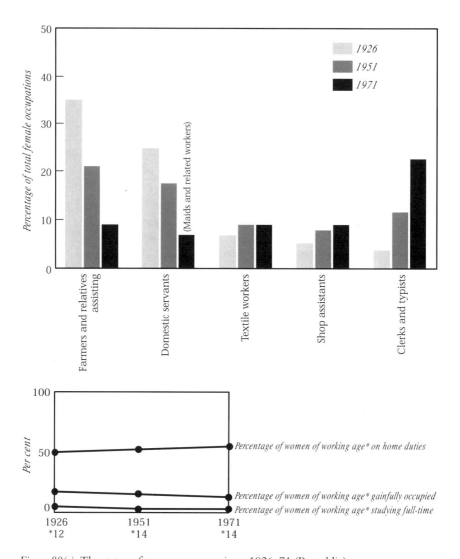

Figure 80(a) The status of women: occupations: 1926–71 (Republic).

Note: Women's occupations had changed so much between 1971 and 2003 that it was not possible to compare information contained in Figure 80a with that shown in Figure 80b. These two figures indicate just how much the status of women has changed.

and a puritanical and materialistic society kept the sexes apart. By 1926, the year of the first census of the Irish Free State, only about 75 per cent of women in their forties were married; half of these had husbands about ten years their senior. Figure 80a shows the pattern of female employment in the Republic between 1926 and 1971, a period that saw the vast majority of working women restricted to a small number of badly paid occupations with no career prospects.

Important advances were made in the 1970s, mainly because of pressure from without and below. Rather late and rather feebly, the Republic had to come to terms with the women's movement of the 1960s and 1970s. The marriage bar for women in public-service jobs was lifted and, through a series of EU regulations, women were granted equal opportunities with men. Between 1971 and 1991 the number of women in the workforce grew by 100,000; in the next six years the number of women at work grew by over 120,000 to reach 512,800 by 1997, just under half of the workforce.

The profile of women's jobs also changed. From being mainly shop assistants, domestic servants, clerical workers, textile workers and labourers on family farms until 1970, they made significant inroads over the next thirty years into such professions as law, medicine, administration and the media, and there are high-profile female entrepreneurs and executives (Figure 80b). However, in 2004 women are still concentrated in lower-paid and part-time jobs and are not represented in management positions in proportion to their numbers in the workforce. In 1998 only 16.8 per cent of judges were female and at the highest levels of the civil service women occupied just over 10 per cent of posts.

Although revolutionary leaders like Pearse and Connolly had supported the movement for female suffrage, and in consequence women in Ireland had voting equality with men before their counterparts in most European countries, they had until recently little voice in public affairs. Most women who achieved prominence did so because of their family connections. With a few exceptions, until the 1980s female members of the Dáil got there only because of an act of piety by the electorate towards dead relatives and were usually distinguished by silence and conservatism. Nor were they present in other than derisory numbers in the Senate or local government.

However, latterly female participation in the Dáil has risen steadily, if slowly, with women being selected and elected on their own merits. For the twenty-four years after the foundation of the state in 1922, the average Dáil contained just four women – or 3 per cent of all TDs. In 1977 this had gone up to 4 per cent; in 2002 twenty-one women (13 per cent) were elected to the Dáil. This still placed Ireland among the lowest in terms of gender balance in parliament in the EU member states, and the party structures are still male-dominated. However, with the two most recent presidents women, as well as the Tánaiste (deputy prime minister), strong role models are rapidly changing perceptions and there are innumerable confident and successful young Irishwomen at home and abroad.

In Northern Ireland the women's movement attracted far less attention, first because of the Troubles and second because women in the province had historically faced much less discrimination than had women in the Republic. However, change is evident in the growing number of women coming to the fore in politics. In the 2003 assembly elections, seventeen of the 108 elected were women.

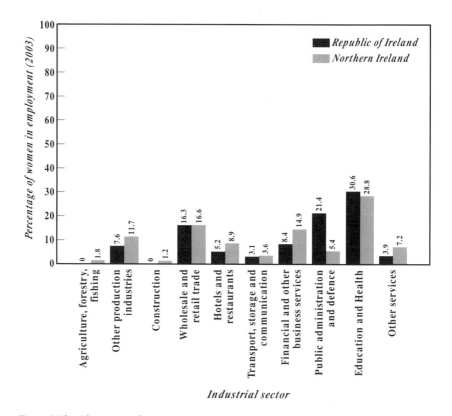

Figure 80(b) The status of women: occupations: 2003.

Sources Adapted from Republic of Ireland Central Statistics Office and Northern Ireland Department of Enterprise, Trade and Investment.

81   SECULARIZATION OF IRISH SOCIETY: 1960–2000

Until the late 1960s the Republic of Ireland largely accorded to de Valera's idealized image of an overwhelmingly Catholic society with large families and simple tastes. The marriage rate was low compared to the rest of Europe, but the unmarried were celibate rather than cohabiting. Every adult could be filed under single, married or widowed.

Liberalization from the 1960s onwards, the steady erosion of the authority of the church and rising prosperity have radically changed the way people live. In the 1970s contraception was legalized (if to a limited extent); in the 1990s came divorce, the legalization of homosexuality and the constitutional right to information about, and freedom of travel to procure, abortion.

Ireland is now more like the rest of the EU: smaller families, more cohabiting couples, more divorced and separated people and more single-parent families –

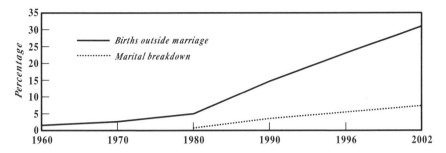

Figure 81 Marital breakdown[1] and births outside marriage[2] in the Republic: 1960–2002.

Notes:

1 Marital breakdown is the number of separated and divorced persons as a percentage of the total number of ever-married persons.

2 Births outside marriage are a percentage of total births.

16 per cent of all families in 1996. The number of families with four or more children almost halved between 1981 and 2002; between 1980 and 1998, the percentage of births outside marriage increased from 5 per cent to 28 per cent; and in just six years, between 1996 and 2002, the number of cohabiting couples rose by 35 per cent.

In the same six-year period, rates of divorce and separation increased by over half (see Figure 81). The number of divorced people trebled, from 9,800 in 1996 to 35,100 in 2002 (2.4 per cent of all marriages) – reflecting the legalization of divorce following the 1995 referendum. There are, however, significant regional differences. In 2002 Limerick City, at 15.4 per cent, had the highest rate of marital breakdown (through separation, desertion or divorce), followed by Dublin City (13.95 per cent). Cavan (5.95 per cent) and Galway county (6.14 per cent) had the lowest.

In Northern Ireland, where on the whole despite the population's conservatism social legislation has been dictated by Westminster, social change has been far more gradual than in the south or, indeed, the rest of the United Kingdom. At 48.5 per cent, for instance, the number of those married exceeds the Republic (47.1 per cent), England (43.5 per cent), Scotland (44.3 per cent) and Wales (44.5 per cent).

82   IMMIGRATION: 1921–2004

Since independence, Ireland has had a more monotone ethnic profile than its European neighbours: white, Catholic and largely ethnically Irish in the south; white, Protestant and Catholic and largely ethnically Irish or Ulster-Scots in the north. As Ireland never had an empire and had a slow economy with high unemployment, unlike many EU countries it did not have a post-Second-World-War influx of immigrants. Certainly immigration was a feature of Irish life – in 1946, 2.2 per cent of the population were foreign-born, but the majority of these were British-born and easily assimilated. Immigrants from America, Canada and Australia also entered Ireland on a regular basis – about 30,000 between 1924 and 1950 – but these were frequently of Irish origin (since 1956, citizenship is available to anyone with an Irish-born grandparent) and, again, were easily assimilated.

Until very recently, Ireland's attitude to refugees has been mean-spirited. The first refugee crisis the new state had to face was asylum applications from European Jews fleeing Nazism. Application numbers are not known, but certainly amounted to hundreds, if not thousands. From 1939 to 1945, approximately 140 were admitted on a temporary basis, with the Irish Refugee Coordinating Committee stipulating that these refugees should be Christians with Jewish blood or 'non-Aryan Christians' as opposed to professing Jews – a distinction not made by other European countries granting asylum.

After Ireland became a signatory to the 1951 UN Convention relating to the status of refugees, it was compelled to offer asylum in specific cases. The Hungarian rising of 1956 aroused great sympathy, especially among the anti-Communist clergy, and 530 Hungarians were warmly welcomed to the country. Thereafter Ireland generally had to be pressured by the UN High Commission for Refugees or NGOs: in 1972, 1979 and 1985 respectively, 120 Chileans, 220 Vietnamese and twenty-five Baha'is were granted refugee status; only the Vietnamese were allowed to bring their families.

In the early 1970s, as many European states began to close their doors to immigrants, the Irish Department of Justice issued the Aliens Order (1975) which effectively harmonized Irish visa requirements for Third World countries with those of other EU member states. It was a precaution, but the number of asylum applications remained negligible. In 1987, the first year in which figures were recorded, there were only fifty applications, but from the late 1990s these escalated. Between 1995 and 1996 numbers more than doubled, from 424 to 1,179 and Ireland now had a problem; the 1996 Refugee Act provided for a refugee appeal board. By 1999 about 90 per cent of asylum applications were being refused, and the 1999 Immigration Act put firm restrictions in place. Despite their history of emigration, Irish people were not noticeably welcoming to immigrants – a 1999 poll indicated that 69 per cent of people wanted the 'absolute minimum' allowed in, and immigrants complained of widespread racism. As a consequence of the Belfast (Good Friday) Agreement (86) a constitutional amendment was passed which conferred citizenship on anyone born on the island of Ireland, but in a referendum in 2004, by 79.2 per cent to 20.8 per cent, this automatic entitlement was removed.

To the figures for asylum seekers (of whom in 2004 37 per cent were Nigerian, 6 per cent Romanian, 4 per cent Somalian and 3 per cent each Chinese and Sudanese) should be added the numbers seeking naturalization and, of course, the illegal immigrants, difficult to quantify. In 1998 an estimated 21 per cent of immigrants were non-EU and non-UK, though at least half of these were Australians, New Zealanders and Canadians. In the 2002 census, a nationality

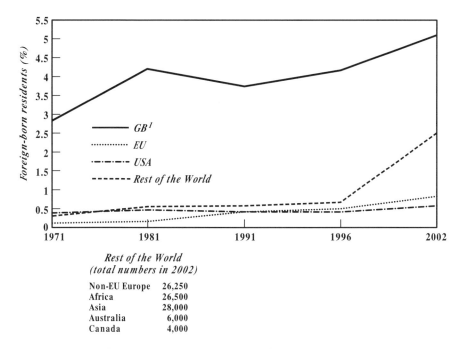

Figure 82 Foreign-born residents in the Republic of Ireland: 1971–2002 (as a percentage of total population).

Note:
1 Figures for Great Britain (GB) are excluding Northern Ireland.

question was included for the first time, allowing a more accurate demographic profile to emerge: 92.9 per cent of the population had Irish nationality. The remainder were mostly UK (2.7 per cent) and other EU (0.8 per cent), but the figures for Africans (0.5 per cent), Asians (0.6 per cent) and non-EU Europe (0.6 per cent) were quite sizeable, while American residents were relatively modest at 0.3 per cent. A further 1.3 per cent refused to state their nationality.

Although absolute numbers remain small, Ireland is approaching fellow EU member states in having a more multicultural society.

In 2002 Northern Ireland had a more homogenous ethnic profile – 99.15 per cent claimed to be white. The largest non-white ethnic group was Chinese at 0.25 per cent. Proportions of other groups were negligible – Indian (0.09 per cent), Pakistani (0.04 per cent), sub-Saharan African (0.03 per cent). This left Northern Ireland significantly less multicultural than the rest of the United Kingdom. Some immigrants have become involved in paramilitaries, with Italian names prominent in the IRA and Egyptian in the UDA. Although political frontmen for paramilitaries have condemned racist behaviour, in 2004 there was an upsurge in racist attacks by loyalists (and some republicans) commonly involved in sectarian violence.

83   SPORT

The island of Ireland has a long and varied tradition of involvement in organized sport, from athletics and team sports to swimming and sailing. When it hosted the Special Olympics (for people with learning disabilities) in 2003, 80,000 people attended the opening and closing ceremonies.

Ireland has provided many world-class competitors. From the Republic, athletes include Ronnie Delaney, Eamon Coughlan, John Treacy, Sonia O'Sullivan, Catherine McKiernan and Gillian O'Sullivan. Boxers from Northern Ireland have included Rinty Monaghan, Barry McGuigan and Wayne McCullough, and from the south Mike McTigue, Steve Collins and Michael Carruth. The cyclists Sean Kelly and Stephen Roche (who in 1987 won the Tour de France, the Giro d'Italia and the World Road Championship) are both from the Republic, as are the three Irish rowers who in 2001 – in the country's best-ever result – won three world championships; and the snooker players Alex Higgins and Dennis Taylor, both world champions, like the Grand Prix motor-racing star, Eddie Irvine, are from Northern Ireland. The Republic's Michelle Smith de Bruin won three Olympic gold medals (and one bronze) in swimming in 1996, but was later discredited in a drug-testing controversy.

Ireland has a long history of success in showjumping, which is organized on a cross-border basis; since 1929 it has won more than seventy Nations Cups and many individual prizes, the best result ever being Northern Ireland's Dermot Lennon's victory in 2001 in the World Showjumping Championships. Cian O'Connor was stripped of his 2004 Olympic gold medal after his horse tested positive for drugs, but the International Equestrian Federation proclaimed him innocent of deliberate wrong-doing.

Horses

Hunting with hounds can be traced back almost two millennia and is still enormously popular: more than 70,000 people are estimated to participate actively in the sport, which is an important focus for social life in rural Ireland. From hunting emerged the passion for horse-racing, which has been hugely popular in Ireland since the eighteenth century and has formed the basis for a multi-million-euro horse-breeding business encouraged by generous tax incentives.

More than 300 race meetings are held annually on the flat and over jumps at twenty-seven different courses, the most famous of which are The Curragh, Fairyhouse and Leopardstown. Irish horses, jockeys and trainers also compete with enormous success around the world.

On the flat, breeder John Magnier and trainer Vincent O'Brien and, later, Aidan O'Brien have seen Coolmore in County Tipperary take on and beat the might and wealth of the sheiks of the Middle East, while top-class jockeys such as Pat Taaffe (who won three successive Cheltenham Gold cups riding the legendary Arkle in the 1960s), Pat Eddery and Kieran Fallon became familiar winners at Cheltenham, Aintree and elsewhere on the international circuit.

Golf

The Royal Belfast, the first Irish golf club, was established in 1881. Ten years later, when the Golfing Union of Ireland was founded, there were ten clubs and courses, which by 1950 had increased to 179 and by the twenty-first century to over 350. Irish professional golfers such as Christy O'Connor helped to popularize the game in Ireland, open it up as a career for the ambitious (like Padraig Harrington and, from Northern Ireland, Darren Clarke) and advertise it as a tourist attraction. Predominantly a game for the well-off, golf is a money-spinner for Ireland, attracting millions of golf tourists to such world-famous courses as Ballybunion, Portmarnock and Royal Portrush; in 2006, the K Club in County Kildare will host the Ryder Cup.

Gaelic games

Team sports are numerous and, with the exception of soccer, are all organized cross-border: basketball, bowls, cricket, hockey, rugby, soccer and even, of late, ice hockey, but the biggest, by far, are Gaelic games. Mainly football and hurling, these games are indigenous and are played only in Ireland and in Irish communities abroad, almost exclusively by Catholics. Their history has been traced back in some way to the Middle Ages but their modern period dates from 1884, when Michael Cusack founded the Gaelic Athletic Association for the Preservation and Cultivation of National Pastimes (later shortened to the Gaelic Athletic Association – GAA); it was later taken over by Fenians (32), who alienated the clergy and lost many members. From 1901, the IRB took control and reinstated rules excluding from membership those playing or watching 'imported games', as well as policemen and soldiers. The first ban was lifted in 1971; the second had come to relate to the British security forces only and remained in place until 2001. Unsurprisingly, unionists perceive the GAA to be viscerally tribal and both nationalist and sectarian.

In 1925 the organization of athletics was hived off to a separate organization and the GAA concentrated solely on football, hurling, camogie (for women) and handball.

Gaelic football is often described as a cross between soccer and rugby, though it is much older than either: the game is played with a round ball, and each team has fifteen players; one point is scored if the ball is either kicked or punched over rugby-style crossbars, and three if the ball is kicked into the net, below the crossbar. Hurling is played on the same style of pitch with the same number of players and scoring system and is similar to, but wilder than, hockey; players carry a stick and the ball is about the same size and texture as a cricket ball. Camogie, its sister sport, has been widely played since the GAA at the beginning of the twentieth century decided to invent a game for women.

The GAA, which is in its essence rural (Dublin has won disproportionately few championships), has more than 2,500 affiliated clubs (minor and senior) in

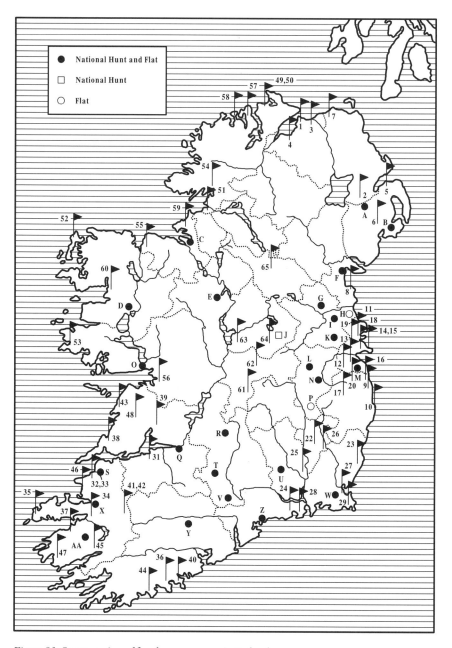

Figure 83 Sport: main golf and race courses in Ireland.

Source Adapted from http://www.europegolf.com/courses/ireland and http://www.hri.ie

Golf courses

1 Castlerock	32 Ballybunion (Cashen)	
2 Malone	33 Ballybunion (Old)	
3 Portstewart	34 Beaufort	
4 Roe Park	35 Caenn Sibeal (Dingle)	
5 Royal Belfast	36 Cork (Little Island)	
6 Royal County Down	37 Dooks	
7 Royal Portrush	38 Doonbeg	
(Dunluce)	39 Dromoland	
8 Baltray (Co. Louth)	40 Fota Island	
9 Carlton House (Mark	41 Killarney (Killeen)	
O'Meara Course)	42 Killarney (Mahony's	
10 Druids Glen	Point)	
11 European Club	43 Lahinch	
12 Island	44 Old Head of Kinsale	
13 K Club	45 Ring of Kerry	
14 Luttrellstown	46 Tralee	
15 Portmarnock	47 Waterville	
16 Portmarnock Hotel &	48 Woodstock	
Golf Links	49 Ballyliffin (Glashedy)	
17 Powerscourt	50 Ballyliffin (Old)	
18 Rathsallagh	51 Bundoran	
19 Royal Dublin	52 Carne (Belmullet)	
20 St. Margaret's	53 Connemara	
21 Tulfarris	54 Donegal (Murvagh)	
22 Carlow	55 Enniscrone	
23 Courtown	56 Galway Bay	
24 Faithlegg	57 Portsalon	
25 Mount Juliet	58 Rosapenna	
26 Mount Wolseley	59 Rosses Point (Co. Sligo)	
27 Rosslare	60 Westport Golf Club	
28 St. Helens Bay	61 Birr	
29 Waterford Castle	62 Esker Hills	
30 Seafield Golf & Country	63 Glasson	
	64 Mullingar	

Racecourses

A	Down Royal
B	Downpatrick
C	Sligo
D	Ballinrobe
E	Roscommon
F	Dundalk
G	Havan
H	Laytown
I	Bellewstown
J	Kilbeggan
K	Fairyhouse
L	Naas
M	Leopardstown
N	Punchestown
O	Galway
P	Curragh
Q	Limerick
R	Thurles
S	Listowel
T	Tipperary
U	Gowran Park
V	Clonmel
W	Wexford
X	Tralee
Y	Cork
Z	Tramore
AA	Killarney

Figure 83 – continued

Ireland alone and has been a cohesive force in local communities. The club is usually composed of players from a small geographical area, traditionally the 'parish', though the games are played at schools and universities also. Most of the clubs are affiliated to the local county, which picks its team from club members. The counties compete in both football and hurling for, respectively, the Sam Maguire and Liam McCarthy cups, with the finals played in September at the GAA's landmark stadium, Croke Park, in Dublin.

Kerry, Cork, Dublin and Meath have historically been strong in football, but recently teams such as Down, Armagh and Tyrone have shifted the balance of power to Northern Ireland. Hurling, however, is still the preserve of a few counties, particularly Cork, Kilkenny and Tipperary, with the occasional challenge by Clare, Galway and Offaly; it is also played passionately in the Glens of Antrim and the Ards Peninsula in County Down.

Cricket

The quintessential gentleman's game of cricket pre-dates rugby and was imported from England by settlers and the army and boys back from English schools; the oldest club is Phoenix, which was formed in 1830. Cricket was widely played in many parts of rural Ireland on a casual, mainly social, basis in the mid-nineteenth century, but the Land War, the rise of the GAA, the First World War, the disappearance of British troops and republican hostility killed it off in many areas.

One exception was west Tyrone and Derry, which saw the formation of numerous clubs in the 1870s and 1880s: many of these clubs – Sion Mills, Limavady, Ardmore and Strabane – are still flourishing today. Cricket benefited from the spread of the linen industry in Ulster as the mill owners encouraged the game among workers and often provided grounds near the factories in such places as Waringstown, Doncloney and also Sion Mills.

These days the majority of the country's 140 or so clubs are based in Northern Ireland, around Belfast and the north-west; Leinster has forty and Munster (which for administrative purposes stretches from Waterford to Galway) twenty-one. Though cricket in Ireland predates rugby and ranks about fourth in Europe, it still has to attain any international standing. In the Republic, however, Commonwealth immigrants are boosting the sport. The Irish Civil Service Cricket Club, founded in 1863, was failing when it was discovered by Indian immigrants. Now under an Indian captain and up from one to four teams, its players also include Australians, New Zealanders, South Africans, Sri Lankans and Pakistanis.

The Irish Cricket Union, the governing body, has set its sights on emulating fellow minnows Kenya and Bangladesh in attaining full One Day International status. The real breakthrough would come, however, with qualification for the Cricket World Cup via the International Cricket Council Trophy – a feat missed by just 30 runs in 1999.

Rugby

The first rugby club in Ireland was founded in Trinity College, Dublin, in 1854. The Irish Rugby Football Union was formed in 1879 by the amalgamation of two rival unions and by 1885 comprised twenty-six clubs in Ulster, Leinster and Munster. Traditionally upper and middle class, the domestic game and the national team are cross-border.

Some of the oldest clubs in Ireland still play in the league, including Lansdowne (founded in 1873), Wanderers (1869) and Queen's University (1869).

Internationally, Ireland has historically been one of the weaker sides in the Six (formerly Five) Nations Championships (an annual competition between Ireland, England, Scotland, Wales, France and now Italy). Ireland's only Grand Slam was in 1948, and until 2004 their last triple crown (beating England, Scotland and Wales) had come in 1985. Recently standards have risen; in the World Cup 2003, Ireland reached the quarter-finals. Irish stars such as Brian O'Driscoll, Willie John McBride and Keith Wood have also played an important role in the tours of the southern hemisphere made by the British and Irish Lions – the rugby touring team that draws for its members on Ireland, England, Scotland and Wales.

Soccer

Since a split in Irish soccer in the 1920s, the Football Association of Ireland runs international and domestic soccer in the Republic. In Northern Ireland the Irish Football League organizes domestic football, while the international aspect is handled by the Irish Football Association.

Since the late 1980s – almost mirroring Northern Ireland's decline – the Republic has acquitted itself well on the international stage. Domestically, the Republic is also more professional, but the main clubs, such as Bohemians, Shelbourne and Shamrock Rovers, are no match for the English league when it comes to resources and popularity. In Northern Ireland, the situation is even worse; even such traditionally strong teams as Linfield and Glentoran are in trouble.

British teams like Arsenal, Chelsea, Everton, Tottenham Hotspur and – above all Manchester United – are immensely popular on both sides of the border and among both communities. But mirroring the sectarian overtones that have disfigured the game since the Troubles started Celtic – despite its mixed-player base – is widely supported by Catholics and Rangers by Protestants.

Ireland has produced great players like Johnny Carey, George Best, Pat Jennings, Liam Brady, Niall Quinn, Johnny Giles, Roy Keane and Damien Duff, all of whom have emigrated to English clubs. It is they – along with British players with some Irish ancestry – who dominate the national teams.

Hockey

Hockey has been played in Ireland since the late nineteenth century, and again has flourished on an all-Ireland basis. The men's and women's hockey associations amalgamated in 2000 to form the Irish Hockey Association, based in Dublin. There are nearly 200 clubs and 277 schools affiliated to the IHA. Hockey is particularly strong in Dublin, Cork and Greater Belfast. Ireland is currently ranked about 18 in the men's game out of 143 countries affiliated to the Federation of International Hockey; the women's team is ranked 14.

Basketball

Basketball, which was formally established in the Republic in 1947, is thriving: in 2003 the Irish Basketball Association relaunched itself as Basketball Ireland, to which the Ulster Basketball Association is affiliated. Basketball is now one of the biggest participation sports in Ireland, with more than 10,000 people playing club basketball: including schools and non-aligned players, it is estimated that around 150,000, male and female (and the disabled), play the game at some level. In the fourteen to eighteen age group it is second only to soccer.

Basketball Ireland runs a busy league and cup programme island-wide throughout the year. It is currently reviewing the game's structure with a view to increasing the standard of coaching and thus the standard of players.

XI Northern Ireland

In 1838 the Railway Commissioners of Ireland, surveying the whole country, said of the northern population: 'They are a frugal, industrious and intelligent race, inhabiting a district for the most part inferior in natural fertility to the southern portion of Ireland, but cultivating it better.' This is a traditional view of the Ulster people, taken by writers and analysts who were largely Protestant, and there is no denying the importance in Ulster of the Protestant work ethic. Travellers, philanthropists and entrepreneurs coming to Ireland in the nineteenth century to try to solve its problems were wont to remark approvingly on the efficiency of the northern population compared to that of the rest of the country.

Although there were English planters, Ulster is very much the creation of the Scots. There is an irony in this, in that the Irish were early colonists in Scotland when in the fifth century they set up the kingdom of Dál Riada. Even in pre-plantation days, intercourse between the province and western Scotland was always frequent. The bond between the two countries was emphasized in the fourteenth century with the Bruce invasion, and during the next two centuries the Scots mercenary soldier (the galloglas) became a familiar feature in Irish military encounters.

Despite John de Courcy's success in subduing limited areas of the province, the old Gaelic families continued to dominate Ulster throughout the medieval period. Ulster had remained independent after the rest of Ireland had been effectively conquered and did not really change until after the Nine Years War, when its strategic inviolability came to an end. By the early seventeenth century garrisons were set up throughout the province, and it was ready for the planters. It was rural; apart from Carrickfergus, there were no towns as we know them before the plantation. That this plantation succeeded when the Tudor plantations failed was mainly due to the Scots' familiarity with Ulster and to their desperation: western Scotland had always had a higher population than it could prosperously accommodate, and even without government incentives the Ulster land attracted them. Most of the immigrants were landless and hungry, as well as hard, brave and stubborn – qualities that would distinguish those of their descendants – like Davy Crockett – who became legendary frontiersmen in the United States.

The seeds of future tragedy were sown during the seventeenth century. There were not enough settlers to work the land, so a large Catholic population remained to act as labourers or to occupy the inferior land, while – unlike in the other provinces of Ireland – there were enough settlers to make up a proportion of the population too substantial ever to be shifted or absorbed. The industrious Scots proved efficient at clearing forests, farming land and founding towns and industries.

With the outbreak of war between Charles I and the Scots, their Presbyterian brethren in Ulster, who had suffered under Sir Thomas Wentworth, supported them. When the 1641 rebellion broke out it was led by Ulster Catholics and the planters had their homes burned and some suffered torture and murder. About 12,000 men, women and children died out of a total Protestant population of about 40,000 (16). 'Here, if anywhere, the mentality of siege was born', said A. T. Q. Stewart. The horrors of the rising were not forgotten, indeed were exacerbated in the Protestant memory; in Portadown, scene of the catastrophic Drumcree confrontations of the 1990s, Orange banners portray how eighty or so men, women and children were driven off a bridge in 1641 and were piked, shot or drowned. With the joining in alliance with the Irish of the Old English, who were also Roman Catholics, the religious element became the important feature distinguishing the royalists from the parliamentarians.

During the seventeenth century Ulster gradually became the most prosperous province in Ireland. Although domestic industries were not unique to Ulster, they were taken more seriously there and the craftsmanship was superior. Immigrants like the Huguenots and the Quakers came to the north in comparatively large numbers and brought with them an expertise in textiles and dedication to their work (40). With the Ulster Custom, which gave security of tenure and compensation to tenants, there was stability in Ulster that was lacking in the rest of the country.

The religious division intensified with the war in Ireland between James II and William of Orange (17). Bitterness about their suffering coupled with pride in their courage and affection for William, the victor at the Boyne, persists in the songs that are still sung by Ulster Protestants about the relief of Londonderry, while for Irish Catholics the defeat of the Stuarts represented the beginning of a period of serious religious persecution and mass emigration.

Despite their loyal support for the winning side, the Ulster Presbyterians experienced discrimination during the eighteenth century and many of them emigrated. For those remaining, history and prejudice prevented any kind of alliance with their fellow victims, the Catholics. Being angry too with England and the established church, they became a very isolated people. Their increasing militarism was evident during the vicious sectarian clashes of the eighteenth century between agrarian secret societies like the Catholic Defenders and the Protestant Peep O'Day Boys; one such confrontation would lead to the foundation in 1795 of the Orange Order. While many Presbyterians were initially enthusiastic supporters of the French Revolution and a radical element joined the United Irishmen in pursuit of religious equality and electoral reform, most

Ulster Protestants saw themselves as a bulwark against lawlessness. The 1798 rebellion – and the stories of anti-Protestant atrocities – as well as Emmet's rising of 1803 kept alive the fears of the Orange movement, as did the pressure first for Catholic emancipation, then for repeal of the union and finally for home rule. Towards the end of the nineteenth century, fear of a sell-out over home rule became more and more potent and was brilliantly summed up by Rudyard Kipling in his 'Ulster 1912':

> The blood our fathers spilt,
> Our love, our toils, our pains,
> Are counted us for guilt,
> And only bind our chains.
> Before an Empire's eyes,
> The traitor claims his price.
> What need of further lies?
> We are the sacrifice.

In this poem are expressed the virtues and the deficiencies of the Ulster Protestants. Their history is that of a proud, industrious and courageous people, short on imagination and intellectual flexibility, developing a prosperous way of life out of devastation and misery. Having for centuries viewed Catholics as a fifth column, they saw their worst fears reinforced by the violence of the years before partition. Northern Ireland suffered from the 'double minority' problem: Catholics were afraid of the majority in the six counties, while Protestants were afraid of the majority in the thirty-two. The vicious republican campaign of the late twentieth century that brought so much misery further poisoned relationships between the two tribes (87). Whatever prospect there might have been of wooing Protestants into a united Ireland, a campaign of intimidation had no chance of success against a people notorious for their passion for principle and their capacity to endure suffering.

84   RELIGIOUS DIVISIONS

After a long period of vicious sectarian confrontations between Catholic and Protestant agrarian secret societies, on 21 September 1795, 300 Defenders attacked Dan Winter's tavern at the Diamond (a hamlet near Loughgall in County Armagh), both because it was a meeting-place for Peep O'Day Boys and because it was a strategically important location. Forty Defenders were killed and the rest routed by armed Protestants who had served in the Volunteers (18); subsequently in a local inn, a Protestant group decided to found a defensive association called the Orange Society (later Order) dedicated to defending the crown and the Protestant religion. The first members were mainly farmers, traders and peasants: all Protestant denominations and constitutional political parties were welcome to join, but not Catholics, because of the 'memory of the bloody Massacre which they Committed on Our Forefathers'. For fearful Protestants, an organization that transcended their religious, political and social differences – for the membership included labourers and gentry – was a tremendous breakthrough in uniting against those they believed wanted them exterminated. Orange societies offered mutual protection against violence and revolution as well as an escape from the mundane through rituals, passwords and the excitement and swagger of parades, music and ceremonies.

A typical oath of one of the early clubs was: 'To the glorious, pious, and immortal memory of the great and good King William, not forgetting Oliver Cromwell, who assisted in redeeming us from popery, slavery, arbitrary power, brass-money and wooden shoes.' Government policy in the 1790s (in the words of an English general) was to 'increase the animosity between Orangemen and the United Irish'. That Defenders flocked to join the United Irishmen (19) and therefore undermine its anti-sectarianism helped to further sectarian polarization, and fear and loathing was increased by the spreading far and wide of baseless allegations that Orangemen took an oath to extirpate Catholics. Throughout its existence the leadership of the Orange Order has been at pains to stress that it celebrates religious and civil liberties, and though anti-Catholicism is not anti-Catholic.

The society's usefulness in providing recruits for the yeomanry led to its acceptance by the middle classes and the gentry. Southern landlords swiftly followed this lead and encouraged their Protestant tenants to form lodges. As Figure 84a shows, by the time the 1798 rebellion broke out, there were Orange lodges in almost every county. The Order's success in reviving the Orange spirit of 1690 made it a natural ally of the government in putting down the 1798 rebellion. In November 1798 the Grand Lodge of Ireland – the ruling body – was set up in Dublin and Lord Donegall's brother-in-law, Thomas Verner, an Armagh landowner, became Grand Master. Landlords saw Orangeism not only as usefully defensive, but also as a way of constraining hotheads, but its fervour and the brutal sectarianism of many of its plebian supporters often made it an embarrassment later. After its suppression in the 1830s it was abandoned by the gentry and the middle classes until its revival in the 1880s to resist home rule.

Sectarian clashes between Orangemen and Ribbonmen (the successors to the Defenders) gave the order an increasingly violent reputation, as did the confrontations with Catholic Irish immigrants as Orangeism spread into England and Scotland. Equating Catholicism with sedition, Orangemen were bitterly opposed to Catholic emancipation and even more fearful of Daniel O'Connell's campaign for repeal of the union. Economic as well as political differences were fought out on the ground. During the nineteenth century, industrialization attracted Catholics to Belfast; 10 per cent of the population in 1800, they were 30 per cent in 1830. Competition for jobs and houses exacerbated religious tensions, and serious riots in Belfast were often experienced from then on; religious segregation in employment and housing followed.

The Orange Order was the vital force in resisting home rule for a united Ireland and its leaders dominated the Northern Irish parliament from its inception. Sectarianism flourished. Unionists were never strong enough to do without the link with the Orange Order, which ensured Catholic hostility:

between 1921 and 1969, of the fifty-four Unionists who reached cabinet rank in Northern Ireland, only three were not Orangemen. David Trimble's high profile during the first Drumcree crisis in 1995 won him votes later that year in the election for leadership of the Ulster Unionist Party. Like other modernizers in his party, he wanted but failed to achieve separation from the Orange Order, but in 2005 its anti-Agreement leadership (86) announced it was breaking the link.

Although – particularly in rural areas – many Catholics were friendly with individual Orangemen, there is an atavistic hostility born of a violent history, which was very evident during the confrontations over Orange parades in the mid-1990s. Since the violence over parades (particularly Drumcree) – much of which was orchestrated for political purposes by the Republican leadership – because of a combination of brilliant republican propaganda and its own hopelessness at public relations, the Orange Order has secured a worldwide reputation for bigotry which its members bitterly resent.

As far as religious divisions are concerned, the census of 2001 showed 53 per cent of the population to be Protestant and 44 per cent to be Catholic. Figure 84b shows the Catholic/Protestant make-up of parliamentary constituencies throughout Northern Ireland. (The high proportion of Catholics near the border is mirrored by the comparatively high proportion of Protestants on the other side. Donegal, Cavan and Monaghan are respectively 9.3 per cent, 8.3 per cent and 8 per cent Protestant; the figure for the Republic as a whole is 3.7 per cent.)

Sectarianism has been exacerbated by segregated schooling; church leaders have been more concerned with maintaining rigid control over their flocks than with encouraging integration. Religious differences are not the major cause of the violence in Northern Ireland, but they provide the labels that differentiate the tribes. Cardinal Ó Fiach – a hate figure for many Protestants because of his republican sympathies – remarked rightly that most of the religious bigotry in Northern Ireland was Protestant while most of the political bigotry was Catholic.

Religious minorities have suffered discrimination on both sides of the border. In the Republic, from the perspective of Protestants, Home Rule really did mean Rome Rule. They saw the Protestant population fall by 34 per cent between 1911 and 1926 because of sectarian persecution and continue to fall throughout the century primarily because in mixed marriages the children were brought up Catholic. Until recently, Catholic morality prevented non-Catholics from following their consciences in such matters as divorce and contraception; and in a Gaelic, Catholic state, there was marked hostility to the British tradition from which most Protestants came (40). In Northern Ireland, the prevailing Protestant ethos imposed on Catholics such restrictions as Sunday observance, as well as actively discriminating against them in housing, employment and politics; in areas where Catholics had any control, they retaliated in kind. Protestants resent the fact that anti-Catholic discrimination in the North has been exaggerated, while anti-Protestant discrimination in the south has been forgotten. These days, equality legislation in both jurisdictions has largely made discrimination a thing of the past.

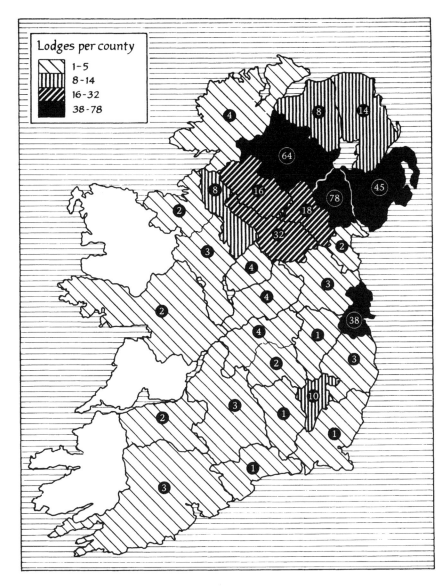

Figure 84(a) The Orange Order, May 1798.

Despite the efforts of centrist political and church leaders, nationalist and unionist parties remain respectively almost exclusively Catholic and Protestant and in deprived areas sectarianism continues to flourish to such an extent that there is virtual apartheid in public housing.

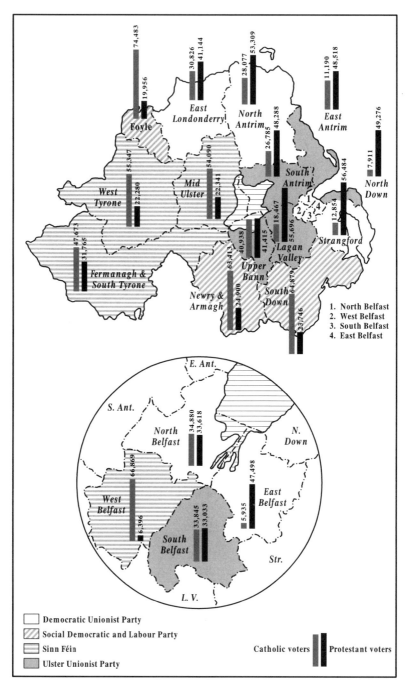

Figure 84(b) Religion and politics by constituency: General Election 2001 (in 2005 the DUP gained East Antrim, South Antrim, Lagan Valley and Upper Bann; the SDLP gained South Belfast; SF gained Newry and South Armagh).

85   GOVERNMENT: 1921–69

The six north-eastern counties of Ireland – Antrim, Down, Armagh, Tyrone, Fermanagh and Londonderry – became the state of Northern Ireland as a result of the Government of Ireland Act of 1920. In extent it is 5,452 square miles – only about 17 per cent of the whole island; the population of Northern Ireland used to hover at around 50 per cent of that of the Republic, but it is now around 43 per cent, having grown at around 0.5 per cent annually during the decade from 1991 as opposed to the 0.9 per cent growth in the Republic. The unionists accepted six counties rather than the nine (the six plus Cavan, Donegal and Monaghan) of Ulster because of the religious and hence the political split. Protestants in the nine were in a majority of 900,000 to 700,000 Catholics; in the six they were in a majority of 820,000 to 430,000, thus ensuring a substantial unionist majority. The Northern Ireland parliament (which from 1932 would be located at Stormont) – like that of the south – was closely modelled on Westminster, although – again like the south – the upper house was ineffective. The prime ministers were: Sir James Craig (from 1927 Lord Craigavon; 1921–40); John Andrews (1940–43), Sir Basil Brooke (from 1952 Lord Brookeborough; 1943–63); Terence O'Neill (1963–9); James Chichester-Clark (1969–71); Brian Faulkner (1971–2).

As in the south, the early years of Northern Ireland were bloody and the minority suffered disproportionately. Between July 1920 and July 1922, 557 people were killed: 303 Catholic and 172 Protestant civilians and eighty-two members of the security forces. Although Catholic civilians made up just a quarter of the population of Belfast, 257 of them died as against 159 Protestants; around 10,000 Catholics were driven from their jobs, more than 20,000 from their homes and around 500 had their businesses destroyed.

Northern Irish nationalists did not really accept that partition was there to stay. Unlike southern Protestants, who emigrated or accepted their clergy's advice to accept the fait accompli with a good grace, in Northern Ireland Catholics were encouraged by their politicians and clergy to make the state unworkable. Until 1925 nationalist MPs refused to take their seats in the local parliament (and between 1932 and 1945 they frequently abstained) and Catholics in general refused to help in setting up the new state's institutions – so leaving themselves at a permanent disadvantage which they then deeply resented. The police force, the Royal Ulster Constabulary (RUC), and the part-time police, the 'B' Specials – armed to combat IRA terrorism – were seen as instruments of oppression; the local government franchise was property- not population-related; gerrymandering was common; proportional representation for elections to the Northern Ireland parliament was abolished in 1929 to assure majoritarian rule; the Catholic community opted out of the state secular education system so children were segregated; and discrimination in housing and employment continued.

Unquestionably many unionists set out from the beginning to discriminate in favour of the Protestant majority, primarily through fear of what they saw as the disloyal minority, the ever-present threat from the IRA, the inclination of British governments to negotiate with their enemies behind their backs, and the pretensions of the state across the border. With the Ulster Protestant bluntness that so offends nationalists, whose rhetoric is more subtle and more ambiguous, in 1934 Lord Craigavon said in a speech: 'in the South they boasted of a Catholic state. They still boast of Southern Ireland being a Catholic state. All I boast of is that we are a Protestant parliament and a Protestant state.' He was telling the truth about the south: the following year de Valera's 1937 constitution enshrined Catholic morality (41) and increased unionist paranoia by claiming the whole territory of Ireland. Yet it is only Craigavon's last sentence that is remembered and quoted.

Those unionist politicians who tried a more inclusive approach were opposed by the Orange Order leadership and extreme Protestants, and received little cooperation or encouragement from Catholics. Politics – which was almost exclusively male – settled into a sectarian rut. One-party government was a leisurely affair: the local parliament met for only a couple of months each year and there was no constructive opposition to call ministers to account. The Government of Ireland Act reserved substantial powers (particularly in foreign affairs, finance and defence) to Westminster, where thirteen seats were allocated to Northern Ireland (reduced to twelve in 1948 with the abolition of university representation; now eighteen).

Between 1922 and 1966 nine Westminster constituencies always returned unionists (as did Queen's University). Of the sixty-two Northern Irish MPs at Westminster during this period, fifty-six were members of the Ulster Unionist Party. Mainly from business or the professions, unrepresentative of their own supporters and out of touch with their grass roots, they had little impact either at Westminster or in Northern Ireland: the politicians who mattered were in the Northern Ireland parliament at Stormont. Figure 85 shows the distribution of their support among the Stormont constituencies that existed between 1929 and 1968, during which period unionists never took fewer than thirty-four of the fifty-two seats at any election.

Massive unemployment (25 per cent on average) during the 1930s, coupled with bad housing brought widespread sectarian riots that died down as employment prospects improved towards the end of the decade. The Second World War brought an economic boom that reduced unemployment dramatically. From 1945 onwards, there were fundamental changes in the Northern Irish economy, as the traditionally important linen and shipbuilding industries declined and the governments encouraged industrial development geared to broadening the state's industrial base.

The post-war British Labour government agreed to subsidize the extension to Northern Ireland of the new health and social welfare benefits; the Education Act of 1947 (which took ten years to implement) brought free post-primary education. By the mid-1950s Northern Irish Catholics, though still suffering from discrimination, were materially far better off than their counterparts in the Republic (a state of affairs that prevailed until the 1970s); a

West Belfast - Irish

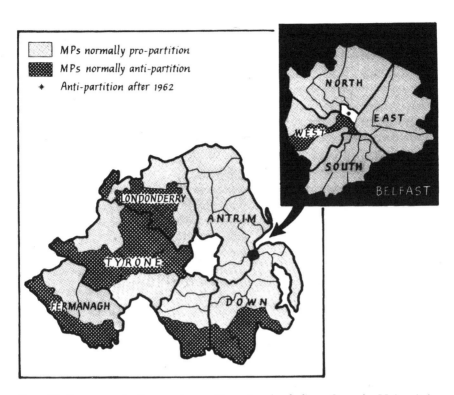

Figure 85 Government: Stormont constituencies (excluding Queen's University), 1929–68.

recognition of this led to the failure of the IRA to gain support for their 1956–62 offensive.

In 1963, Lord Brookeborough – who had shown no more imagination than his predecessors in dealing with the minority – retired. His successor, Terence O'Neill, had a policy of promoting reconciliation between the two communities and the two states. Although his efforts brought about much improved relations with the Republic, his domestic policies left the Catholic community unsatisfied. In 1967 came the foundation of the Northern Ireland Civil Rights Association (NICRA), which called, *inter alia*, for a universal franchise for local-government elections, the ending of electoral gerrymandering and of discrimination in housing and employment, and the disbanding of the 'B' Specials. Many Protestants believed the NICRA to be an IRA front, but it was a confused mixture of nationalists, liberals and student radicals with some IRA sympathizers thrown in. On 5 October 1968, a banned civil rights march in Londonderry turned into a series of confrontations with the RUC who were televised batoning demonstrators (including nationalist Stormont MPs). From being a backwater, Northern Ireland suddenly acquired an international reputation for oppression and brutality. Though the government agreed to a number of reforms, they came too late to stop the agitation and the bad publicity: instead they split NICRA. The radical student movement, the People's Democracy, whose leaders included Bernadette Devlin (who won a Westminster seat in 1969) pressed on. Against the advice of NICRA, in January 1969 they organized a march from Belfast to Derry which was attacked violently at Burntollet Bridge by Protestant extremists, bitterly resentful of what they saw as O'Neill's compromising with traitors.

The year 1969 saw a hardening on both sides. In the Stormont election of that year twenty-four pro-O'Neill and twelve anti-O'Neill Official Unionists were returned. Unable to control the growing dissension in the Unionist Party and under violent personal attack from popular Protestant hardliners like the Reverend Ian Paisley, O'Neill resigned, and his successor, James Chichester-Clark, took over the hopeless task of attempting reconciliation.

Sporadic violence took a new and nasty turn in August 1969 when rioting led to a three-day battle in the Bogside in Derry between the RUC and the Catholic community. An invasion of the Falls area in Belfast by an angry Protestant mob led to seven deaths, with 3,000 Catholics losing their homes. On 14 August the British government sent in the army to protect Catholics. The honeymoon was brief.

86   SEARCHING FOR PEACE

For a military account of the 'Troubles', see 24; for major casualties, see 87. Throughout all those years of murder, maiming, suffering and bereavement, desperate attempts went on behind the scenes in Belfast, Dublin, London and Washington to find a peaceful solution.

In March 1971 Chichester-Clark gave way to Brian Faulkner, who commanded the support of moderate unionists. However, the credibility of the Northern Irish parliament was eroded when the newly formed moderate nationalist Social Democratic and Labour Party (SDLP) withdrew from it in a protest in July; abstentionism by one side or the other has continued to be a feature of Northern Ireland politics. The following month, in response to escalating violence and Protestant pressure, internment was introduced. Botched by the intelligence services and restricted to nationalists, it failed to reduce the bloodshed and served only to alienate the Catholic community further; it ended in 1975.

As a consequence of the mayhem that followed the killing by British soldiers of thirteen unarmed republican and nationalist demonstrators on Bloody Sunday in January 1972, in March Edward Heath's Conservative government prorogued Stormont and imposed direct rule from Westminster. A secret meeting in July between British ministers and an IRA delegation that included Gerry Adams and Martin McGuinness demonstrated that reasoned negotiation was impossible.

The following year the British government announced its plans for a power-sharing executive to be formed from an elected assembly. It held a tripartite conference (Britain, Northern Ireland and the Republic) at Sunningdale in December, where under pressure from the SDLP and both governments Faulkner agreed to the setting up of a Council of Ireland, which he thought was just an advisory body and the SDLP saw as the springboard to a united Ireland. Members of the Faulkner Unionists, the SDLP and the new centrist Alliance Party took office as members of the Executive on 1 January 1974, but the ambiguity over the Council of Ireland was to be its downfall; many unionists believed the SDLP interpretation. In the February 1974 Westminster elections anti-Sunningdale candidates polled 51 per cent of the vote and in May, after a massive loyalist strike and a weak response from the British government, the Executive collapsed, Protestant paramilitary organizations emerged and sectarian murder and violence became rife.

The then politically naive IRA became convinced that the British were prepared to negotiate withdrawal and declared an indefinite ceasefire in February 1975, which limped along with various breaches until it ended in practice in September 1975 and in theory in March 1976. Strengthened but disillusioned, the IRA settled in for a long war and began to reinforce its political arm, Sinn Féin.

In May 1975 elections were held for a seventy-eight-member Constitutional Convention which the British Labour government of Harold Wilson hoped would make constructive proposals about how Northern Ireland should be governed. Yet again, a majority of electors opposed power-sharing, and this was reflected in the composition of the Convention and the proposals put by the majority to the British government in November 1975; these were rejected. In March 1976, the Convention was dissolved, as it was clear that there was no prospect of agreement between the SDLP, which wanted power-sharing and the United Ulster Unionist Council (UUUC composed of Official Unionists, the Orange Order, the Vanguard Unionist Party and Ian Paisley's Democratic Unionist Party). After this the British government decided that there should be a settled period of direct rule before any new constitutional initiatives. In May 1977, Paisley led a loyalist strike to demand the implementation of the Convention report failed which both because of a lack of support from the unionist community (which did not feel constitutionally threatened) and decisive action by the Secretary of State. The UUUC dissolved, as the Official Unionists refused to cooperate with those who had supported the strike.

In September 1976, after a government decision to treat all prisoners the same, the republican 'blanket protest' began. This campaign by IRA and INLA prisoners in the Maze (Long Kesh) prison to secure special category status, with such privileges as free association, no uniforms and no prison work, escalated from wearing blankets rather than prison clothing, to smearing their excrement on cell walls rather than 'slop out' ('the dirty protest'), and in October 1980, against the wishes of the republican leadership, to a hunger strike that lasted until mid-December. On 1 March 1981 the hunger strike was restarted by Bobby Sands, who became the first of ten republicans to die between May and August; Sands was followed by Francis Hughes, Raymond McCreesh, Patsy O'Hara (INLA), Joe McDonnell, Martin Hurson, Kevin Lynch (INLA), Kieran

Doherty, Thomas McElwee, and Michael Devine (INLA). While still on hunger strike, Sands was put forward as a candidate in a Westminster by-election; with the SDLP withdrawing, Sands was elected with a 1,446-vote majority over the Official Unionist candidate. When a pro-prisoners campaigner won the seat in the by-election following Sands's death, Sinn Féin announced it would hence-forward contest all elections. The emotional impact of the hunger strikes con-vulsed nationalist Ireland, won international sympathy for republicans and a huge increase in Irish-American funds, and further polarized Northern Ireland.

In 1982, an election was held for a Northern Ireland Assembly to agree on how powers could be devolved ('rolling devolution'). At the October elections Sinn Féin won 10.1 per cent first preference votes to 18.8 per cent for the SDLP; neither party took its seats and after an inglorious career the assembly was dissolved in June 1986. By then, as a result of deep anxiety in both the British and Irish governments about the growth of popular support for the IRA, the Anglo-Irish Agreement – inspired by the SDLP leader John Hume and negotiated in great secrecy – was signed at Hillsborough, Co. Down, on 15 November 1985. In exchange for agreeing that there would be no change in the status of Northern Ireland without the consent of a majority of its citizens, the Irish government, through the Anglo-Irish Intergovernmental Conference and Maryfield Secretariat, was given a consultative role in the administration of Northern Ireland.

The agreement was bitterly opposed by the unionist population of Northern Ireland, who feared a sell-out, and by republicans, who saw it as copper-fastening partition. In the words of Paul Bew, it 'ushered in an era of direct rule with a green tinge', but it also marginalized Sinn Féin, whose vote slumped from 13.4 per cent in 1983 to 11.4 per cent in 1987 and 10 per cent in 1992. Throughout this period the IRA was largely being contained by the security forces and the supply of Irish-American money on which it relied was steadily falling.

Disappointed that despite the agreement and the enormous sums of money being poured into the economy the killings and bombings continued, the British attempted a further peace initiative. Secretary of State Peter Brooke, and his successor Patrick Mayhew, using an approach suggested by John Hume, initiated three-stranded talks: on relations between the two communities in Northern Ireland; on relations north and south of the Irish border in Ireland; and on relations between Dublin and London. Although the UUP cautiously cooperated, they were ultimately rebuffed by Dublin, which was supporting Hume's strategy of wooing republicanism into talks through the secret dialogue he had begun with Sinn Féin leader Gerry Adams in 1988.

In 1993, as a result of much behind-the-scenes negotiation, the Downing Street Declaration agreed by both governments stated that the two govern-ments were committed to work towards a new political framework for Northern Ireland, confirmed an earlier statement that Britain had 'no selfish strategic or economic interest in Northern Ireland', accepted that the people of Ireland should democratically determine their own constitutional future, reiterated the principle that constitutional change required the consent of

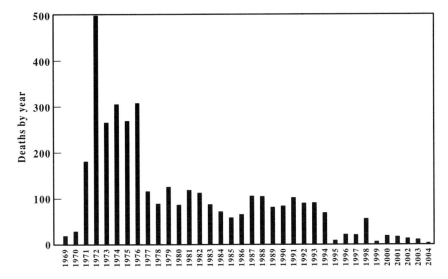

Figure 86 The Troubles, 1969–2004.

the majority of the people of Northern Ireland and invited 'democratically mandated parties which establish a commitment to exclusively peaceful methods and which have shown that they abide by the democratic process' to join the dialogue. The following August, the IRA declared a 'cessation' (24), followed by the Combined Loyalist Military Command in October.

Unlike the much-quoted South African model of peace-making, this peace process made peace not from the centre out but from the extremes in: inclusiveness was the mantra. For that reason, the insistence by both governments that decommissioning of weapons was a prerequisite for entering talks was dropped and continued criminal paramilitary activity was largely overlooked.

The Belfast (preferred unionist term) or Good Friday (preferred nationalist) Agreement was accepted by the talks' participants (Alliance, UUP, SDLP, Sinn Féin, the Women's Coalition and two small loyalist parties – but not the DUP) on 10 April 1998: key points were a Northern Ireland Assembly, devolved government operated by a power-sharing executive, a British-Irish Council and cross-border bodies. From the unionist perspective, the key attraction was the acceptance by republicans – who had fought for decades for a united Ireland – of the principle of consent. The republican leadership, who had proved to be superb negotiators, won innumerable concessions like prisoner release and radical police reform, but in the eyes of some of their followers, they had sold out their principles for the sake of seats in Stormont.

In the subsequent referenda, the Republic voted overwhelmingly in favour of the agreement; on a turnout of 81 per cent in Northern Ireland, 71.1 per cent voted Yes and 28.9 per cent No; though, disturbingly, it appeared that only about 55 per cent of Protestants were in favour. John Hume and David Trimble (who dragged unwilling unionism along the peace path) won the Nobel Peace Prize later that year.

Although an executive which included two Sinn Féin ministers did eventually come into being in 1999, the refusal of the IRA to decommission fully and stop its criminality led to temporary suspensions, the most recent in October 2002. Since then endless negotiations have failed to break the stalemate and in elections for the Assembly in 2003, the European parliament in 2004 (53) and Westminster in 2005, the centre lost steadily to the hardliners. Nationalism is now led by Sinn Féin, and unionism by Ian Paisley's DUP which will not share power until the IRA decommissions fully and disbands. Still, despite the impasse, few people are murdered these days.

Since the beginning of the Troubles, the British prime ministers have been Harold Wilson, Labour, (1964–70), Edward Heath, Conservative, (1970–74), Harold Wilson, Labour, (1974–76), James Callaghan, Labour, (1976–79), Margaret Thatcher, Conservative, (1979–90), John Major, Conservative, (1990–97) and Tony Blair, Labour, (1997–). Initially, Northern Ireland was the responsibility of the home secretary (James Callaghan (1967–70) and Reginald Maudling (1970–72)), but from then on responsibility went to secretaries of state for Northern Ireland: William Whitelaw (1972–73), Francis Pym (1973–74), Merlyn Rees (1974–76), Roy Mason (1976–79), Humphrey Atkins (1979–81), James Prior (1981–84), Douglas Hurd (1984–85), Tom King (1985–89), Peter Brooke (1989–92), Patrick Mayhew (1992–97), Marjorie (Mo) Mowlam (1997–99), Peter Mandelson (1999–2001), John Reid (2001–2) and Paul Murphy (2002–4).

From 6 December 1999 to 15 October 2002, excluding various periods of suspension, David Trimble of the UUP was First Minister, first with Seamus Mallon and then later Mark Durkan of the SDLP as his Deputy. The Executive was finally suspended on 15 October 2002.

87   KILLINGS: 1969–2005

> Bear in mind these dead:
> I can find no plainer words.
> (*John Hewitt, 'Neither an*
>   *elegy nor a manifesto'*)

There were thousands of bombs and tens of thousands of shootings, almost 3,700 deaths, tens of thousands of injured and hundreds of thousands of people touched by suffering. Here is a list of those events in Ireland that killed five or more, as well as a few that have lived on in the public consciousness or are of particular importance to one or the other community. The use of bold for famous names and places is for ease of reference. (See 24 for an account of paramilitary activity in Ireland and England and on the Continent.)

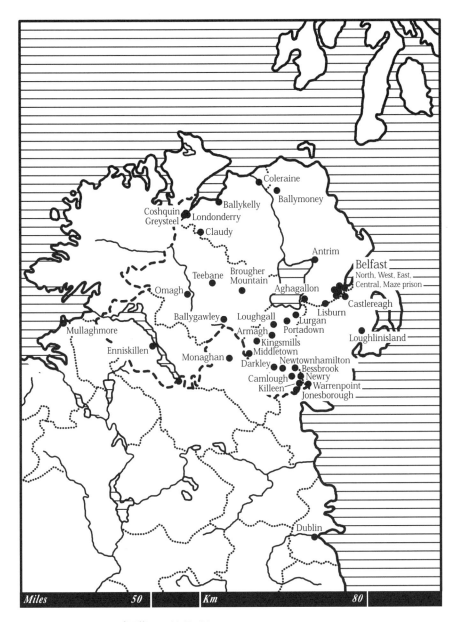

Figure 87 Location of Killings: 1969–99.

1970

Londonderry

On 26 June, along with his two young daughters, Thomas McCool died with two other IRA members when the bomb they were making blew up.

1971

Brougher Mountain, County Tyrone

On 9 February, two BBC engineers and three building workers were killed by an IRA landmine.

Belfast (north)

On 9 March, three young **Scottish soldiers** – two of them brothers – were lured from a bar, taken by the IRA to a mountain road and shot in the head: they became folk heroes for loyalist 'tartan gangs'.

Belfast (north)

On 4 December, a loyalist bomb in the Tramore Bar (known as **McGurk's**), killed fifteen Catholics – ten men, three women and two children – and injured thirteen.

Belfast (west)

On 11 December, apparently in retaliation for the McGurk's bomb, two men (one Catholic) and two babies were killed and nineteen were injured by an IRA bomb in a Shankill Road furniture showroom.

1972

Londonderry

On 30 January, which became known as **Bloody Sunday**, thirteen Catholic men died, one was fatally wounded and seventeen were injured when soldiers of the Parachute Regiment fired on an illegal parade. International outrage followed, the British embassy in Dublin was burned down, the IRA had a huge propaganda victory and a massive increase in recruitment, and OIRA bombed the Parachute Regiment's headquarters in Aldershot in retaliation (24). The sequence of events is still disputed, despite the labours of Lord Savile's inquiry, which was set up in 1998, has cost well over £150 million and has not yet reported.

Belfast (central)

On 4 March, an IRA bomb in the **Abercorn Restaurant** on a Saturday afternoon killed two young Catholic women and injured seventy, some of whom were horribly mutilated.

Belfast (central)

On 20 March, an IRA bomb killed seven (two police, four civilians and a member of the UDR) and injured 150.

Belfast (west)

On 22 April, Francis Rowntree, aged eleven, was killed by a **rubber bullet**, as were two men in the next thirteen months: **a plastic bullet** killed Stephen Geddis, aged eleven, on 29 August 1975 and between then and 1989, thirteen others, eight aged under eighteen. Rubber baton rounds and their plastic successors are regarded by the security forces as essential for riot control; in 1985 an opinion poll showed 87 per cent of Catholics considered them offensive weapons and disapproved, while 86 per cent of Protestants considered them defensive and approved. Despite a long-running campaign against them, no effective substitute has yet been found.

Londonderry

On 21 May, William Best of the Royal Irish Rangers, a nineteen-year-old serving in Germany, was abducted and murdered by the Official IRA while visiting his family in the Creggan estate: 200 women marched on OIRA headquarters in protest and there were 5,000 at **Ranger Best**'s funeral. On 29 May, OIRA announced an end to their military campaign.

Belfast (east)

On 28 May, an IRA bomb exploded prematurely, killing four IRA men and four civilians – two men, a girl and a woman.

Belfast (west)

On 9 July, two Protestant civilians and one member of the Territorial Army were shot dead by the IRA; later that day, after widespread shooting followed the breakdown of an IRA ceasefire, one sixteen-year-old and one fourteen-year-old boy, one thirteen-year-old girl, a priest and a civilian were shot dead by British army snipers.

Belfast (central)

On 21 July, which became known as **Bloody Friday**, the IRA detonated twenty bombs at different locations within 75 minutes, killing two soldiers and eight civilians (four men, two women and one boy) and injuring 130.

Claudy

On 31 July, an IRA bomb caused the deaths of five men, two women, one boy and one girl; several others were injured.

Newry

On 22 August, three IRA men were among the nine (four customs officials; two lorry drivers) killed when their bomb went off prematurely at Newry customs clearing station; six others were injured.

Armagh (south)

On 2 October, Seamus Wright and Kevin McKee from Belfast were the first of those abducted and later murdered whose bodies were then hidden; they would become known as the **Disappeared. Jean McConville**, a widowed mother of ten (abducted 7 December 1972), and an English military intelligence officer, **Robert Nairac** (14 May 1977), about whose activities there is much controversy, are the most famous victims. The others were Eamon Molloy (1975, precise date unknown), seventeen-year-old Columba McVeigh (1 November 1975), Brendan Megraw (8 April 1978), eighteen-year-old John McClory and his retarded friend Brian McKinney (25 May 1978), Gerald Evans (27 March 1979), Charles Armstrong (16 August 1981), Danny McIlhone (1981, precise date unknown), Seamus Ruddy (1 May 1985), Sean Murphy (4 December 1981) and Gareth O'Connor (11 May 2003). Under intense pressure from the Families of the Disappeared, founded in 1994, who made the issue international and secured President Clinton's backing, the IRA admitted murdering Wright, McKee, McConville, Molloy, McVeigh, Megraw, McClory, McKinney and McIlhone; the remains of Molloy, McClory and McKinney were recovered with IRA help; Murphy's and McConville's remains were found accidentally. Nairac was killed by the IRA, Ruddy in France by the INLA; no one has admitted to Murphy's murder, though he died in an IRA-controlled area, and the IRA have been blamed for the disappearance of O'Connor, who had Real IRA connections.

Londonderry

On 20 December, five Catholic men were murdered in the Top of the Hill Bar in a UDA/UFF gun attack.

1973

Omagh

On 17 May, an IRA bomb killed five soldiers.

Coleraine

On 12 June, an IRA car bomb outside an off-licence killed six pensioners: Francis Campbell, his wife Dinah, his sister Elizabeth and another man and two women; three others seriously injured lost limbs.

Belfast (north)

On 26 June, **Senator Paddy Wilson**, an SDLP politician, and a ballroom dancer, Irene Andrews, were shot and stabbed to death in what the judge called 'a psychotic outburst'; the UDA/UFF murderers included John White, later a prominent figure in the peace process.

1974

Monaghan

On 11 March, **Billy Fox**, a Protestant Fine Gael senator, was shot dead by panicking members of the IRA in an area close to the border where the IRA assassinated many Protestants – civilian and otherwise.

Belfast (south)

On 2 May, six Catholic men were killed and eleven people injured when the UVF bombed the Rose and Crown bar on the **Ormeau Road**.

Dublin

On 17 May, in an attack later described by the loyalist spokesman David Ervine as 'returning the serve', three UVF car bombs in the city centre killed twenty-five people. The first, in Parnell Street at 5.28 p.m., killed John and Anne O'Brien and their baby daughters, in addition to four men (one an Italian) and two young women; the second, in Talbot Street at 5.30, killed one man, thirteen women (one French) and an unborn child; the third, at 5.32 in South Leinster Street, killed two women.

Monaghan

On 17 May, at 7.00 p.m., six men and one woman died after a UVF car bomb exploded in the city centre. Over 250 people were injured that day in Dublin and Monaghan.

1975

Belfast (west)

On 5 April, five Protestant men (one a paramilitary) were killed and sixty-one injured – almost certainly by the IRA – in the **Mountainview Tavern** in the Shankill Road.

Belfast (east)

On 12 April, two men and four women, all Catholic, were killed by a UVF bomb in the Strand bar in the **Short Strand**.

Newry

On 31 July, at Buskill, near Newry, a UVF gang, some of whom were members of the UDR, stopped the popular **Miami Showband** on their way home from Banbridge to the Irish Republic, put a bomb in their van which exploded and killed two bombers, and then shot dead three members of the band (two Catholics and one Protestant) and wounded two others.

Belfast (west)

On 13 August, five Protestants (one UVF member, two male and two female civilians – one a seventeen-year-old) died and almost sixty were injured after an IRA bomb and gun attack on the Bayardo Bar in the Shankill Road.

Newtownhamilton

On 1 September, two IRA gunmen killed five Protestant male civilians (including a father and son) and injured six in nearby **Tullyvallen** Orange hall.

1976

Armagh (south)

On 4 January, UVF gunmen killed the brothers John, Brian and Anthony (aged seventeen) Reavy at their family home; later UVF gunmen killed the brothers Barry and Declan O'Dowd and their uncle Joe at their family home and seriously injured their father.

Kingsmills, County Armagh

On 5 January there was a revenge attack for the murder of the Reaveys and the O'Dowds, when IRA gunmen (using the cover name Republic Action Force) stopped a textile workers' bus, ascertained each man's religion, told the only Catholic to leave and shot ten civilian Protestants dead and injured one seriously.

Belfast (west)

On 5 June, allegedly in retaliation for an earlier IRA bomb attack on a North Belfast pub that killed two Protestant civilians, four UVF gunmen killed five male civilians, three Protestant and two Catholic, in the Chlorane Bar.

Antrim

On 2 July, allegedly in retaliation for the IRA murder of three Protestant civilians – a man, a mother of three and her seventeen-year-old brother – in Walker's Bar, Templepatrick, a week earlier, one Catholic male civilian and five male Protestant civilians died after a UVF gun attack on the Catholic-owned Ramble Inn near Antrim town.

Dublin

On 21 July, the British Ambassador, **Christopher Ewart-Biggs**, and a civil servant, Judith Cook, were killed by an IRA landmine. Brian Cubbon, who was seriously injured, survived to become Permanent Secretary of the Home Office; **Richard Sykes**, who reported on the assassinations for the Foreign Office, was murdered with his valet in The Hague, where he was ambassador, on 22 March 1979.

Belfast (west)

On 10 August the getaway car driven by an IRA man fatally shot by a soldier mounted a pavement and crushed to death eight-year-old Joanne **Maguire** and her two little brothers; their severely injured mother Anne never recovered and after several attempts killed herself on 21 January 1980. Her sister **Mairead Corrigan**, a Catholic, with a Protestant, **Betty Williams**, founded the Women's Peace Movement (later the **Peace People**) in 1976 which gained huge local and international support and won them a joint Nobel Peace Prize, but soon disintegrated.

1977

Londonderry

On 2 February, the IRA shot dead **Jeffrey Agate**, the English managing director of the local Du Pont plant, just one of several murders of businessmen whom the IRA decreed to be legitimate targets because they were attempting to stabilize the economy; Seamus McAvoy, a builder, was the first of four murdered in 1985 by the IRA for working or providing materials for the army or police; in July 1986 the IRA declared that anyone providing any services whatsoever to the security forces would be targeted as 'collaborators'; a quarry-owner and an electrician were the first to be shot. In the south, the IRA also kidnapped and held to ransom businessmen including **Ben Dunne** (rescued 1981) and **Don Tidey** (rescued 16 December 1983 in a gun battle in which one soldier and a garda cadet were killed).

Dublin

On 5 October a member of OIRA murdered **Seamus Costello**, the able and ruthless lifelong violent republican and socialist, chief of staff of INLA, chairman of the Irish Republican Socialist Party (IRSP), its political wing, and a Wicklow County councillor.

Belfast (south)

On 7 October, the IRA shot dead Desmond Irvine, the secretary of the Prison Officers Association; twenty-nine **prison officers** were killed overall during the Troubles.

1978

Castlereagh

On 17 February, seven women and five men, all Protestant civilians except for one member of the RUC Reserve and including three married couples, were burned to death by an IRA-planted incendiary bomb while attending the annual dinner-dance of the Irish Collie Club at **La Mon House**, a country hotel; more than thirty were injured.

1979

Belfast

On 20 February, eleven members of the **Shankill Butchers**, a loyalist gang which had continued to operate even after their leader, **Lenny Murphy** (himself murdered by the IRA in November 1982), was jailed in 1976, were convicted of nineteen murders – some of loyalists – and ninety-three other offences. Between July 1972 and May 1977 they operated out of UVF drinking dens in the Shankill Road area and got their name because they tortured and mutilated many of the Catholics they killed.

Mullaghmore, County Sligo

On 27 August, an IRA bomb killed **Lord Mountbatten**, the Queen's cousin, his fourteen-year-old grandson, his daughter's mother-in-law and a fifteen-year-old local; three others were seriously injured.

Warrenpoint

On 27 August, six members of the Parachute Regiment were killed by a 500-pound bomb as an army convoy passed Narrow Water, near Warrenpoint, and IRA gunmen located a few hundred yards away across the border opened fire: an uninvolved English civilian was killed in crossfire. As a helicopter was taking off with the wounded, an 800-pound bomb was detonated and killed four more paras and two of the Queen's Own Highlanders. Several other soldiers were very badly injured.

1981

Middletown, County Armagh

On 21 January, the eighty-six-year-old **Sir Norman Stronge**, former speaker of the Stormont parliament, and his son, were shot dead by the IRA in Tynan Abbey, their home near the border; the mansion was then burned down.

Camlough, South Armagh

On 19 May, five soldiers were killed by an IRA landmine.

Belfast (south)

On 14 November, IRA gunmen shot dead the **Reverend Robert Bradford**, an Ulster Unionist MP, as well as a caretaker at the community centre where Bradford was holding a political surgery.

1982

Ballykelly, County Londonderry

On 7 December, an INLA bomb attack on the **Droppin Well** public house during a disco killed eleven soldiers and five civilians, of whom four were women; thirty were injured.

1983

Darkley

On 20 November, three church elders were shot dead and seven worshippers injured when INLA gunmen opened fire on Darkley Pentecostal Church, a wooden building.

Belfast (south)

On 7 December, the IRA shot dead **Edgar Graham**, an Ulster Unionist Assembly member and academic lawyer, outside Queen's University library. Other **lawyers** killed by the IRA have included William Doyle (1983) and the judge **Lord (Maurice) Gibson** (1987); Tom Travers, a Catholic magistrate, was wounded and his daughter killed in a gun attack in 1984 as they left Mass; three members of the Hanna family were killed in 1988 by a bomb intended for Judge Eoin Higgins. Loyalists murdered **Pat Finucane** (1989) and **Rosemary Nelson** (1999), two high-profile solicitors who represented many republicans.

1985

Newry

On 28 February, seven policemen and two policewomen were killed in an IRA mortar attack on their police station; thirty-seven were injured, of whom twenty-five were civilians.

1987

Killeen, County Armagh

Judge Maurice **Gibson** and his wife Cicely were blown up by a remote-controlled IRA bomb.

Loughgall

On 8 May, the SAS ambushed and killed eight members of the IRA's east Tyrone brigade as they attacked a police station; one civilian was killed and his brother injured as he drove into the area.

Enniskillen

On 8 November, an IRA bomb killed six men and five women – all civilians except for one police reservist and including three married couples – as they waited for a Remembrance Sunday ceremony to begin at the war memorial. Among the sixty-three injured was a headmaster who would die after thirteen years in a coma; among the dead was Marie **Wilson**, whose father **Gordon** won acclaim for forgiving her murderers, was appointed to the Irish Senate, and worked for peace; when he finally met IRA representatives to ask them to stop he was 'disappointed and indeed saddened' by their response.

1988

Belfast (west)

On 16 March, at the huge funerals of **Mairead Farrell**, Sean Savage and Danny McCann, shot by the SAS in Gibraltar on 6 March while unarmed but planning a bomb attack, a UFF assassin, **Michael Stone,** killed two civilians and a member of the IRA in a gun and grenade attack; sixty were injured.

On 19 March, two plainclothes **corporals** were seized, stripped and badly beaten by a mob that thought them loyalist gunmen when their car strayed into the cortège at the funeral of the IRA man killed by Stone; they were then shot dead by the IRA.

Lisburn

On 15 June, following a charity run, six soldiers were killed by an IRA bomb under their van.

Ballygawley, County Tyrone

On 20 August, eight soldiers were killed by an IRA landmine and nineteen were injured.

1989

Belfast

On 12 February, **Pat Finucane** was shot dead in front of his family by the UFF (see 1983, 1997).

Jonesborough

On 20 March, RUC Chief Superintendent **Harry Breen** and Superintendent **Bob Buchanan** were machine-gunned to death by the IRA on their way home after meeting gardaí in Dundalk (see 1997).

1990

Coshquin, near Derry

On 24 October, with the IRA holding his family hostage, **Patsy Gillespie** was forced to drive a van bomb to the army base in the canteen of which he worked; when it was detonated by remote control, he and five soldiers were killed and seventeen civilians were injured. Two other 'human bombs' were sent to other targets the same day. One killed a soldier near Newry but the sixty-eight-year-old driver escaped with a broken leg; the third did not detonate.

1992

Teebane, near Cookstown

On 17 January, eight Protestant building workers were killed by an IRA land-mine on their way home from working on an army base; the other six were badly injured.

Belfast (south)

In retaliation for Teebane, on 5 February five Catholics, including a fifteen-year-old boy, were killed by two UFF gunmen in the **Sean Graham** betting shop on the Ormeau Road; twelve were injured.

1993

Belfast (west)

On 23 October, when his bomb went off prematurely, IRA man Thomas Begley died in a fish shop in the **Shankill Road**, along with Protestant civilians, including four women and two schoolgirls; a married couple, a father and daughter and a mother and daughter; fifty-seven were injured. There was outrage when Gerry Adams carried Begley's coffin.

Greysteel, County Londonderry

On 30 October, two UDA/UFF gunmen killed six men and two women in the Rising Sun lounge in retaliation for the Shankill bombing; nineteen people were injured.

1994

Loughlinisland, County Down

On 18 June, as they watched an Ireland v. Italy World Cup football match on television in the Heights Bar, six Catholic men were killed and five wounded by the UVF.

1996

Aghagallon, near Lurgan

On 8 July, at the height of the Drumcree confrontation, **Michael McGoldrick**, who had just graduated from Queen's university, was murdered in his taxi by renegade UVF members, almost certainly on the orders of their leader, **Billy Wright** (see 1997).

1997

Bessbrook

On 12 February, Lance-bombardier **Stephen Restorick**, the last soldier to be killed before the second IRA ceasefire, was shot in the back by a member of the notorious South Armagh brigade as he manned a checkpoint.

Portadown

On 8 May, **Robert Hamill** died eleven days after being beaten by a loyalist mob. His death became a cause célèbre owing to allegations that police in a nearby landrover had failed to intervene. As a result of political pressure, **Judge Peter Cory** was asked to produce a report on suspected state collusion north and south; on his recommendation public inquiries are being held in the UK into the deaths of **Hamill**, **Finucane** (1989), **Billy Wright** (1997) and **Rosemary Nelson** (1999) and in the Republic of Ireland into the deaths of **Breen** and **Buchanan** (1989) but not of the **Gibsons** (see 1987).

Maze prison

On 27 December, **Billy Wright** was killed in a prison van by three INLA gunmen, founder of the LVF (see 1996).

1998

Ballymoney

On 12 July, **Jason** (aged eight), **Mark** (nine) and **Richard Quinn** (ten) died when their home was petrol-bombed by loyalists at the height of the Drumcree stand-off.

Omagh

On 15 August, the Real IRA murdered twenty-nine shoppers – five men, fourteen women (one pregnant with twins) and nine children, of whom two were Spanish and one English; bereaved families have mounted a civil case against the Real IRA and five alleged bombers.

1999

Newry

On 27 January, **Eamon Collins**, an ex-member of the IRA who had become a high-profile and vocal critic, author of *Killing Rage*, was battered and stabbed to death by the IRA.

Lurgan

On 15 March, **Rosemary Nelson** was killed by a loyalist booby-trap bomb (see 1983 and 1997).

2000

Belfast

On 13 October, **Joe O'Connor**, a senior member of the Real IRA, was shot, almost certainly by the IRA, whose sovereignty he was challenging in their west Belfast heartland.

2005

Belfast

On 30 January, **Robert McCartney** was stabbed and kicked to death in West Belfast by members of the IRA. His five sisters and his partner launched a campaign for justice which took them to the White House and caused much damage to the reputation of Sinn Féin and the IRA in Irish-America and elsewhere.

XII Literature

88 MODERN IRISH LITERATURE

It is convenient to study Gaelic and Anglo-Irish literature as two separate cultural developments. To do this without distortion, it is vital to be alive to the common inspiration of many writings in both English and Irish. An appreciation of Gaelic folklore and literature was necessary to Yeats, Joyce, O'Connor and many other lesser writers; to place such writers solely in the context of an Anglo-Irish tradition is to ignore the real roots of their inspiration.

The seventeenth century in Ireland witnessed the decline of an oral and written Gaelic literature and the rise of a great tradition of writing in English. Political upheaval had finally ended the poets' position of privilege; the bardic tradition was dying, with the ruin of its aristocratic patrons. Seventeenth- and eighteenth-century poets were often reduced to manual labour or begging to survive. Dáibhidh Ó Bruadair (c. 1625–98), Séamus Dall Mac Cuarta (c. 1650–1732), Aodhagán Ó Rathaille (1670–1728) and Eoghan Ruadh Ó Súilleabháin (1748–84), the most famous poets of this period, all experienced great physical deprivation and died in poverty, railing against a society that no longer acknowledged their privileged position.

The main feature of their poetry lay in their use of satire. For some, it could be a stiletto; for others, a bludgeon, but in all cases their language showed traces of a great rhetorical tradition. A unique example of the genre came with Brian Merriman (c. 1747–1805), with whom Frank O'Connor considered 'Irish literature in the Irish language may be said to have died'. In his poem *The Midnight Court*, Merriman chose a broader satiric target than his predecessors were wont to do, in flaying the marrying habits of the Irish. The earthy humour of the text, so true to the spirit of Irish folklore, led to its exclusion, for many years, from the accepted canon of Irish literature.

The economic and social disasters of the nineteenth century, combined with the decline of the Irish language, brought a swift end to the Gaelic poetical tradition. The only other Gaelic poets with a reputation were the itinerant Antóin Ó Raiftearai – Anthony Raftery – (c. 1784–c. 1835) and Eibhlín Dhubh Ní Chonaill (c. 1743–c. 1800) – Eileen O'Leary, an aunt of Daniel O'Connell's – whose lament 'Caoineadh Airt Uí Laoghaire' for her murdered husband,

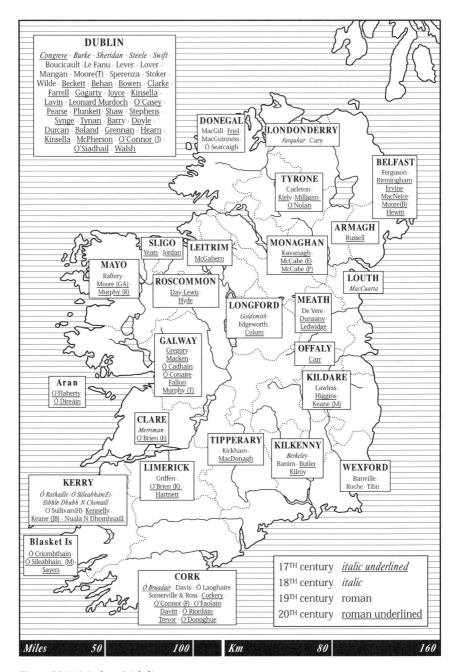

DUBLIN
Congreve · Burke · Sheridan · Steele · Swift ·
Boucicault ·Le Fanu · Lever · Lover ·
Mangan · Moore(T) · Sperenza · Stoker ·
Wilde · Beckett · Behan · Bowen · Clarke ·
Farrell · Gogarty · Joyce · Kinsella ·
Lavin · Leonard Murdoch · O'Casey ·
Pearse · Plunkett · Shaw · Stephens ·
Synge · Tynan · Barry · Doyle ·
Durcan · Boland · Grennan · Hearn ·
Kinsella · McPherson · O'Connor (J) ·
O'Siadhail · Walsh

DONEGAL
MacGill · Friel ·
MacGuinness ·
Ó Searcaigh

LONDONDERRY
Farquhar · Cary

BELFAST
Ferguson ·
Birmingham ·
Ervine ·
MacNeice ·
Moore(B) ·
Hewitt

TYRONE
Carleton ·
Kiely · Milligan ·
O'Nolan

ARMAGH
Russell

SLIGO
Yeats · Jordan

LEITRIM
McGahern

MONAGHAN
Kavanagh ·
McCabe (E) ·
McCabe (P)

MAYO
Raftery ·
Moore (GA) ·
Murphy (R)

ROSCOMMON
Day·Lewis·
Hyde

LONGFORD
Goldsmith ·
Edgeworth ·
Colum

LOUTH
MacCuarta

MEATH
De Vere ·
Dunsany ·
Ledwidge

GALWAY
Gregory ·
Macken ·
Ó Cadhain ·
Ó Conaire ·
Fallon ·
Murphy (T)

OFFALY
Carr

Aran
O'Flaherty ·
Ó Direáin

KILDARE
Lawless ·
Higgins ·
Keane (M)

CLARE
Merriman ·
O'Brien (E)

TIPPERARY
Kickham ·
MacDonagh

KILKENNY
Berkeley ·
Banim · Butler ·
Kilroy

WEXFORD
Banville ·
Roche · Tibn

LIMERICK
Griffen ·
O'Brien (K) ·
Hartnett

KERRY
Ó Rathaille · Ó Silleabhán(E)·
Eibhln Dhubh N Chonaill ·
O'Sullivan(H) · Kennelly ·
Keane (JB) · Nuala N Dhomhnaill

Blasket Is
Ó Criomhthain ·
Ó Sileabháin (M) ·
Sayers

CORK
Ó Bruadair · Davis · Ó Laoghaire ·
Somerville & Ross · Corkery ·
O'Connor (F) · O'Faolain
Davitt · Ó Riordáin ·
Trevor · O'Donoghue

17TH century *italic underlined*
18TH century *italic*
19TH century roman
20TH century roman underlined

Miles 50 100 Km 80 160

Figure 88(a) Modern Irish literature.

Art O'Leary, is the most famous keening poem in the language – though it may possibly be the work of a number of different women. Humphrey O'Sullivan (1780–1837) was among the rare prose writers. The work of these people was not published until the Gaelic Revival at the end of the century, which was preceded by an antiquarian interest in the older language, which provided materials on which Yeats and his co-workers were to draw so fruitfully.

The twentieth century saw a number of distinguished autobiographical works in Irish, written by members of the fast-vanishing Gaeltachts: an tAthair Peadar Ó Laoghaire (1839–1920), *My Own Story*; Tomás Ó Criomhthain (1856–1937), *The Islandman*, Peig Sayers (1873–1958), *Peig*, Muiris Ó Súileabháin (1904–50), *Twenty Years A-Growing*, were all voices from a world of little or no property that had received scant attention in the novels of the Ascendancy and of nationalist writers alike. They are evocative and realistic constructions of a vanished world, recorded elsewhere only in the collections of the Irish Folklore Commission.

The Gaelic Revivalists succeeded in making Irish a compulsory school subject, but did not succeed in halting the erosion of the Gaeltachts (which held only 2.2 per cent of the population by 2002); as literature depends on a vibrant oral culture, Gaelic writing has inevitably suffered. However, it has never died out and is kept alive, to a rather remarkable degree, by a small number of dedicated writers. Outstanding among creative works are the short stories of Martín O'Caidhin (1907–70) (also known for his novel *Cré na Cille*), Pádraic O'Conaire (1883–1928) and Liam O'Flaherty (1896–1984), who was better known for his work in English. Brian O'Nolan (1911–66) whose comic tour-de-force *At Swim-Two-Birds* was written in English as Flann O'Brien, produced as Myles na gCopaleen, *An Béal Bocht*, a fine contribution to the distinguished Gaelic satirical tradition. In recent years poetry has kept writing in Irish alive with Sean Ó Ríordáin (1916–77), Máirtín Ó Direáin (1910–88), Michael Hartnett (1941–99) – again better known for his work in English – Nuala Ní

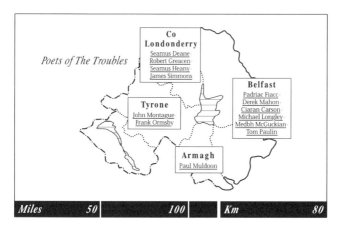

Figure 88(b) Poets of the Troubles.

Dhomhnaill (b. 1952 in Lancashire but brought up in Dingle), Cathal Ó Searcaigh (b. 1956), Michael Davitt (b. 1950) and Mebh McGuckian (b. 1950) – all well known and several of them award-winning poets.

While creative work in the native language decayed, a distinctive literature emerged, which is termed 'Anglo-Irish'. Many of the great eighteenth-century names are essayists, whose contemporary reputations were often based equally on achievements outside literature. Foremost among them were the polemicist and satirist Jonathan Swift (1667–1745), the journalist Richard Steele (1672–1729) and the orator Edmund Burke (1729–97), while in George Berkeley (1685–1753) Ireland produced its only philosopher of world renown. Later great essayists included the playwright George Bernard Shaw (1856–1950) and the undervalued Hubert Butler (1990–90). The begetters of the great and still flourishing tradition of Irish drama were the fine comic writers William Congreve (1670–1729), George Farquhar (1677–1707), Oliver Goldsmith (1728–74) and Richard Brinsley Sheridan (1751–1816) – all of whom were mainly from the Protestant middle class. Later came Dionysius Boucicault (1820–90), a master of the melodrama.

Early in the nineteenth century, descendants of the native Irish, now the emerging Catholic middle classes, demonstrated attitudes that diverged from those of their more prosperous Protestant contemporaries. This perspective was already evident in the work of Humphrey O'Sullivan, who wrote in Irish a diary Pepysian in its concern for detail and solidly middle class in outlook and aspiration. Writers in this tradition include William Carleton (1794–1869), Michael (1796–1874) and John (1798–1842) Banim, Gerald Griffin (1803–40) and Charles Kickham (1828–82).

The concerns of these writers provide an interesting contrast to those of what is often pejoratively described as the 'Ascendancy' or 'landlord' tradition. Foremost among these were Maria Edgeworth (1767–1849), Samuel Lover (1797–1868), Charles Lever (1806–72), Emily Lawless (1845–1913), George Birmingham (1865–1950) and Somerville and Ross (Edith Somerville 1858–1949 and Violet Martin 1862–1915). Many of these writers were later resented for appearing to laugh at 'Irishness' and their reputations suffered accordingly, but recently their work has been judged more objectively.

Two distinctive novelists who fit into the broader English-language of gothic writing were Sheridan Le Fanu (1814–73) and Bram Stoker (1847–1912) who proved themselves masters of mystery and horror. And impossible to pigeon-hole is Lafcadio Hearn (1850–1905), Japanophile and writer of ghost stories, born in Greece but brought up in Dublin.

The nationalist tradition in Anglo-Irish literature is generally seen to begin with Thomas Moore (1779–1852), whose *Irish Melodies* proved immensely popular, both musically and politically. Aubrey de Vere (1814–1902) and, more notably, Sir Samuel Ferguson (1810–86) based much of their poetic work on Irish history and tradition, thus providing a link with the later Irish literary renaissance. With the exception of James Clarence Mangan (1803–49), the Young Ireland movement yielded writers like Thomas Davis (1814–45) and

Speranza, Lady Wilde (1826–96), whose poetry was more noted for its nationalistic fervour than for its quality. This was true also of later poets in this tradition, although Patrick Pearse (1879–1916), Joseph Mary Plunkett (1887–1916) and Thomas MacDonagh (1878–1916) had some talent. Francis Ledwidge (1887–1917), who died, aged 29, in the battle of Ypres, has given his name to a region in his home country of Meath.

The single most important literary development of the late nineteenth and early twentieth centuries was the emergence of the movement which was centred round William Butler Yeats (1865–1939), probably the greatest English-language poet of the twentieth century. It drew its inspiration from Gaelic literature and folklore. This has been called variously the Irish Renaissance, the Celtic Twilight and the Celtic Revival. Lady Gregory (1859–1932) made a lasting contribution with her collections of folk beliefs and songs, her versions of the Irish sagas, her plays and her role in the founding of the Abbey Theatre. Both Yeats and Lady Gregory provided plays for the Abbey, the most famous of which was Yeats's *Cathleen ni Houlihan*, but the most important works for the new theatre were by their younger contemporaries, John Millington Synge (1870–1909) and Seán O'Casey (1884–1964). Rioting greeted the unsentimental portrayal of Ireland in Synge's *Playboy of the Western World* and O'Casey's *The Plough and the Stars*. Other notable members of the Irish Renaissance were George Russell (1867–1933) who wrote as Æ and was an important poet and mystic; the novelist George Moore (1852–1933), an acerbic chronicler of the movement; Oliver St John Gogarty (1878–1957), poet and socialite; and Kathleen Tynan (1861–1931), prolific and popular poet and novelist. Contemporaries who made important contributions to the appreciation of Gaelic literature were Douglas Hyde (1860–1949), outstanding for his work as President of the Gaelic League, and Daniel Corkery (1878–1964), author of *The Hidden Ireland*.

The writers of the Irish Renaissance took the conscious decision to remain in Ireland, where the Abbey provided a forum for their work. Since the time of Swift and Burke, the more usual practice for Irish writers had been to take their talent to England. This was the path chosen by Oscar Wilde (1856–1900), George Bernard Shaw (1856–1950) and eventually by O'Casey himself, who left Dublin for London in 1926, never to return. Padraic Colum (1881–1972), playwright and poet, also opted for America; and the most famous Irish exile, James Joyce (1882–1941), lived in Trieste and Zurich but is most identified with Paris, where he lived from 1920 to 1939. Samuel Beckett (1906–89) followed Joyce to Paris (acting for a time as his secretary), and switched to French to write his most famous play, *Waiting for Godot*.

With *Ulysses* Joyce changed modern literature. Although he is not among Ireland's four Nobel Prize winners for Literature (these are Yeats, Shaw, Beckett and Seamus Heaney), he has the greatest reputation of any twentieth-century writer and has engendered an industry to rival Shakespeare's: Bloomsday (16 June), the day on which *Ulysses* is set, is celebrated in cities across the world; Dublin has a Joyce museum, a Joyce centre, two public statues to Joyce and plaques on the street indicating places mentioned in *Ulysses*.

The effect of Joyce and Yeats on their successors was paralysing. For a time the only literary form that really flourished in Ireland was the short story. Popularized by Lord Dunsany (1878–1957), it reached its zenith with Frank O'Connor (1903–66), but Seán O'Faolain (1900–91), Liam O'Flaherty (1896–1984), Benedict Kiely (b. 1919), Mary Lavin (1912–96) and later William Trevor (b. 1928) and John McGahern (b. 1935) were authors of international standing. O'Faolain was also founder and editor of the magazine *The Bell*, which for many years raised a lonely standard for literature while church and state did their best to close down debate. During the 1930s, 1940s and 1950s it was joked, bitterly, that the mark of quality in a writer was inclusion on the Irish censorship list.

For a time the short story was seen as the quintessentially 'Irish' form: again, with *Dubliners*, Joyce was the master in this field. In recent years, however, Irish writers have tended to ignore the short story, while all other literary forms are flourishing. O'Flaherty, Kate O'Brien (1897–1974), Elizabeth Bowen (1900–73), Iris Murdoch (1919–99), Brian Moore (1921–99), and later Edna O'Brien (b. 1932) and Julia O'Faolain (b. 1932, daughter of Seán) were distinguished novelists, all of whom lived mainly outside Ireland. The three names that still dominate are Trevor, McGahern and John Banville (b. 1945), with Colm Tóibín (b. 1955) and Joseph O'Connor (b. 1963) coming up fast. The work of Roddy Doyle (b. 1958) and Patrick McCabe (b. 1955) has translated particularly well to the screen: Doyle's *The Commitments* and *The Snapper* and McCabe's *The Butcher Boy* have been made into acclaimed films. Neil Jordan (b. 1950) is a novelist turned immensely successful film scriptwriter and director.

Between Yeats and Seamus Heaney (b. 1939), the outstanding names in Irish poetry are Patrick Kavanagh (1906–67), Austin Clarke (1896–1974) and John Hewitt (1906–87). However, these were not part of any movement. Louis MacNeice (1907–63) and Cecil Day Lewis (1905–72) were two of the four most celebrated English-language poets of the 1930s (the others being W. H. Auden and Stephen Spender) but they left Ireland as young men and have been identified more with the British poetic tradition. However, the 'Troubles' in Northern Ireland have either coincided with, or brought forth, a remarkable range of poets (Figure 88b). Most celebrated among these is Heaney but notable Northern Irish contemporaries include Robert Greacen (b. 1920), John Montague (b. 1929 in New York but raised in Tyrone), James Simmons (1933–2001) and some of the most famous poets writing today: Michael Longley (b. 1939), Seamus Deane (b. 1940), Derek Mahon (b. 1941), Tom Paulin (b. 1949 in Leeds, but raised in Belfast), Derek Mahon (b. 1941), Ciaran Carson (b. 1948) and Paul Muldoon (b. 1951) (see Figure 88b). These are disparate poets who in no way form a movement, but they are geographically close and all have dealt with the Northern Irish conflict, often obliquely and indirectly. Northern Ireland now has the strongest poetic culture on the island, although southern poets have also been resurgent, chief among them – in English – Padraic Fallon (1905–74), Richard Murphy (b. 1927), Thomas Kinsella (b. 1928), Brendan Kennelly (b. 1936), Eamon Grennan (b. 1941), Paul Durcan (b. 1944), Eavan

Boland (b. 1944), Bernard O'Donoghue (b.1945) and Micheal O'Siadhail (b. 1947). To quote Kavanagh: 'The standing army of Irish poets never falls below 10,000'.

Brendan Behan (1923–64), like O'Casey, drew his inspiration from the Dublin slums. He was succeeded by a brilliant crop of playwrights, notably Hugh Leonard (b. 1926), John B. Keane (1928–2002), Brian Friel (b. 1929), Eugene McCabe (b. 1930 in Glasgow but has spent most of his life in Monaghan), Tom Murphy (b. 1935) and Tom Kilroy (b. 1943). These were joined by Sebastian Barry (b. 1955), Billy Roche (b. 1949) and Frank McGuinness (b. 1953), whose *Observe the Sons of Ulster Marching towards the Somme* is a rare dramatic depiction of the unionist tradition (albeit from a Catholic dramatist). The most recent names are Conor McPherson (b. 1971), Martin McDonagh (b. 1971 in London but writes about Ireland), Enda Walsh (b. 1967) and Marina Carr (b. 1964).

Despite generous tax concessions to artists, many Irish writers continue to live principally abroad – mainly in London or the United States. However, where émigré writers from Congreve to Wilde tended not to write directly about Ireland, contemporary writers follow Joyce in living abroad but writing about home. The great achievement of writers, living and dead, is to have taken Ireland to a worldwide audience.

Select bibliography

The objectives of this bibliography are twofold. Its primary purpose is to give the general reader some guidelines on future reading on particular topics covered during the course of the book; it is in no way intended to be comprehensive. Its secondary purpose is to acknowledge my debts to various writers on whose work I have relied heavily. In recent years there has been an explosion of writing on Irish history and literature, so many outstanding books will not appear here.

General

The *New History of Ireland*, published in the 1980s, 1990s and 2000s, now stretches to eight volumes, including a chronology and a volume of maps and lists. The individual volumes are: *Medieval Ireland, 1169–1534* (ed. Art Cosgrave, 1987); *Early Modern Ireland, 1534–1691* (ed. T. W. Moody, F. X. Martin and F. J. Byrne, 1991); *Eighteenth Century Ireland, 1691–1800* (ed. T. W. Moody and W. E. Vaughan, 1986); *Ireland under the Union, I: 1801–1870* (ed. W. E. Vaughan, 1986); *Ireland under the Union, II: 1870–1921* (ed. W. E. Vaughan, 1996); *Ireland, 1921–84* (ed. J. R. Hill, 2003); *Chronology of Irish History to 1976* (ed. T. W. Moody. F. X. Martin and F. J. Byrne, 1982); *Maps, Genealogies and Lists* (ed. T. W. Moody, F. X. Martin and F. J. Byrne, 1984).

The six volumes of the *New Gill History of Ireland*, published in the 1980s and 1990s, succeeded the eleven volumes of the 1970s *Gill History of Ireland* (many of which are still well worth reading). Individual volumes are: Michael Richter, *Medieval Ireland: the enduring tradition* (1988); Sean Lennon, *Sixteenth Century Ireland: the incomplete conquest* (1994); Brendan Fitzpatrick, *Seventeenth Century Ireland: the war of religion* (1988); Edith Mary Johnston, *Eighteenth Century Ireland: the long peace* (1974); D. G. Boyce, *Nineteenth Century Ireland: the search for stability* (1990); Dermot Keogh, *Twentieth Century Ireland: nation and state* (1994).

The *Helicon History of Ireland* is a series of nine brief volumes – a good schools survey.

S. J. Connolly (ed.) *The Oxford Companion of Irish history* (1998) is a useful reference book; James Lydon, *The Making of Ireland: from ancient times to the present* (1998), and Roy Foster (ed.) *The Oxford Illustrated History of Ireland* (2002) are good one-volume overviews. Ciaran Brady (ed.), *Interpreting Irish History: the debate on historical revisionism, 1938–1994* (1994) is a fine introduction to historiographical debate.

The medieval period

Dáibhí O'Cróinín, *Early Medieval Ireland 400–1200* (1995); A. J. Otway-Ruthven, *A History of Medieval Ireland* (1968); James Lydon, *The Lordship of Ireland in the Middle Ages* (1972), and *Ireland in the Later Middle Ages* (1973); Robin Frame, *Ireland and Britain, 1170–1450* (1998).

The modern period

Marcus Tanner, *Ireland's Holy Wars: the struggle for a nation's soul 1500–2000* (2001); J. C. Beckett, *The Making of Modern Ireland, 1603–1923* (1966); R. F. Foster, *Modern Ireland 1600–1972: politics and society* (1988); W. E. H. Lecky, *Ireland in the Eighteenth Century* (1892); F. S. L. Lyons, *Ireland since the Famine* (1971); J. J. Lee, *Ireland 1912–1985* (1989); Alvin Jackson, *Ireland 1798–1998: politics and war* (1999) and *Home Rule: an Irish history, 1800–2000* (2003); Diarmaid Ferriter, *The Transformation of Ireland 1900–2000* (2004).

Historical geography

T. W. Freeman, *Pre-Famine Ireland: a study of historical geography* (1957); *Ireland: a general and regional geography* (1972); Walter Fitzgerald, *The Historical Geography of Early Ireland* (1925); F. H. A. Aalen, *Man and Landscape in Ireland* (1978); J. P. Haughton (ed.) *Atlas of Ireland* (1979); B. J. Graham and L. J. Proudfoot (eds) *An Historical Geography of Ireland* (1993).

Area and local studies

See the important and continuing 'History and Society' series of Geography Publications: each volume consists of interdisciplinary essays on the history of a specific Irish county. Series editor: William Nolan. See also Diarmuid Ferriter, *Lovers of Liberty? Local government in twentieth century Ireland* (2001).

Cartography

General cartography

H. G. Fordham, *Some Notable Surveyors and Map Makers of the Sixteenth–Eighteenth Centuries and Their Work* (1929); G. R. Crone, *Maps and their Makers* (1953); John Noble Wilford, *The Mapmakers* (1981).

Ireland

John Speed, *The History of Great Britaine under the Conquests of ye Romans, Saxons, Danes and Normans* (1611); Robert Dunlop, 'Sixteenth century maps of Ireland' in *English Historical Review* xx (1905); T. J. Westropp, 'Early Italian maps of Ireland, 1300–1600' in *Proceedings of the Royal Irish Academy* XXX (1913); G. A. Hayes-McCoy, *Ulster and other Irish Maps c. 1600* (1964); J. H. Andrews, 'John Norden's Maps of Ireland' in *Proceedings of the Royal Irish Academy* 100C (2000); Tim Robinson, *The Burren: a map of the uplands of north-west Clare* (1977); *Mapping South Connemara* (1985).

See also the excellent Ordnance Survey maps of Irish counties.

Military

General

Thomas Bartlett and Keith Jeffrey (eds) *A Military History of Ireland* (1996) is the most comprehensive study to date. See also: J. J. O'Connell, *The Irish Wars: a military history of Ireland from the Norse invasions to 1798* (c. 1928); G. A. Hayes-McCoy, *Irish Battles: a military history of Ireland* (1969). Eileen McCracken, *The Irish Woods since Tudor Times* (1971); Samuel Clark and James S. Donnelly (eds) *Irish Peasants: violence and political unrest, 1780–1914* (1983); C. H. E. Philpin, *Nationalism and Popular Protest in Ireland* (1987); and Emmett O'Byrne, *War, Politics and the Irish of Leinster* 1156–1606 (2003), provide interesting angles.

Vikings

P. G. Foote and D. M. Wilson, *The Viking Achievement* (1970); A. Walshe, *Scandinavian Relations with Ireland during the Viking Period* (1922).

Norman and medieval

G. H. Orpen, *Ireland under the Normans, 1169–1333* (1911–20); O. Armstrong, *Edward Bruce's Invasion of Ireland* (1923); Brendan Smith, *Colonisation and Conquest in Medieval Ireland: the English in Louth, 1170–1330* (1999); Tom McNeill, *Castles in Ireland: feudal power in a Gaelic world* (1997), covers Norman to late Tudor.

Tudor

Cyril Falls, *Elizabeth's Irish Wars* (1950); G. A. Hayes-McCoy, 'Strategy and tactics in Irish warfare, 1593–1601' in *Irish Historical Studies* 7 (1941).

United Irishmen

Sir Henry McNally, *The Irish Militia, 1793–1816* (1949); Thomas Pakenham, *The Year of Liberty. The great Irish rebellion of 1798* (1969); Marianne Elliott, *Partners in Revolution: the United Irishmen and France* (1982); Nancy J. Curtin, *The United Irishmen: popular politics in Ulster and Dublin, 1791–1798* (1994); Patrick M. Geoghegan, *Robert Emmet: a life* (2002).

Independence and civil war

Owen Dudley Edwards and F. Pyle (eds) *1916: the Easter Rising* (1968); Peter Hart, *The I.R.A. and its Enemies: violence and community in Cork 1916–1923* and *The I.R.A. at War 1916–1923* (2003); Carlton Younger, *Ireland's Civil War* (1968); Charles Townshend,

The British Campaign in Ireland, 1919–1921 (1975); David Fitzpatrick, *Politics and Irish Life, 1913–1921: provincial experience of war and revolution* (1977); Oliver Coogan, *Politics and War in Meath, 1913–1923* (1983); Michael Hopkinson, *Green against Green: the Irish Civil War* (1988) and *The Irish War of Independence* (2002); Donal J. O'Sullivan, *The Irish Constabularies 1822–1922* (1999); David Fitzpatrick, *Harry Boland's Irish Revolution* (2003); Francis Costello, *The Irish Revolution and its Aftermath 1916–1923: Years of Revolt* (2003).

Republican and loyalist paramilitarism

J. Bowyer Bell, *The Secret Army: the IRA*, revised third edition (1997), and *The IRA, 1968–2000: analysis of a secret army* (2000); Richard English, *Armed Struggle (2003);* Peter Taylor, *Provos: the IRA and Sinn Féin* (1997), *Loyalists* (1999) and *Brits: the war against the IRA* (2001); Steve Bruce, *God Save Ulster! The Red Hand – Protestant Paramilitaries in Northern Ireland* (1992); Martin Dillon, *The Shankill Butchers: a case study of mass murder* (1990); Toby Harnden, *Bandit Country* (1999); Jack Holland and Susan Phoenix, *Phoenix: policing the shadows* (1996); Chris Ryder, *The RUC 1922–2000: a force under fire* (2000); David McKittrick, Seamus Kelters, Brian Feeney and Chris Thornton, *Lost Lives* (2004). And see below on Northern Ireland.

Politics

Early and medieval

Eoin McNeill, *Celtic Ireland* (1921) and *Phases of Irish History* (1919); Francis John Byrne *Irish Kings and High-Kings* (1973); Ben Jarski, *Early Irish Kingship and Succession* (2000); Brendan Smith (ed.) *Britain and Ireland 900–1300: insular responses to medieval European change* (1999); Robert Dudley Edwards, 'Anglo-Norman relations with Connacht, 1169–1224' in *Irish Historical Studies* 2 (1938); H. G. Richardson and G. O. Sayles, *The Irish Parliament in the Middle Ages* (1952); James Lydon, *England and Ireland in the Later Middle Ages* (1981).

Tudor, Stuart and Jacobite

Nicholas Canny, *The Elizabethan Conquest of Ireland* (1976); D. B. Quinn, 'Henry VIII and Ireland, 1509–34' in *Irish Historical Studies* 12 (1960); Ciaran Brady, *The Chief Governors: the rise and fall of reform government in Tudor Ireland, 1536–1588* (1994); A. Clarke, *The Old English in Ireland* (1966); H. F. Kearney, *Stafford in Ireland, 1633–41* (1959); J. M. Simms, *Jacobite Ireland, 1685–1691* (1969).

Eighteenth century

Robert E. Burns, *Irish Parliamentary Politics in the Eighteenth Century*, I: *1714–1730* (1989), II: *1730–1760* (1990); R. B. McDowell, *Ireland in the Age of Imperialism and Revolution, 1760–1801* (1979); Thomas Bartlett, *The Fall and Rise of the Catholic Nation* (1992); James Kelly, *Prelude to Union* (1992); Jacqueline Hill, *From Patriots to Unionists* (1997); Patrick M. Geoghegan, *The Act of Union* (1999); Edith Mary Johnston-Liik, *History of the Irish Parliament 1692–1800*, six volumes (2002).

Nineteenth century

K. Theodore Hoppen, *Elections, Politics and Society in Ireland, 1832–1885* (1984);
K. B. Nowlan, *The Politics of Repeal* (1963); Oliver McDonagh, *O'Connell* (1991);
J. H. Whyte, *The Independent Irish Party, 1850–59* (1958); Conor Cruise O' Brien,
Parnell and his Party, 1880–1890 (1957); F. S. L. Lyons, *Parnell* (1977); Paul Bew, *Charles
Stewart Parnell* (1980).

Nationalist Ireland 1890–1921

Maurice Golding, *Faith of our Fathers: the formation of Irish nationalist ideology 1890–1920*
(1982) and *Pleasant the Scholar's Life: Irish intellectuals and the construction of the nation state*
(1993); Patrick Maume, *The Long Gestation: Irish nationalist life, 1891–1918* (1999);
Michael Laffan, *The Resurrection of Ireland: the Sinn Fein party, 1916–1923* (1999); David
Fitzpatrick, 'The geography of Irish nationalism, 1910–1921' in *Past and Present* lxxviii
(Feb. 1978) and *The Two Irelands 1912–1939* (1998); Arthur Mitchell, *Revolutionary
Government in Ireland: Dáil Eireann, 1919–22* (1993); Brian Farrell, *The Founding of Dail
Eireann: parliament and nation building* (1971).

Independent Ireland

John M. Regan, *The Irish Counter-revolution 1921–1936: treatyite politics and settlement in
independent Ireland* (1999); Richard Dunphy, *The Making of Fianna Fail Power in Ireland,
1923–48* (1995); Brian Farrell, *The Irish Parliamentary Tradition* (1973); John A. Murphy,
Ireland in the Twentieth Century (1975); Ronan Fanning, *Independent Ireland* (1983); M. A.
Busteed, *Voting Behaviour in the Republic of Ireland* (1990); Basil Chubb, *The Government
and Politics of Ireland* (third edition, 1992); John Coakley, *Politics in the Republic of Ireland*
(1999); Conor Cruise O'Brien, *States of Ireland* (1972) and *Ancestral Voices: religion and
nationalism in Ireland* (1994). See also the 'How Ireland voted' series, which monitor each
election.

Labour history

Arthur Mitchell, *Labour in Irish Politics, 1890–1930* (1974); David Fitzpatrick, 'Strikes in
Ireland, 1914–21' in *Saothar* vi (1980), 26–39; John W. Boyle, *The Irish Labour Movement
in the Nineteenth Century* (1988); Pádriag Yeates, *Lockout: Dublin 1913* (2000); Emmet
O'Connor, 'Agrarian unrest and the labour movement in county Waterford 1917–1923'
in *Saothar* vi (1980), 40–58, *Syndicalism in Ireland 1917–1923* (1988) and *A Labour
History of Ireland, 1824–1960* (1992).

Useful primary sources for the modern period

Alan O'Day and John Stephens (eds) *Irish Historical Documents since 1800* (1992);
Arthur Mitchell and Padraig O'Snodaigh, *Irish Political Documents 1869–1916* (1989)
and *1916–1949* (1985); Brian M. Walker (ed.) *Parliamentary Election Results in Ireland,
1801–1922* (1978) and *Parliamentary Election Results in Ireland, 1918–92: Irish elections to
parliaments and parliamentary assemblies at Westminster, Belfast, Dublin, Strasbourg* (1992).

Religion

Early and medieval

J. F. Kenny, *Sources for the Early History of Ireland: ecclesiastical* (1929); M. and L. de Paor, *Early Christian Ireland* (1958); Kathleen Hughes, *The Church in Early Irish Society* (1966); A. Gwynn, *The Twelfth Century Reform* (1968); A. Gwynn and N. Hadcock, *Medieval Religious Houses: Ireland* (1970).

Reformation

Robert Dudley Edwards, *Church and State in Tudor Ireland* (1935); Brendan Bradshaw, *The Dissolution of the Religious Orders* (1974).

Protestants

Toby Barnard, *A New Anatomy of Ireland: the Irish Protestants, 1649–1770* (2003).

Church of Ireland

W. A. Phillips (ed.) *The History of the Church* (1933–4); Alan Ford, James McGuire and Kenneth Milne (eds) *As by Law Established: the Church of Ireland since the Reformation* (1995).

Dissenters

J. C. Beckett, *Protestant Dissent in Ireland 1687–1780* (1948); David Hempton and Myrtle Hill, *Evangelical Protestantism in Ulster Society 1740–1890* (1992).

Catholicism

M. Wall, *The Church under the Penal Laws 1691–1760* (1961); J. Brady and P. J. Corish, *The Church under the Penal Code* (1971). The dominating name for late nineteenth-century church history is Emmet Larkin; see *inter alia*: *The Consolidation of the Roman Catholic Church in Ireland, 1860–1870* (1987) and *The Roman Catholic Church and the Creation of the Modern Irish State, 1878–1886* (1975). For the twentieth century, David Miller, *Church, State and Nation in Ireland, 1898–1921* (1973), and John Whyte, *Church and State in Ireland, 1923–1979* (1980), are the key texts while Tom Inglis, *Moral Monopoly: the rise and fall of the Catholic church in modern Ireland* (1998) and Louise Fuller, *Irish Catholicism since 1950* (2002), are excellent guides to the more recent period. See also Dermot Keogh, *Ireland and the Vatican: the politics and diplomacy of church-state relations 1922–1960* (1995).

Other

Dermot Keogh, *Jews in Twentieth Century Ireland* (1998).

The Irish abroad

General

Patrick O'Sullivan (ed.) *The Irish World Wide: history, heritage, identity* is an indispensable six-volume series. The individual volumes are: *Patterns of Migration* (1992); *The Irish in the New Communities* (1992); *The Creative Migrant* (1994); *Irish Women and Irish migration* (1995); *Religion and Identity* (1996); *The Meaning of the Famine* (1997). For good succinct accounts, see David Fitzpatrick, *Irish Emigration, 1801–1921* (1984); D. H. Akenson, *An Irish Diaspora* (1990); Andy Bielenberg, *The Irish Diaspora* (2000); Thomas O'Connor (ed.), *The Irish in Europe, 1580–1815* (2001); Thomas O'Connor and Mary Ann Lyons (eds), *Irish Migrants in Europe after Kinsale*, 1602–1820 (2003).

The Irish in North America and Canada

John Mannion, *Irish Settlements in Eastern Canada: a study of cultural transfer and adaptation* (1974); David Noel Doyle, *Ireland, Irishmen and Revolutionary America, 1760–1820* (1981); Kerby A. Miller, *Emigrants and Exiles: Ireland and the Irish exodus to North America* (1985); Bruce Elliot, *Irish Migrants in the Canadas* (1988); Arthur Gribben (ed.) *The Great Famine and the Irish Diaspora in America* (1999); Andrew J. Wilson, *Irish America and the Ulster Conflict, 1968–1995* (1995).

The Irish in Australia

Oliver McDonagh, *The Sharing of the Green: a modern Irish history for Australians* (1996).

The Irish in Britain

Donald M. MacRaild, *Irish Migrants in Modern Britain, 1750–1922* (1995).

The Irish in the British Empire

Keith Jeffrey (ed.) *An Irish Empire?* (1996); David Murphy, *Ireland and the Crimean War* (2002).

The Fenians

T. W. Moody (ed.), *The Fenian Movement* (1968); Patrick Quinlivan and Paul Rose, *The Fenians in England, 1865–1872: a sense of insecurity* (1982); R. V. Comerford, *The Fenians in Context: Irish politics and society 1848–82* (1985); Amos Keith, *The Fenians in Australia, 1865–1880* (1988).

International relations

P. Keatinge, *The Formulation of Irish Foreign Policy* (1973) and *A Place among the Nations: issues in Irish foreign policy* (1978); Michael Kennedy, *Ireland and the League of Nations,*

1919–1946 (1996); Joseph Morrison Skelly, *Irish Diplomacy at the United Nations, 1945–1965* (1997); Michael Kennedy and Joseph Morrison Skelly (eds) *Irish Foreign Policy, 1919–66: from independence to internationalism* (2000); R. Fanning, M. Kennedy, D. Keogh and E. O'Halpin, *Documents in Irish Foreign Policy,* four volumes (1998, 2000, 2002, 2004), covering 1919–36 – important source material.

European Union

Brigid Laffan, 'The European Union and Ireland' in Neil Collins (ed.) *Political Issues in Ireland Today* (1999); Rory O'Donnell (ed.) *Europe: the Irish experience* (2000).

Land

Seventeenth century

T. W. Moody, *The Londonderry Plantation* (1939); J. G. Simms, *The Williamite Confiscation in Ireland, 1690–1703* (1958); Philip S. Robinson, *The Plantation of Ulster: British settlement in an Irish landscape, 1600–1670* (1984).

Nineteenth century

Robert Dudley Edwards and T. D. Williams (eds) *The Great Famine: studies in Irish history, 1845–1852* (1956); Paul Bew, *Land and the National Question in Ireland, 1858–82* (1978); David Fitzpatrick, 'The disappearance of the Irish agricultural labourer 1841–1912' in *Irish Economic and Social History* vii (1980); Mary Daly, *The Famine in Ireland* (1986); Christine Kinealy, *This Great Calamity: Irish famine, 1845–52* (1994); W. E. Vaughan, *Landlords and Tenants in Mid-Victorian Ireland* (1994); Philip Bull, *Land, Politics and Nationalism: a study of the Irish land question* (1996); Peter Gray, *Famine, Land and Politics* (1999).

Twentieth century

Dan Bradley, *Farm Labourers: Irish struggle, 1900–1976* (1988); Cormac Ó Gráda, three brief working papers, published 1989: *Irish Agricultural History: recent research*; *Irish Agriculture North and South since 1900*; *Snapshots of Irish Agricultural History: output and productivity pre-famine and post-famine*; Seamus Lafferty, Patrick Cummins and James A. Walsh, *Irish Agriculture in Transition; a census atlas of agriculture in the Republic of Ireland* (1991); Mary Daly, *The First Department: a history of the department of agriculture* (2002).

Infrastructure

Colm O Lochlainn, 'Irish roadways' in *Féilsgribhinn Eoin Mhic Neill* (1940); K. B. Nowlan, *Travel and Transport in Ireland* (1973); Sean D. Barett, *Transport Policy in Ireland in the 1990s* (1991); Ruth Delany, *Ireland's Royal Canal 1789–1992* (1992) and *The Grand Canal of Ireland* (1995); David Turnock, *An Historical Geography of Railways in Great Britain and Ireland* (1998); John Mangan and Kevin Hannigan, *Logistics and Transport in a Fast-Growing Economy* (2000).

The economy

General

L. M. Cullen, *An Economic History of Ireland since 1660* (1972) and *Anglo-Irish Trade, 1660–1800* (1968); Mary Daly, *A Social and Economic History of Ireland since 1800* (1981); Cormac Ó Gráda, *Ireland: a new economic history, 1780–1939* (1994) and *Ireland before and after the Famine* (1993); Liam Kennedy, *Colonialism, Religion and Nationalism in Ireland* (1996).

Pre-seventeenth century

A. K. Longfield, *Anglo-Irish Trade in the Sixteenth Century* (1929); H. F. Kearney, 'The Irish wine trade, 1614–15' in *Irish Historical Studies* 36 (1955).

Independent Ireland

Ronan Fanning, *The Irish Department of Finance, 1922–1958* (1978); J. Meenan, *The Irish Economy since 1922* (1970); Cormac Ó Gráda, *A Rocky Road: the Irish economy since 1920* (1997); Cormac Ó Gráda and Kevin Bourke, *Irish Economic Growth, 1945–88* (1994).

Celtic Tiger

Denis O'Hearn, *Inside the Celtic Tiger* (1998); Paul Sweeny, *The Celtic Tiger* (1999); Brian Nolan, Philip J. O'Connell and Christopher T. Whelan, *Bust to Boom: the Irish experience of growth and inequality* (2000).

Social change

General

James S. Donnelly Jnr. and Kerby A. Miller, *Irish Popular Culture 1650–1850* (1998); L. M. Cullen, *Six Generations: everyday life and work in Ireland from 1790* (1970); Terence Brown, *Ireland: a social and cultural history 1922–1985* (1985). See also Mary Daly's and J. J. Lee's social and economic histories, mentioned above, and the Censuses of Ireland (starting 1841 and appearing every decade since). There are innumerable, useful, general websites, e.g. www.coso.ie; www.eurostat.com; www.orac.ie

Early Ireland

E. O'Curry, *Manners and Customs of the Early Irish* (1873); P. W. Joyce, *Social History of Ancient Ireland* (1903); M. Dillon (ed.) *Early Irish Society* (1954).

Towns and general settlement patterns

R. A. Butlin, *The Development of the Irish Town* (1977); Terry Barry (ed.) *A History of Settlement in Ireland* (2000).

Population patterns

K. H. Connell, *The Population of Ireland* (1950); W. E. Vaughan and A. J. Fitzpatrick (eds) *Irish Historical Statistics: population, 1821–1971* (1978).

Recent migration

Russell King, *Contemporary Irish Migration* (1991); Ethel Crawley and Jim McLaughlin (eds) *Under the Belly of the Tiger: class, race, identity and culture in global Ireland* (1997); Marshall Tracy, *Racism and Immigration in Ireland: a comparative analysis* (2000). For immigrants/refugee information: www.justice.ie; www.irishrefugeecouncil.ie

Education

Robert E. Ward, *An Encyclopedia of Irish Schools 1500–1800* (1995); John Colahan, *Irish Education: its history and structure* (1981); Mary Daly, *The Origins of Popular Literacy in Ireland: language change and educational development 1700–1920* (1990); T. J. McElligot, *Secondary Education in Ireland, 1870–1921* (1981); D. H. Akenson, *A Mirror to Kathleen's Face: education in independent Ireland, 1922–1960* (1976); E. Randles, *Post-Primary Education in Ireland, 1957–70* (1976).

Status of women

Margaret MacCurtain and D. O'Corrain (eds) *Women in Irish Society* (1978); Margaret MacCurtain and Mary O'Dowd, *Women in Early Modern Ireland* (1991); Maryann Gialanella Valiulis and Mary O'Dowd (eds) *Women and Irish History* (1997); Mary Daly, *Women and Work in Ireland* (1997); Catriona Clear, *Women of the House: women's household work in Ireland 1926–1961* (2000).

Irish language

Brian O'Cuiv (ed.) *A View of the Irish Language* (1969).

Northern Ireland

T. W. Moody, *The Ulster Question, 1603–1973* (1974); Jonathan Bardon, *A History of Ulster* (1992); Flann Campbell, *The Dissenting Voice: Protestant democracy in Ulster from plantation to partition* (1991); Marianne Elliott, *The Catholics of Ulster* (2000); Kevin Haddick-Flynn, *Orangeism – the making of a tradition* (1999); Ruth Dudley Edwards, *The Faithful Tribe: an intimate portrait of the loyal institutions* (2000); John Bowman, *De Valera and the Ulster Question, 1917–1973* (1982); Liam Kennedy and Philip Ollerenshaw (eds) *An Economic History of Ulster, 1820–1940* (1985); Paul Bew, Peter Gibbon and Henry Patterson, *Northern Ireland, 1921–1996: political forces and social classes* (1996); Malachi O'Doherty, *The Trouble with Guns: republican strategy and the Provisional IRA* (1998); Brian Feeney, *Sinn Fein: a hundred turbulent years* (2002); Paul Bew and Gordon Gillespie, *Northern Ireland: a chronology of the Troubles, 1968–1999* (1999); Ed Moloney, *A Secret History of the IRA* (2002); Brian Rowan, *The Armed Peace: life and death after the cease-fires*

(2004); Dean Godson: *Himself Alone: David Trimble and the ordeal of unionism* (2004); Frank Millar, *David Trimble: the price of peace* (2004). And see above on republican and loyalist paramilitarism.

Literature

Reference and anthologies

D. J. O'Donoghue, *The Poets of Ireland: a biographical dictionary* (1912); Seamus Deane (ed.) *The Field Day Anthology of Irish Writing* (1991 – and see subsequent volumes); Robert Hogan (ed.) *Dictionary of Irish Literature* (1996); Robert Welch (ed.) *Oxford Companion to Irish Literature* (1996).

General criticism

George Watson, *Irish Identity and the Literary Revival: Synge, Yeats, Joyce, O'Casey* (1979); Robert Welch, *Irish Poetry from Moore to Yeats* (1980); R. F. Foster, *W. B. Yeats: a life*, two volumes, Vol. 1: *The Apprentice Mage* (1997), Vol. 2: *The Arch-Poet* (2003); Hugh Kenner, *A Colder Eye: the modern Irish writers* (1983); James M. Cahalan, *Great Hatred, Little Room: the Irish historical novel* (1983) and *The Irish Novel: a critical history* (1988); Seamus Deane, *A Short History of Irish Literature* (1986); Norman Vance, *Irish Literature: a social history* (1990); John Wilson Foster, *Colonial Consequences: essays in Irish literature and culture* (1991); W. J. McCormack, *The Battle of the Books: two decades of Irish cultural debate* (1986); *From Burke to Beckett: ascendancy, tradition and betrayal in literary history* (1994); Edna Longley, *The Living Stream: literature and revisionism in Ireland* (1994); Declan Kiberd, *Inventing Ireland* (1995), and *Irish Classics* (2000); P. J. Mathews (ed.) *New Voices in Irish Criticism* (2000).

Index

Were every name and place to be indexed, this section would be ridiculously long and – since the book has a clear table of contents and is heavily cross-referenced - not much more helpful. I have therefore excluded names and places that can be found just once and in an obvious place, so, for example, if you want a sport or a sportsman, see 'Sport' (83), or a literary person, see 'Literature' (XII), or those involved with the 1916 rising, see 'The 1916 rising' (20), or individual victims of the Troubles or places where atrocities occurred (in Ireland), see 'Killings' (87) - though the index has, for instance, an item on 'The Disappeared'. Otherwise, common sense has ruled and the index contains items people might be expected to look up.

Page numbers in *italics* refer to the maps